U0583987

Truth and Actuality

真理与事实

[印度]克里希那穆提 [英]大卫·博姆 ——— 著

Sue ——— 译

九州出版社 JIUZHOUPRESS | 全国百佳图书出版单位

图书在版编目（CIP）数据

真理与事实 /（印）克里希那穆提，（英）大卫·博姆著 ; Sue译. -- 北京 : 九州出版社，2025. 1.

ISBN 978-7-5225-3505-0

Ⅰ. B-53

中国国家版本馆CIP数据核字第2025U09P55号

版权合同登记号：图字 01-2022-6523

"Copyright©1977 Krishnamurti Foundation Trust, Ltd."

Krishnamurti Foundation Trust Ltd.,

Brockwood Park, Bramdean, Hampshire, SO24 0LQ, England.

E-mail: info@kfoundation.org

Website: www.kfa.org

想要了解克里希那穆提的更多信息，请访问：www.jkrishnamurti.org。

真理与事实

作　　者	[印]克里希那穆提 著　[英]大卫·博姆 著　Sue 译
责任编辑	李文君
出版发行	九州出版社
地　　址	北京市西城区阜外大街甲35号（100037）
发行电话	（010）68992190/3/5/6
网　　址	www.jiuzhoupress.com
印　　刷	鑫艺佳利（天津）印刷有限公司
开　　本	880毫米×1230毫米　32开
印　　张	10.75
字　　数	290千字
版　　次	2025年5月第1版
印　　次	2025年5月第1次印刷
书　　号	ISBN 978-7-5225-3505-0
定　　价	88.00元

教一件事，那就是观察你自己，深入探索你自己，然后加以超越。你不是去听从我的教诲，你只是在了解自己罢了。"他的思想，为世人指明了东西方一切伟大智慧的精髓——认识自我。

　　本书的第一部分取自克里希那穆提与理论物理学家大卫·博姆之间的一系列讨论。第二部分为克氏于 1975 年秋在布洛克伍德公园进行的演讲和对话内容的真实记录。第三部分的问答取自克氏于 1975 年和 1976 年在萨能的演讲。

　　克里希那穆提系列作品得到了台湾著名作家胡因梦女士的倾情推荐，在此谨表谢忱。

九州出版社

出版前言

　　克里希那穆提 1895 年生于印度，13 岁时被"通神学会"带到英国训导培养。"通神学会"由西方人士发起，以印度教和佛教经典为基础，逐步发展为一个宣扬神灵救世的世界性组织，它相信"世界导师"将再度降临，并认为克里希那穆提就是这个"世界导师"。而克里希那穆提在自己 30 岁时，内心得以觉悟，否定了"通神学会"的种种谬误。1929 年，为了排除"救世主"的形象，他毅然解散专门为他设立的组织——世界明星社，宣布任何一种约束心灵解放的形式化的宗教、哲学和主张都无法带领人进入真理的国度。

　　克里希那穆提一生在世界各地传播他的智慧，他的思想魅力吸引了世界各地的人们，但是他坚持宣称自己不是宗教权威，拒绝别人给他加上"上师"的称号。他教导人们进行自我觉察，了解自我的局限以及宗教、民族主义狭隘性的制约。他指出打破意识束缚，进入"开放"极为重要，因为"大脑里广大的空间有着无可想象的能量"，而这个广大的空间，正是人的生命创造力的源泉所在。他提出："我只

EDITOR'S NOTES AND INSCRIPTIONS

编者按语及题记

In Part I the discussions are taken from a series between J. Krishnamurti and David Bohm, professor of Theoretical Physics at London University. Part II is the Authentic Report of Talks and Dialogues at Brockwood Park which took place in the autumn of 1975. The Questions and Answers in Part II come from Talks at Saanen given in 1975 and 1976.

"What is the relationship between truth and reality? Reality being, as we said, all the things that thought has put together. Reality means, the root meaning of that word is, things or thing. And living in the world of things, which is reality, we want to establish a relationship with a world which has no things—which is impossible."

"Actuality means 'What is'... Are you facing in yourself what actually is going on.. You don't take actuality and look at it."

"Man has been concerned throughout the ages to discover or live in 'Truth'."

C. AND G. WD.

　　本书的第一部分取自克里希那穆提与伦敦大学的理论物理学教授大卫·博姆之间的一系列讨论。第二部分为 1975 年秋在布洛克伍德公园进行的演讲和对话内容的真实记录。第三部分的问答取自 1975 年和 1976 年在萨能的演讲。

　　"真理与现实之间的关系如何？正如我们之前所说，现实即为思想所造的一切物品。'现实'的意思，这个词的词根义，指的是物品。活在这个充满了物品即现实的世界上，我们想要与空无一物的世界建立联系——这是不可能的。"

　　"事实的意思是'现在如何'……你正面对着你内心此刻实际发生的事情吗……你不肯拿起事实来看一看。"

　　"人类世世代代以来一直都注重探索'真理'或者活在'真理'之中。"

C 与 G·WD

C目录
CONTENTS

PART I
第一部分

Discussions between J. Krishnamurti and Professor David Bohm

Discussions between J. Krishnamurti and Professor David Bohm

J. 克里希那穆提与大卫·博姆教授之间的讨论

CHAPTER 1
第 1 章

REALITY, ACTUALITY, TRUTH

现实、事实与真理

Krishnamurti: I was thinking about the question of what is truth and what is reality and whether there is any relationship between the two, or whether they are separate. Are they eternally divorced, or are they just projections of thought? And if thought didn't operate, would there be reality? I thought that reality comes from "res", thing, and that anything that thought operates on, or fabricates, or reflects about, is reality. And thought, thinking in a distorted, conditioned manner is illusion, is self-deception, is distortion. I left it there, because I wanted to let it come rather than my pursuing it.

Dr Bohm: The question of thought and reality and truth has occupied philosophers over the ages. It's a very difficult one. It seems to me that what you say is basically true, but there are a lot of points that need to be ironed out. One of the questions that arises is this: if reality is thought, what thought thinks about, what appears in consciousness, does it go beyond consciousness?

K: Are the contents of consciousness reality ?

Dr B.: That's the question; and can we use thought as equivalent to consciousness in its basic form ?

K: Yes.

Dr B: I wonder whether, just for the sake of completeness, we should include in thought also feeling, desire, will and reaction. I feel we should, if we are exploring the connection between consciousness, reality and truth.

　　克里希那穆提（以下简称为"克"）：我之前在想"什么是真理"和"什么是现实"这两个问题，以及这两者之间是不是存在某种关系，抑或它们是彼此分开的。它们永远都是分开的呢，还是它们只是思想的投射？如果思想不运作，那么现实还会存在吗？我认为"现实"这个词来自"物品""东西"，而思想操控、构造或考虑的任何东西，都是现实。以一种扭曲而受限的方式进行的思考或者思想，是幻觉，是自欺，是歪曲。到这儿我就打住了，因为我想让问题自己呈现，而不是我去追究它。

　　博姆博士（以下简称"博姆"）：关于思想、现实和真理的问题，世世代代以来一直占据着哲学家们的头脑。这是一个很难解答的问题。在我看来，你所说的基本上是对的，但是还有很多个难点需要得到解决。其中出现的一个问题是：如果现实就是思想，那么思想所思考的东西，出现在意识中的东西，会超越意识吗？

　　克：意识的内容是现实吗？

　　博姆：这就是问题所在；而我们可以把思想等同于意识的基本形态吗？

　　克：可以。

　　博姆：只不过为了尽可能考虑周全，我想知道我们是不是应该把感情、欲望、意志和反应也包括在思想之内。如果我们要探索意识、现实和真理之间的联系，我觉得上述这些内容应该包括进来。

K: Yes.

Dr B: One of the points I'd like to bring up is: there is thought, there is our consciousness, and there is the thing of which we are conscious. And as you have often said, the thought is not the thing.

K: Yes.

Dr B: We have to get it clear, because in some sense the thing may have some kind of reality independent of thought; we can't go so far as to deny all that. Or do we go as far as some philosophers, like Bishop Berkeley, who has said that all is thought? Now I would like to suggest a possibly useful distinction between that reality which is largely created by our own thought, or by the thought of mankind, and that realty which one can regard as existing independently of this thought. For example, would you say Nature is real?

K: It is, yes.

Dr B: And it is not just our own thoughts.

K: No, obviously not.

Dr B: The tree, the whole earth, the stars.

K: Of course, the cosmos. Pain is real.

Dr B: Yes. I was thinking the other day, illusion is real, in the sense that it is really something going on, to a person who is in a state of illusion.

K: To him it is real.

Dr B: But to us it is also real because his brain is in a certain state of electrical and chemical movement, and he acts from his illusion in a real way.

K: In a real way, in a distorted way.

Dr B: Distorted but real. Now it occurred to me that one could say that even the false is real but not true. This might be important.

克：是的。

博姆：我想提出的一点是：思想、我们的意识以及我们意识到的东西，都是存在的。而正如你经常说到的那样：思想并非事物本身。

克：是的。

博姆：我们得把这一点弄清楚，因为从某种意义上来说，事物本身也许具有某种独立于思想而存在的现实性；我们无法否认这一点。或者，我们会不会像某些哲学家，比如，伯克利主教①那样，认为一切皆为思想？现在我想提出一种也许有些帮助的划分方法，来区分两种现实：一种是主要由我们自己的思想或者由人类的思想制造出来的现实，另一种是可以被认为是独立于这种思想而存在的现实。比如说，你会不会说大自然是现实存在的？

克：是的，没错。

博姆：它并非只是我们自己的思想。

克：没错，显然不是。

博姆：树木，整个地球，还有星辰。

克：当然，整个宇宙。疼痛是现实存在的。

博姆：前两天我在想，幻觉从某种意义上讲也是现实存在的，对一个处于幻觉状态的人来说，它就是实际发生着的事情。

克：那对他来说是现实存在的。

博姆：但是那对我们来说也是现实存在的，因为他的大脑处于某种电子和化学活动状态之中，而他又以一种现实的方式根据自己的幻觉采取着行动。

克：以某种现实的方式，某种扭曲的方式。

① 爱尔兰哲学家，英国圣公会主教，反对托马斯·霍布斯的唯物主义。（译者注）

K: I understand. For instance: is Christ real?

Dr B: He is certainly real in the minds of people who believe in Him, in the sense we have been discussing.

K: We want to find out the distinction between truth and reality. We said anything that thought thinks about, whether unreasonably or reasonably, is a reality. It may be distorted or reasoned clearly, it is still a reality. That reality, I say, has nothing to do with truth.

Dr B: Yes, but we have to say besides, that in some way reality involves more than mere thought. There is also the question of actuality. Is the thing actual? Is its existence an actual fact? According to the dictionary, the fact means what is actually done, what actually happens, what is actually perceived.

K: Yes, we must understand what we mean by the fact.

Dr B: The fact is the action that is actually taking place. Suppose, for example, that you are walking on a dark road and that you think you see something. It may be real, it may not be real. One moment you feel that it's real and the next moment that it's not real. But then you suddenly touch it and it resists your movement. From this action it's immediately clear that there is a real thing which you have contacted. But if there is no such contact you say that it's not real, that it was perhaps an illusion, or at least something mistakenly taken as real.

K: But, of course, that thing is still a reality that thought thinks about. And reality has nothing to do with truth.

Dr B: But now, let us go further with the discussion of "the thing". You see, the root of the English word "thing" is fundamentally the same as the German "bedingen", to condition, to set the conditions or determine. And indeed we must agree that a thing is necessarily conditioned.

博姆：扭曲但现实存在的方式。于是我就想到，我们可以说即使是虚假的东西也是现实存在的，但它并不正确。这点也许很重要。

克：我明白。比如说，基督是现实存在的吗？

博姆：他在某些信仰他的人心目当中当然是现实存在的，这种现实指的就是我们刚刚所探讨的那个含义。

克：我们想搞清楚真理和现实之间的区别。我们说过思想思考的任何东西，无论合理与否，都是一种现实。它无论是扭曲的还是清晰合理的，都依然是一种现实。我认为，这种现实与真理毫无关系。

博姆：是的，但我们不得不说，除此之外，在某些方面，现实所涉及的不仅仅只有思想，还有事实的问题。那个东西是实际的吗？它的存在是一个实际的事实吗？根据词典，"事实"意味着实际做的事情，实际发生的事情，实际感知到的事情。

克：是的，我们必须了解我们所说的事实指的是什么。

博姆：事实是实际发生的行动。比如说，假设你正走在一条黑漆漆的路上，然后你觉得自己看到了什么东西。也许真有什么东西，也许并不真的有什么。你一会儿觉得真有，一会儿又觉得不是真的。但是随后你突然碰到了什么，它抵抗你的动作。从这个行动你立刻就能清楚地知道你刚刚摸到了一个真的东西。但是如果没有这种接触，你就会说那不是真的，那也许只是一个幻觉，或者至少把什么东西误以为是真的了。

克：但是，那个东西无疑依然是思想所思考的一个现实。而现实与真理毫无关系。

博姆：但是现在让我们更进一步地讨论一下"东西"这个问题。你看，英文里"东西"（thing）这个词基本上和德语里的"bedingen"这个词有着同样的意思，就是去制约、去设下条件或者决定。而我们确实

K: It is conditioned. Let's accept that.

Dr B: This is a key point. Any form of reality is conditioned. Thus, an illusion is still a form of reality which is conditioned. For example, the man's blood may have a different constitution because he's not in a balanced state. He is distorting, he may be too excited, and that could be why he is caught in illusion. So every thing is determined by conditions and it also conditions every other thing.

K: Yes, quite.

Dr B: All things are interrelated in the way of mutual conditioning which we call influence. In physics that's very clear, the planets all influence each other, the atoms influence each other, and I wanted to suggest that maybe we could regard thought and consciousness as part of this whole chain of influence.

K: Quite right.

Dr B: So that every thing can influence consciousness and it in turn can work back and influence the shapes of things, as we make objects. And you could then say that this is all reality, that thought is therefore also real.

K: Thought is real.

Dr B: And there is one part of reality influencing another part of reality.

K: Also, one part of illusion influences another part of illusion.

Dr B: Yes, but now we have to be careful because we can say there is that reality which is not made by man, by mankind. But that's still limited. The cosmos, for example, as seen by us is influenced by our own experience and therefore limited.

K: Quite.

Dr B: Any thing that we see, we see through our own experience, our own

必须同意这一点，即一样东西必然是受到了制约的。

克：它受到了制约。我们先接受这一点。

博姆：这是很关键的一点。任何一种形式的现实都受到了制约。因此，幻觉也是受到了制约的现实的一种表现形式。比如说，有个人的血液成分可能有些与众不同，因为他的健康状况不佳。他身上存在某种扭曲，他也许太激动了，而那也许就是他陷入幻觉的原因。所以每种东西都取决于各种条件的制约，而它同时也在制约着其他的东西。

克：是的，没错。

博姆：一切事物都以互相制约的方式发生着联系，我们称之为影响。这点在物理学上是显而易见的，行星们都彼此相互影响着，原子也相互影响，而我想提出的是，也许我们可以认为思想和意识是这整个相互影响的链条的一部分。

克：非常正确。

博姆：所以每种东西都能影响意识，意识反过来也能影响事物的形态，就像我们制造出各种东西那样。于是你就可以说，这都是现实，所以思想也是现实存在的。

克：思想是现实存在的。

博姆：而一部分现实也在影响着另一部分现实。

克：同样，一部分幻觉也在影响着另一部分幻觉。

博姆：是的，但这里我们得小心一点儿，因为我们可以说还存在着一些并非由人、由人类所制造的现实。但那依然非常有限。比如说，我们所看到的宇宙，由于被我们自己的经验所影响，因而是有限的。

克：确实如此。

博姆：我们看到的任何东西，都是透过我们自己的经验、我们自

background. So that reality cannot possibly be totally independent of man.

K: No.

Dr B: It may be relatively independent. The tree is a reality that is relatively independent but it's our consciousness that abstracts the tree.

K: Are you saying that man's reality is the product of influence and conditioning?

Dr B: Yes, mutual interaction and reaction.

K: And all his illusions are also his product.

Dr B: Yes, they are all mixed together.

K: And what is the relationship of a sane, rational, healthy, whole man, to reality and to truth?

Dr B: Yes, we must consider that, but first may we look at this question of truth. I think the derivation of words is often very useful. The word "true" in Latin, which is "verus", means "that which is". The same as the English "was" and "were", or German "wahr". Now in English the root meaning of the word "true" is honest and faithful; you see, we can often say that a line is true, or a machine is true. There was a story I once read about a thread that ran so true; it was using the image of a spinning-wheel with the thread running straight.

K: Quite.

Dr B: And now we can say that our thought, or our consciousness, is true to that which is, if it is running straight, if the man is sane and healthy. And otherwise it is not, it is false. So the falseness of consciousness is not just wrong information, but it is actually running crookedly as a reality.

K: So you're saying, as long as man is sane, healthy, whole and rational, his thread is always straight.

Dr B: Yes, his consciousness is on a straight thread. Therefore his reality –

己的背景看到的。所以这种现实不可能完全独立于人而存在。

克：没错。

博姆：它也许只是相对独立的。树是一种相对独立的现实，但正是我们的意识把树抽象化了。

克：你是说，人的现实是影响和制约的产物？

博姆：没错，是互动和反应的产物。

克：而他所有的幻觉也是他自身的产物。

博姆：是的，它们统统混杂在一起。

克：那么，一个清醒的、理智的、健全的、完整的人，与现实和真理有着怎样的关系呢？

博姆：是的，我们必须考虑这个问题，但是我们可不可以先来看看真理这个问题？我认为词语的各种变形通常很有帮助。拉丁语里的"真实"（"true"）这个词，也就是"verus"，意思是"现在如何"。英语里的"曾是"（"was"和"were"）和德语里的"wahr"也是同样的情况。而英语里"真实"（"true"）这个词的词根义是诚实和可信；你看，我们经常说"某条线是正确的"或者"某部机器是正确的"。我曾经读到过一个故事，讲的是一条运行得很正确的线；故事用的画面是一部纺车上有一根笔直的线。

克：好的。

博姆：那么我们可以说，如果我们的思想或者我们的意识是笔直运行的，如果这个人是清醒的、健全的，那么思想或意识就是忠于事实的。否则它就不是真实的，是虚假的。所以说，意识的虚假之处不仅仅在于错误的信息，而是它实际上是作为一种现实在扭曲地运行着。

克：所以你说的是，只要人是清醒的、健全的、完整的、理智的，

K: —is different from the reality of a man whose thread is crooked, who is irrational, who is neurotic.

Dr B: Very different. Perhaps the latter is even insane. You can see with insane people how different it is—they sometimes cannot even see the same reality at all.

K: And the sane, healthy, whole, holy man, what is his relationship to truth?

Dr B: If you accept the meaning of the word, if you say truth is that which is, as well as being true to that which is, then you have to say that he is all this.

K: So you would say the man who is sane, whole, is truth?

Dr B: He is truth, yes.

K: Such a man is truth. He may think certain things which would be reality, but he is truth. He can't think irrationally.

Dr B: Well, I wouldn't say quite that, I'd say that he can make a mistake.

K: Of course.

Dr B: But he doesn't persist in it. In other words, there is the man who has made a mistake and acknowledges it, changes it.

K: Yes, quite right.

Dr B: And there is also the man who has made a mistake but his mind is not straight and therefore he goes on with it. But we have to come back to the question: does truth go beyond any particular man; does it include other men, and Nature as well?

K: It includes all that is.

Dr B: Yes, so the truth is one. But there are many different things in the field of reality. Each thing is conditioned, the whole field of reality is

那么他的那条线就始终是笔直的。

博姆：是的，他的意识处于一条直线上。所以他的现实——

克：——就完全不同于一个神经质的、不理智的、线是歪曲的人的现实。

博姆：完全不同。后者甚至有可能是疯狂的。你可以看到对那些疯子来说是多么不一样——他们有时甚至会完全看不到同一个现实存在的东西。

克：那么一个清醒的、健全的、完整的、神圣的人，他与真理是什么关系呢？

博姆：如果你接受了"真理"这个词的意思，如果你说真理就是事实以及忠于事实，那么你就不得不说他就是这一切。

克：所以你会说清醒、完整的人就是真理？

博姆：他就是真理，是的。

克：这样的一个人就是真理。他也许会思考某种将会成为现实的事情，但他就是真理。他不可能不理智地思考。

博姆：哦，我可能不太会这么说，我会说他可能会犯错。

克：当然。

博姆：但他不会坚持这个错误。换句话说，有一种人犯了错之后会承认，然后改掉。

克：是的，没错。

博姆：还有一种人犯了错，但由于他的头脑不够直接，因此会继续错下去。但我们得回到这个问题上来了：真理是不是超越任何特定的个人的；它是不是也包括了其他人以及大自然在内？

克：它包含了真实的一切。

conditioned. But clearly, truth itself cannot be conditioned or dependent on things.

K: What then is the relationship to reality of the man who is truth?

Dr B: He sees all the things and, in doing this, he comprehends reality. What the word "comprehends" means is to hold it all together.

K: He doesn't separate reality. He says, "I comprehend it, I hold it, I see it".

Dr B: Yes, it's all one field of reality, himself and everything. But it has things in it which are conditioned and he comprehends the conditions.

K: And because he comprehends conditioning, he is free of conditioning.

Dr B: It seems clear then that all our knowledge, being based on thought, is actually a part of this one conditioned field of reality.

K: Now another question. Suppose I am a scholar, I'm full of such conditioned and conditioning knowledge. How am I to comprehend truth in the sense of holding it all together?

Dr B: I don't think you can comprehend truth.

K: Say I have studied all my life, I've devoted all my life to knowledge, which is reality.

Dr B: Yes, and it is also about a bigger reality.

K: And suppose you come along and say, "Truth is somewhere else, it's not that". I accept you, because you show it to me, and so I say, "Please help me to move from here to that".

Dr B: Yes.

K: Because once I get that, I comprehend it. If I live here, then my comprehension is always fragmented.

Dr B: Yes.

博姆：是的，所以真理是一个整体。但是在现实的范围内就有各种不同的东西了。每种东西都是受制约的，现实的整个领域都受到了制约。然而，显然真理本身无法被制约，它也不依赖于任何东西。

克：那么本身就是真理的人与现实有什么关系呢？

博姆：他看到了所有的东西，在这个过程中，他理解了现实。"理解"这个词的意思是从整体上完全地把握了现实。

克：他并不把现实划分开来。他说："我理解了它，把握了它，看到了它。"

博姆：是的，那是一整个现实的领域，包括了他自己和一切。但现实中有受到制约的东西，而他理解了那些制约。

克：而由于他理解了制约，所以他摆脱了制约。

博姆：那么，这一点看起来就清楚了，那就是：由于我们所有的知识都是基于思想的，所以它实际上是这整个受限的现实领域的一部分。

克：那么就有了另外一个问题。假设我是一个学者，我装满了这些受制约的同时又具有制约作用的知识。那么我如何才能从整体上完全把握真理，如何才能这样地去理解真理呢？

博姆：我认为你无法理解真理。

克：比如说，我毕生都致力于研究，我把自己的一生奉献给了知识，也就是现实。

博姆：是的，这也涉及一个更大范围的现实的问题。

克：然后假设你走过来，说："真理在别的地方，那不是真理。"我接受了你说的话，因为你指给我看了，于是我说："请帮我从这里走到那里。"

博姆：嗯。

K: Therefore my knowledge tells me, "This is reality but it is not truth". And suppose you come along and say, "No, it is not". And I ask: please tell me how to move from here to that.

Dr B: Well, we've just said we can't move...

K: I'm putting it briefly. What am I to do?

Dr B: I think I have to see that this whole structure of knowledge is inevitably false, because my reality is twisted.

K: Would you say the content of my consciousness is knowledge?

Dr B: Yes.

K: How am I to empty that consciousness and yet retain knowledge which is not twisted—otherwise I can't function—and reach a state, or whatever it is, which will comprehend reality. I don't know if I'm making myself clear.

Dr B: Yes.

K: What I'm asking is: my human consciousness is its content, which is knowledge; it's a messy conglomeration of irrational knowledge and some which is correct. Can that consciousness comprehend, or bring into itself, truth?

Dr B: No, it can't.

K: Therefore, can this consciousness go to that truth? It can't either. Then what?

Dr B: There can be a perception of the falseness in this consciousness. This consciousness is false, in the sense that it does not run true. Because of the confused content it does not run true.

K: It's contradictory.

Dr B: It muddles things up.

K: Not, "muddles things up"; it is a muddle.

克：因为一旦我到达了那里，我就理解了真理。如果我待在这儿，那么我的理解就是支离破碎的。

博姆：是的。

克：所以我的知识告诉我说："这是现实，但不是真理。"然后假设你过来说："不，这不是。"于是我就说：请告诉我如何从这里走到那里。

博姆：哦，我们刚才说了我们不能走向……

克：那我简单点儿说：我该怎么办呢？

博姆：我想我们必须看到，这整个知识的结构不可避免地是虚假的，因为我的现实是扭曲的。

克：你会不会说我意识的内容就是知识？

博姆：会。

克：那我怎样才能清空那个意识，同样又保留不扭曲的知识——否则我就无法运转——并且达到某种能够理解现实的状态？我不知道有没有把自己的意思说清楚。

博姆：清楚了。

克：我问的是：我作为人类的意识就它本身的内容，也就是知识；那是一团庞大的不理性的知识，其中只有一部分是正确的。那个意识能够领悟真理或者把真理引入它自身吗？

博姆：不，它不能。

克：那么，这个意识能够到达那个真理吗？它也不能。那然后呢？

博姆：这个意识之中可以有一种对虚假的洞察。这个意识是虚假的，虚假的意思是它并没有正确地运转。它因为自身混乱的内容而无法正确地运转。

Dr B: It is a muddle, yes, in the way it moves. Now then, one of the main points of the muddle is that when consciousness reflects on itself, the reflection has this character: it's as if there were a mirror and consciousness were looking at itself through a mirror and the mirror is reflecting consciousness as if it were not consciousness but an independent reality.

K: Yes.

Dr B: Now therefore, the action which consciousness takes is wrong, because it tries to improve the apparently independent reality, whereas in fact to do this is just a muddle.

I would like to put it this way: the whole of consciousness is somehow an instrument which is connected up to a deeper energy. And as long as consciousness is connected in that way, it maintains its state of wrong action.

K: Yes.

Dr B: So on seeing that this consciousness is reflecting itself wrongly as independent of thought, what is needed is somehow to disconnect the energy of consciousness. The whole of consciousness has to be disconnected, so it would, as it were, lie there without energy.

K: You're saying, don't feed it. My consciousness is a muddle, it is confused, contradictory, and all the rest of it. And its very contradiction, its very muddle, gives its own energy.

Dr B: Well, I would say that the energy is not actually coming from consciousness, but that as long as the energy is coming, consciousness keeps the muddle going.

K: From where does it come?

Dr B: We'd have to say that perhaps it comes from something deeper.

K: If it comes from something deeper, then we enter into the whole field of gods and outside agency and so on.

克：它矛盾重重。

博姆：它把事情搞得一团糟。

克：不是"把事情搞得一团糟"，它就是一团糟。

博姆：它就是一团糟，是的，它的活动方式就是这样的。那么，这团混乱中主要的一点是，当意识反省它自身，这种反省就具备这样的特点：就好像有一面镜子，而意识从那面镜子里看着自己，镜子反映出的意识好像不是意识，而是某种独立存在的现实。

克：是的。

博姆：所以，意识采取的行动是错误的，因为它试图改善那个看起来独立存在的现实，而实际上这么做恰恰是一团糟的做法。

我想这么表达：整个意识就好像一个连接着更深层能量的工具。而只要意识是以那种方式连接起来的，它就会维持自身错误的行动状态。

克：是的。

博姆：所以，一旦看到了这个意识错误地认为自己是独立于思想而存在的，那么需要做的可以说就是切断意识的能量。整个意识都必须被切断，于是它就能够像最初那样毫无能量地待在那里。

克：你是说不要喂养它。我的意识是一团糟，它很混乱，矛盾重重……诸如此类。而正是它自身的这种矛盾和混乱给它自己带来了能量。

博姆：哦，我会说，能量实际上并不是来自意识，而是只要能量还在涌入，意识就会继续混乱下去。

克：那它是从哪里来的呢？

博姆：我们不得不说也许是从某个更深层的地方来的。

克：如果它来自某个更深层的地方，那么我们就会落入那整个关于神明和外在的媒介之类的范畴。

Dr B: No, I wouldn't say the energy comes from an outside agency. I would prefer to say it comes from me, in some sense.

K: Then the "me" is this consciousness?

Dr B: Yes.

K: So the content is creating its own energy. Would you say that?

Dr B: In some sense it is, but the puzzle is that it seems impossible for this content to create its own energy. That would be saying that the content is able to create its own energy.

K: Actually, the content is creating its own energy. Look, I'm in contradiction and that very contradiction gives me vitality. I have got opposing desires. When I have opposing desires I have energy, I fight. Therefore that desire is creating the energy—not God, or something profounder—it is still desire. This is the trick that so many played. They say there is an outside agency, a deeper energy—but then one's back in the old field. But I realize the energy of contradiction, the energy of desire, of will, of pursuit, of pleasure, all that which is the content of my consciousness—which is consciousness—is creating its own energy. Reality is this; reality is creating its own energy. I may say, "I derive my energy deep down", but it's still reality.

Dr B: Yes, suppose we accept that, but the point is that seeing the truth of this...

K: ...that's what I want to get at. Is this energy different from the energy of truth?

Dr B: Yes.

K: It is different.

Dr B: But let's try to put it like this: reality may have many levels of energy.

K: Yes.

博姆：不，我不会说能量来自某个外在的媒介。从某种意义上讲，我更愿意说它来自"我"。

克：那么"我"就是这个意识？

博姆：是的。

克：所以意识在制造它自身的能量。你是这个意思吗？

博姆：从某种意义上讲是这样的，但令人费解的是，这个内容创造它自身的能量似乎是不可能的。

克：实际上，内容确实在创造着它自身的能量。你看，我内心矛盾，而正是这种矛盾给我带来了活力。我抱有互相矛盾的欲望。当我有互相矛盾的欲望时，我就有了能量，我就会斗争。所以是那个欲望产生了能量——不是上帝，也不是什么更深层的东西——那还是个欲望。这是太多人玩儿的把戏了。他们说有个外在的媒介，有个更深层的能量——但是这样的话你就回到了老一套的窠臼中。然而，我认识到了矛盾带来的能量、欲望带来的能量，意志、追求和欢愉带来的能量，那一切都是我意识的内容——也就是意识——是它们产生了自己的能量。现实就是这些，现实在制造自己的能量。我可以说"我是从深处获得了能量"，但那依然属于现实。

博姆：是的，假设我们接受了这一点，可问题是看到了这个真相……

克：……那就是我打算说到的。这种能量与真理的能量是不同的吗？

博姆：是的。

克：是不同的。

博姆：但我们是想这么说：现实也许有很多个不同层面的能量。

克：嗯。

Dr B: But a certain part of the energy has gone off the straight line. Let's say the brain feeds energy to all the thought processes. Now, if somehow the brain didn't feed energy to the thought process that is confused, then the thing might straighten out.

K: That's it. If this energy runs along the straight thread it is a reality without contradiction. It's an energy which is endless because it has no friction. Now is that energy different from the energy of truth?

Dr B: Yes. They are different, and as we once discussed, there must be a deeper common source.

K: I'm not sure. You are suggesting that they both spring out of the same root.

Dr B: That's what I suggest. But for the moment there is the energy of truth which can comprehend the reality and—

K: —the other way it cannot.

Dr B: No, it cannot; but there appears to be some connection in the sense that when truth comprehends reality, reality goes straight. So there appears to be a connection at least one way.

K: That's right, a one-way connection—truth loves this, this doesn't love truth.

Dr B: But once the connection has been made, then reality runs true and does not waste energy or make confusion.

K: You see, that's where meditation comes in. Generally, meditation is from here to there, with practice and all the rest of it. To move from this to that.

Dr B: Move from one reality to another.

K: That's right. Meditation is actually seeing what is. But generally meditation is taken as moving from one reality to another.

博姆：但某一部分能量是沿直线运行的。比如说大脑给所有的思考过程补给能量。那么，如果不管是什么原因大脑不再给混乱的思维过程补充能量的话，那么事情没准儿就理清了。

克：就是这样。如果这种能量沿直线运行，那么它就是没有矛盾的现实。它是一种无穷无尽的能量，因为它没有摩擦。那么，这种能量和真理的能量是不同的吗？

博姆：是的。它们是不同的，而就像我们曾经讨论过的那样，必然存在某种更深层的共同的源头。

克：我不确定是这样的。你是说它们都脱胎于同一个根源。

博姆：那就是我的意思。但是一旦有了能够理解现实的真理的能量，而且——

克：——否则的话就不可能。

博姆：对，不可能；但从某种意义上来说，这两种能量似乎又存在着某种联系，即：当真理领会了现实，现实就会走上直路。所以至少在这一个方向上看起来是有联系的。

克：对，有一种单向的联系——真理喜欢这个，但这个不喜欢真理。

博姆：但是联系一旦建立起来，现实就会按正确的方式运行，同时也不会浪费能量或者制造混乱。

克：你看，这就是冥想开始的地方。人们通常认为，冥想是由此及彼，进行练习等事情，是从这里走向那里。

博姆：从一个现实走向另一个现实。

克：没错。而冥想实际上是看到事实。但人们通常认为冥想是从一个现实走向另一个现实。

CHAPTER 2
第 2 章

Insight And Truth. Gulf
Between Reality And Truth
洞察与真理；现实与真理
之间的鸿沟

Krishnamurti: I am concerned with trying to find out if there is an action which is not a process of thought, an action which is of truth—if I can put it that way—an insight which acts instantly. I want to inquire into that question.

Dr Bohm: Perhaps one action that acts instantly is to see falseness.

K: Yes. It's difficult to take examples. I have an insight into the fact that people believe in God—I'm taking that as an example.

Dr B: What is the nature of your insight, then?

K: The insight into the fact that God is their projection.

Dr B: Yes, and therefore false.

K: I have an insight. If I had a belief in God it would drop instantly. So it is not a process of thought, it is an insight into truth.

Dr B: Or into falseness.

K: Or into falseness, and that action is complete, it's over and done with. I don't know if I'm conveying it: that action is whole, there is no regret, there is no personal advantage, there is no emotion. It is an action which is complete. Whereas the action brought about by thought, the investigation of an analysis whether there is a God or no God, is always incomplete.

Dr B: Yes, I understand that. Then there is another action in which you do use words, where you try to realize the insight. Let's say, you talk to people. Is that action complete or incomplete? Say you have discovered

克里希那穆提：我想试着弄清楚有没有一种行动并非一个思想过程，有没有一种属于真理的行动——如果我可以这么表达的话——有没有一种即刻行动的洞察。我想探究这些问题。

博姆博士：也许即刻产生行动的一种行为就是看到虚假。

克：是的，但这很难举例子。我对"人们信仰上帝"这个事实拥有一种洞察——我拿这个来举例子。

博：那么你的洞察具有怎样的性质？

克：洞察到"上帝是他们的投射"这个事实。

博：是的，因而那是虚假的。

克：我有了一种洞察。如果我之前抱有对上帝的信仰，我就会立刻把它丢掉。所以这不是一个思想过程，而是对真相的洞察。

博：或者对虚假的洞察。

克：或者对虚假的洞察，而那种行动是完整的，它结束了，完成了。不知道我有没有说清楚：那种行动是完整的，其中没有遗憾，没有个人利益，也没有情绪。那是一种完满的行动。然而思想产生的行动，对上帝存在与否的分析研究，始终是不完整的。

博：是的，我明白。然后还有另一种行动，在那种行动中你确实会用到语言，你试着去实现那种洞察。比如说，你与人们谈话。这种行动是完整的还是不完整的？比如说，你发现了关于上帝的真相，而其他

about God. Other people are still calling this a fact, and therefore...

K: But the man speaks from an insight.

Dr B: He speaks from an insight, but at the same time he starts a process of time.

K: Yes, to convey something.

Dr B: To change things. Let's now consider that just to get it clear. It's starting from an insight but it's conveying truth.

K: Yes, but it's always starting from an insight.

Dr B: And in doing that you may have to organise...

K: ...reasonable thinking and so on, of course. And the action of reasoned thought is different from the action of insight.

Dr B: Now what is the difference when insight is conveyed through reasoned thought? To come back again to your insight about God: you have to convey it to other people, you must put it into a reasonable form.

K: Yes.

Dr B: And therefore isn't there still some of the quality of the insight, as you convey it? You must find a reasonable way to convey it. Therefore in doing that, some of the truth of the insight is still being communicated in this form. And in some sense that is thought.

K: No, when conveying to another that insight verbally, one's action will be incomplete unless he has insight.

Dr B: That's right. So you must convey what will give someone an insight.

K: Can you give an insight?

Dr B: Not really, but whatever you convey must somehow do something which perhaps cannot be further described.

K: Yes. That can only happen when you yourself have dropped the

人还在说那是一个事实，因此……

克：但那个人是依据洞察来讲话的。

博：他依据洞察来讲话，但同时他开启了一个时间过程。

克：是的，为了传达某些东西。

博：为了改变一些事情。现在我们来考虑一下这个问题，好让它清楚一些。它是从洞察开始的，却在传达真相。

克：是的，但它始终是从洞察出发的。

博：而在这么做的过程中，你也许不得不组织……

克：进行合理的思考等，当然。而理性思考的行动与洞察的行动是不同的。

博：那么当通过理性的思想来传达真相时，那种不同又在哪里？再回过头来说你对上帝的洞察：你不得不把它传达给人们，你必须把它诉诸某种合理的表达方式。

克：是的。

博：因此在你传达它的过程中，难道不是依然有着某种洞察的品质吗？你必须找到一种合理的方式来传达它。所以在这么做的过程中，那种洞察所包含的某些真相依然在以这种形式交流着。而这从某种意义上来说也是思想。

克：不，当一个人用语言向别人传达那种洞察时，他的行动是不完整的，除非他拥有洞察。

博：没错。所以你必须传达会给别人带来洞察的东西。

克：你能带给别人洞察吗？

博：不能，但无论你传达什么，都必然会或多或少产生一些也许无法进一步描述的影响。

belief in God.

Dr B: But there is no guarantee that it will happen.

K: No, of course not.

Dr B: That depends on the other person, whether he is ready to listen.

K: So we come to this point: is there a thinking which is non-verbal? Would this be what communicates insight?

Dr B: I would say there is a kind of thinking that communicates insight. The insight is non-verbal, but the thinking itself is not non-verbal. There is the kind of thinking which is dominated by the word and there is another kind of thinking whose order is determined, not by the word, but by the insight.

K: Is the insight the product of thought?

Dr B: No, but insight works through thought. Insight is never the product of thought.

K: Obviously not.

Dr B: But it may work through thought. I wanted to say that the thought through which insight is working has a different order from the other kind of thought. I want to distinguish those two. You once gave an example of a drum vibrating from the emptiness within. I took it to mean that the action of the skin was like the action of thought. Is that right?

K: Yes, that's right. Now, how does insight take place? Because if it is not the product of thought, not the process of organized thought and all the rest of it, then how does this insight come into being?

Dr B: It's not clear what you mean by the question.

K: How do I have an insight that God is a projection of our own desires, images and so on? I see the falseness of it or the truth of it; how does it take place?

克：是的。只有当你自己抛开了对上帝的信仰时，那才能发生。

博：但无法保证那肯定会发生。

克：没错，当然无法保证。

博：那取决于另一个人，他是不是愿意聆听。

克：所以我们来到了这一点上：有没有一种思考是非语言的？是它在传达洞察吗？

博：我会说存在一种传达洞察的思考。洞察是非语言的，而思考本身并不是非语言的。有一种思考是被语言掌控的，还有另一种思考，其秩序是由洞察而不是语言决定的。

克：洞察是思想的产物吗？

博：不是，但洞察通过思想来起作用。洞察绝不是思想的产物。

克：显然不是。

博：但它也许会通过思想来起作用。我想说的是，洞察借以发挥作用的思想与另一种思想拥有一种不同的秩序。我想把这两者区分开来。你曾经举过一个鼓的例子：鼓因为自身内在的空无而振动发声。我理解那个例子的意思是，鼓皮的活动就像是思想的活动，这么说对吗？

克：对，没错。那么，洞察是如何发生的？因为如果它不是思想的产物，不是有组织的思想过程以及诸如此类，那么这种洞察是如何产生的？

博：我不太清楚你这个问题的意思。

克：我如何才能拥有这样一种洞察：上帝是我们自身欲望的投射、意象等之类？我看到了它的虚假性或者它的真实性；这是如何发生的？

博：我不知道你该如何描述这个过程。

Dr B: I don't see how you could expect to describe it.

K: I have a feeling inside that thought cannot possibly enter into an area where insight, where truth is, although it operates anywhere else. But truth, that area, can operate through thought.

Dr B: Yes.

K: But thought cannot enter into that area.

Dr B: That seems clear. We say that thought is the response of memory. It seems clear that this cannot be unconditioned and free.

K: I would like to go into this question, if I may: how does insight take place? If it is not the process of thought, then what is the quality of the mind, or the quality of observation, in which thought doesn't enter? And because it doesn't enter, you have an insight. We said, insight is complete. It is not fragmented as thought is. So thought cannot bring about an insight.

Dr B: Thought may communicate the insight. Or it may communicate some of the data which lead you to an insight. For example, people told you about religion and so on, but eventually the insight depends on something which is not thought.

K: Then how does that insight come? Is it a cessation of thought?

Dr B: It could be considered as a cessation.

K: Thought itself realizes that it cannot enter into a certain area. That is, the thinker is the thought, the observer, the experiencer, all the rest of it; and thought itself realizes, becomes aware, that,it can only function within a certain area.

Dr B: Doesn't that itself require insight? Before thought realizes that, there must be an insight.

K: That's just it. Does thought realize that there must be insight?

克：我内心有一种感觉：思想不可能进入一个洞察、真理所在的领域，尽管它在其他各处运转着。但真理那个领域可以借助思想来运转。

博：是的。

克：但思想无法进入那个领域。

博：这一点看起来很清楚。我们说思想是记忆的反应，它无法解除制约并获得自由，这一点似乎是清楚的。

克：我想探讨一下这个问题，如果可以的话：洞察是如何发生的？如果它不是思想的过程，那么没有思想进入的那种心灵品质或者观察的品质是怎样的？因为思想没有进入，所以我有了洞察。我们说，洞察是完整的，它不像思想那样破碎。所以思想无法带来洞察。

博：思想可以传达那种洞察，或者说它可以传达把你引向洞察的某些信息。比如说，人们告诉了你一些有关宗教之类的事情，但最终那种洞察取决于某种并非思想的东西。

克：那么那种洞察是如何出现的？它是思想的止息吗？

博：可以认为是一种止息。

克：思想自身意识到它无法进入某个领域，也就是说，思想者就是思想，还有观察者、体验者等；而思想自身意识到、觉察到它只能在某个领域中运转。

博：它本身难道不就需要洞察吗？在思想认识到那一点之前，必须先有某种洞察。

克：就是这样。思想认识到必须有洞察吗？

博：我不知道，但是我认为在思想认识到任何事情之前，对思想的本质需要有某种洞察。因为在我看来思想本身是无法认识到任何此类

Dr B: I don't know, but I'm saying there would have to be insight into the nature of thought before thought would realize anything. Because it seems to me that thought by itself cannot realize anything of this kind.

K: Yes.

Dr B.: But in some way, we said, truth can operate in thought, in reality.

K: Truth can operate in the field of reality. Now how does one's mind see the truth? Is it a process?

Dr B: You're asking whether there is a process of seeing. There is no process, that would be time.

K: That's right.

Dr B: Let's consider a certain point, that there is an insight about the nature of thought, that the observer is the observed and so on.

K: That's clear.

Dr B: Now in some sense thought must accept that insight, carry it, respond to it.

K: Or the insight is so vital, so energetic, so full of vitality, that it forces thought to operate.

Dr B: All right, then there is the necessity to operate.

K: Yes, the necessity.

Dr B: But you see, generally speaking it doesn't have that vitality. So in some indirect way thought has rejected the insight, at least it appears to be so.

K: Most people have an insight, but habit is so strong they reject it.

Dr B: I'm trying to get to the bottom of it, to see if we can break through that rejection.

K: Break through the rejection, break through the habit, the conditioning, which prevents the insight. Though one may have an insight,

事情的。

克：是的。

博：但我们说过，真理可以通过某种方式在思想中、在现实中运转。

克：真理可以在现实的领域中运转。那么人的心灵如何才能看到真理？那是一个过程吗？

博：你问是不是有一个看到的过程。没有过程，过程就是时间了。

克：没错。

博：让我们来考虑一个点：对思想的本质存在一种洞察，观察者就是被观察者，等等。

克：这一点很清楚。

博：那么从某种意义来说思想必须接受那种洞察，承载它，回应它。

克：或者那种洞察是如此有活力，如此生机勃勃，充满了生命力，乃至它推动着思想去运转。

博：那好，于是就有了运转的必要。

克：是的，必要性。

博：但是你知道，通常说来它没有那种活力。所以思想以某种间接的方式摒弃了那种洞察，至少看起来是这样的。

克：大部分人都有过某种洞察，但习惯是如此强大，以至于他们摒弃了它。

博：我正试着探究到最底层，看看我们能不能打破这种摒弃。

克：打破那种摒弃，打破阻碍着洞察的习惯和制约。尽管你也许有了洞察，但制约是如此强大，你摒弃了那种洞察。这就是实际发生的

the conditioning is so strong, you reject the insight. This is what happens.

Dr B: I looked up the word "habit" and it says, "A settled disposition of the mind", which seems very good. The mind is disposed in a certain fixed way which resists change. Now we get caught in the same question: how are we going to break that "very settled disposition"?

K: I don't think you can break it, I don't think thought can break it.

Dr B: We are asking for that intense insight which necessarily dissolves it.

K: So, to summarize: one has an insight into truth and reality. One's mind is disposed in a certain way, it has formed habits in the world of reality—it lives there.

Dr B: It's very rigid.

K: Now suppose you come along and point out the rigidity of it. I catch a glimpse of what you're saying—which is nonthinking—and I see it.

Dr B: In a glimpse only.

K: In a glimpse. But this conditioning is so strong I reject it.

Dr B: I don't do it purposely; it just happens.

K: It has happened because you helped to create that happening. Is that glimpse, first of all, strong enough to dissolve this? If it is not so strong, then it goes on. Can this conditioning dissolve? You see, I must have an insight into the conditioning, otherwise I can't dissolve it.

Dr B: Maybe we could look at it like this: conditioning is a reality, a very solid reality, which is fundamentally what we think about.

K: Yes.

Dr B: As we said in the previous dialogue, it's actual. Ordinary reality is not only what I think about, but it fits actuality to some extent—the actual fact. That's the proof of its reality. Now, at first sight it seems that this conditioning is just as solid as any reality, if not more solid.

事情。

博：我查了查"习惯"这个词，字典上说它是"心智的一种固定的倾向"，这个解释听起来很不错。心智倾向于某种固定的抗拒改变的方式。现在我们困在了同一个问题上：我们要如何打破那种"非常固定的倾向"？

克：我不认为你能打破它，我认为思想无法打破它。

博：我们要的是那种足以消除它的强烈的洞察。

克：所以概括一下：一个人对真理和现实有了一种洞察。人的心智倾向于某个特定的方式，它在现实世界中形成了各种习惯——它就生活在那里。

博：它很僵化。

克：现在假设你过来指出了它的僵化。我对你说的话有了惊鸿一瞥——那是非思想性的——然后我看到了真相。

博：只有一瞥而已。

克：只有一瞥。但是制约太强大了，所以我摒弃了它。

博：我不是故意这么做的，它就那样发生了。

克：它就那样发生了，因为你协助了事情的发生。首先，那一瞥有没有强大到能够消除这种制约？如果它不够强大，制约就会继续存在下去。这种制约能够被消除吗？你瞧，我必须洞察那种制约，否则我就无法消除它。

博：也许我们可以这样来看：制约是一个现实，一个非常坚固的现实，从本质上讲它就是我们的所思所想。

克：是的。

博：正如我们在之前的对话中所说，它是实际存在的。通常的现

K: Much more solid. Is that conditioning dissolved, does it come to an end through thing?

Dr B: It won't because thinking is what it is.

K: So thinking won't dissolve it. Then what will?

Dr B: We're back again. We see that it's only truth, insight.

K: I think something takes place. I see I'm conditioned and I separate myself from the conditioning, I am different from the conditioning. And you come along and say "No, it isn't like that, the observer is the observed". If I can see, or have an insight, that the observer is the observed, then the conditioning begins to dissolve.

Dr B: Because it's not solid.

K: The perception of that is the ending of the conditioning. The truth is, when there is the realization that the observer is the observed. Then in that realization, which is truth, the conditioning disappears. How does it disappear? What is necessary for the crumbling of that structure?

Dr B: The insight into the falseness of it.

K: But I can have an insight into something that is false and yet I go on that way, accept the false and live in the false.

Dr B: Yes.

K: Now I don't know if I can convey something. I want to bring this into action in my life. I have accepted reality as truth, I live in that - my gods, my habits, everything—I live in that. You come along and say "Look, truth is different from reality" and you explain it to me. How will I put away that tremendous weight, or break that tremendous conditioning? I need energy to break that conditioning. Does the energy come when I see, "the observer is the observed"? As we've said, I see the importance, rationally, that the conditioning must break down, I see the necessity of it: I see how

实不仅仅是我的所思所想，而且它在一定程度上是符合事实的——实际的事实。这就证明了它的现实性。那么，乍一看来，这种制约似乎和任何现实一样牢固，如果不是更牢固的话。

克：要牢固得多。那种制约能够借助物品来消除或者终止吗？

博：不能，因为思想就是那副样子。

克：所以思想不会消除它。那么什么能消除？

博：我们又绕回来了。我们知道只有真理、洞察能将其消除。

克：我认为有些事情发生了。我发现我受到了制约，我把自己跟制约分离了开来，我与制约是不同的。然后你过来说，"不，不是这样的，观察者就是被观察之物"。如果我能看到，或者洞察到观察者就是被观察之物，那么制约就开始消融了。

博：因为它不再牢固。

克：对这一点的洞察就是制约的终结。真相是，当有了那种领悟，观察者就是被观察之物。然后在那种领悟中，也就是真理中，制约就消失了。它是如何消失的？瓦解那个结构需要什么？

博：对它的虚假性的洞察。

克：但是我也洞察到了某种虚假的东西，同时还继续那样生活，接受虚假并活在虚假中。

博：是的。

克：现在我不知道我能否传达某种东西。我想在生活中把这种洞察付诸行动。我接受了现实就是真理，并活在其中——我的神明，我的习惯，一切——我活在那里面。你过来说，"你瞧，真理与现实是不同的"，然后你解释给我听。我要如何才能抛下那巨大的重负，或者打破那种沉重的制约？我需要能量来打破那种制约。当我看到了"观察者就

it operates, the division, the conflict and all the rest of what is involved. Now when I realize that the observer is the observed, a totally different kind of energy comes into being. That's all I want to get at.

Dr B: Yes, it's not the energy of reality then. I see it better when I say, "the thinker is the thought". It's actually the same thing.

K: Yes, the thinker is the thought. Now, is that energy different from the energy of conditioning and the activity of the conditioning and reality? Is that energy the perception of truth?—and therefore it has quite a different quality of energy.

Dr B: It seems to have the quality of being free of, not being bound by the conditioning.

K: Yes. Now I want to make it practical to myself. I see this whole thing that you have described to me. I have got a fairly good mind, I can argue, explain it, all the rest of it, but this quality of energy doesn't come. And you want me to have this quality, out of your compassion, out of your understanding, out of your perception of truth. You say, "Please, see that". And I can't see it, because I'm always living in the realm of reality. You are living in the realm of truth and I can't. There is no relationship between you and me. I accept your word, I see the reason for it, I see the logic of it, I see the actuality of it, but I can't break it down.

How will you help—I'm using that word hesitantly—how can you help me to break this down? It's your job, because you see the truth and I don't. You say, "For God's sake, see this". How will you help me? Through words? Then we enter into the realm with which I am quite familiar. This is actually going on, you understand? So what is one to do? What will you do with me, who refuses to see something which is just there? And you point out that as long as we live in this world of reality, there is going to be

是被观察之物", 能量是不是就到来了? 正如我们之前所说, 我理智地看到了必须打破制约的重要性, 我看到了它的必要性: 我看到了它是如何运作的, 那些分裂、冲突以及其中所涉及的诸如此类的一切。那么, 当我认识到了观察者就是被观察之物, 一种截然不同的能量就产生了。这就是我想说明的意思。

博: 是的, 那就不再是现实的能量了。如果说"思想者就是思想", 我会更明白一些。那实际上是一回事。

克: 是的, 思想者就是思想。那么, 那种能量与制约的能量、制约和现实的活动是不同的吗? 那种能量是不是对真相的洞察? ——因此它具有一种完全不同的能量品质。

博: 它似乎具有摆脱制约而不被制约所局限的品质。

克: 是的。现在我想让它对我自己具有实际的价值。我看到了你向我描述的这整件事情。我有一颗非常好用的头脑, 我可以争辩、解释, 诸如此类, 但那种品质的能量并没有到来。而因为你的慈悲, 因为你的领悟, 因为你对真相的洞察, 你想让我拥有那种品质。你说, "拜托, 请看到这一点"。而我看不到, 因为我一直生活在现实的领域中。你活在真理的国度, 而我不能。你和我之间没有关系。我接受你说的话, 我看到了其中的道理, 我明白其中的逻辑, 我看到了其中的事实, 但我无法打破它。

你如何才能帮助我——我不太愿意用这个词——你如何才能帮我打破它? 这是你的工作, 因为你看到了真相而我没有。你说, "看在老天的份上, 请看到这一点"。你要如何帮助我? 通过语言吗? 那样我们就会进入我非常熟悉的领域。这实际上就在发生着, 你明白吗? 所以你该怎么办? 你会拿我怎么办? 我拒绝去看一件就摆在那里的事情。然后

murder, death—everything that goes on there. There is no answer in that realm for any of our problems. How will you convey this to me? I want to find out, I'm very keen, I want to get out of this.

Dr B: It's only possible to communicate the intensity. We already discussed all the other factors that are communicated.

K: You see, what you say has no system, no method, because they are all part of the conditioning. You say something totally new, unexpected, to which I haven't even given a single moment of thought. You come along with a basketful and I do not know how to receive you. This has been really a problem; to the prophets, to every...

Dr B: It seems nobody has really succeeded in it.

K: Nobody has. It's part of education that keeps us constantly in the realm of reality.

Dr B: Everyone is expecting a path marked out in the field of reality.

K: You talk of a totally different kind of energy from the energy of reality. And you say that energy will wipe all this out, but it will use this reality.

Dr B: Yes, it will work through it.

K: It's all words to me, because society, education, economics, my parents, everything is here in reality. All the scientists are working here, all the professors, all the economists, everybody is here. And you say "Look", and I refuse to look.

Dr B: It's not even that one refuses, it's something more unconscious perhaps.

K: So in discussing this, is there a thinking which is not in the realm of reality?

Dr B: One might ask whether there is such thought, in the sense of

你指出来，只要我们生活在这个现实世界上，就会有谋杀、死亡——有发生在那里的一切。那个领域中没有解决我们任何一个问题的答案。你要如何把这一点传达给我？我想要搞清楚，我非常恳切，我想从中脱离出来。

博：只可能去传达那种热烈度。我们已经讨论了交流的其他所有因素。

克：你知道，你说的没有体系，没有方法，因为它们都是制约的一部分。你说了某种全新的、始料未及的事情，我之前对它甚至想都没想过。你带着一大堆这样的东西走过来，我不知道该如何听取你的话。这真是一个问题；对于先知，对于每一个……

博：在这件事情上似乎没有人真正成功过。

克：没人成功过。一部分是因为教育一直把我们留在了现实的领域里。

博：每个人都期望现实的领域中有一条标明的道路。

克：你说的是一种与现实的能量完全不同的能量。而且你说那种能量将会消除这一切，但它会运用这种现实。

博：是的，它会借助现实来运转。

克：这些对我来说都是词语，因为社会、教育、经济、我的父母，一切都在这里，在现实世界里。所有的科学家都在这里工作，所有的教授、所有的经济学家，每个人都在这里。而你说"你看"，但我拒绝去看。

博：那甚至不是拒绝，而也许更像是某种无意识的事情。

克：所以在讨论这些的过程中，有没有一种思考不在现实的领域内？

the response of the drum to the emptiness within.

K: That's a good simile. Because it is empty, it is vibrating.

Dr B: The material thing is vibrating to the emptiness.

K: The material thing is vibrating. Wait—is truth nothingness?

Dr B: Reality is some thing, perhaps every thing. Truth is no thing. That is what the word "nothing" deeply means. So truth is "no-thingness".

K: Yes, truth is nothing.

Dr B.: Because if it's not reality it must be nothing—no thing.

K: And therefore empty. Empty being - how did you once describe it?

Dr B: Leisure is the word—leisure means basically "empty". The English root of "empty" means at leisure, unoccupied.

K: So you are saying to me, "Your mind must be unoccupied". It mustn't be occupied by reality.

Dr B: Yes, that's clear.

K: So it must be empty, there mustn't be a thing in it which has been put together by reality, by thought - no thing. Nothing means that.

Dr B: It's clear that things are what we think about, therefore we have to say the mind must not think about anything.

K: That's right. That means thought cannot think about emptiness.

Dr B: That would make it into a thing.

K: That's just it. You see, Hindu tradition says you can come to it.

Dr B: Yes, but anything you come to must be by a path which is marked out in the field of reality.

K: Yes. Now, I have an insight into that, I see it. I see my 1nind 1nust be unoccupied, must have no inhabitants, must be an empty house. What is the action of that emptiness in 1ny life?—because I must live here; I don't know why, but I 1nust live here. I want to find out, is that action different

博：一个人也许会问有没有这样的思想，它就像是鼓对内在的空无所做出的回应。

克：这是个很好的比喻。因为它是空的，所以它在振动。

博：物质在对那种空无产生振动。

克：物质在振动。等一下——真理是空无一物吗？

博：现实是某个东西，也许是所有东西。真理是没有东西（nothing）。这就是"空无一物（nothing）"这个词深层的含义。所以真理就是"空无一物"。

克：是的，真理就是空无一物。

博：因为如果它不是现实，它就必然空无一物——没有东西。

克：所以是空的。空无的存在——你有一次是怎么描述它的？

博：就是闲暇这个词——闲暇基本的意思是"空"。"空"这个英语词根的意思是空闲的，未被占据的。

克：所以你对我说，"你的心必须不被占据"。它一定不能被现实占据。

博：是的，这点很清楚。

克：所以它必须是空的，一定不能有任何一件由现实、由思想所造的东西在里面——没有东西。空无一物就是这个意思。

博：显然东西就是我们的所思所想，所以我们不得不说，心一定不能想着任何东西。

克：没错。也就是说思想也不能想着空无。

博：那就会把它变成一样东西。

克：就是这样。你知道，印度教的传统说你可以到达它。

博：是的，但你到达的任何东西都必定是通过在现实领域中标明

from the other action? It must be, and therefore ...

Dr B: It has to be.

K: And how am I to empty my mind of the content which makes up consciousness? How am I to empty the content? Content is reality, my consciousness is reality.

Dr B: Yes, the consciousness is reality. It's not merely consciousness of reality.

K: No, consciousness is reality. And how is that content to be emptied, so that it is not reality?—let's put it that way.

Dr B: Yes, so it would be no thing.

K: How is it to be done?

Dr B: We've often gone into this question of "how" already. There's something wrong with the question.

K: Of course, something is wrong, because the very word "how" means reality, thought and all the rest of it. Do a miracle!

Dr B: That's what we need.

K: How can you bring about a miracle in a man who lives in this consciousness with its content? I'll trying to find out, is there any action which will dissolve the whole content? Consciousness is not of reality, consciousness is reality. That, I think, is the difference.

Dr B: Let's try to make it more clear. Consciousness is ordinarily thought to reflect reality. But it is reality. In some way we should make it clear that consciousness reflects on what is actual. For example, we have the reality of the table in our 1ninds and we may see its actual effect. So that consciousness is some peculiar combination of reality and actuality, so far as I can see.

K: Yes, I accept that.

Dr B: Could I put it that instead we need truth and actuality? Could

的一条道路达到的。

克：是的。现在，我对此有了洞察，我看到了这一点。我看到了我的心必须不被占据，必须没有东西驻扎，必须是一所空房子。那种空无在我的生活中将会如何行动？——因为我必须生活在这里；我不知道为什么，但我必须住在这里。我想要弄清楚，那种行动与另一种行动不同吗？它必须不同，因此……

博：它必须不同。

克：而我要如何清空构成我的意识的心智内容？我要如何清空那些内容？内容就是现实，我的意识就是现实。

博：是的，意识就是现实。它不仅仅是现实的意识。

克：没错，意识就是现实。而那些内容要如何才能清空，于是它不再是现实——让我们先这样表达。

博：是的，于是它就空无一物。

克：这要如何做到？

博：我们经常探讨"如何"这个问题。这个问题本身就不对劲。

克：当然，是有些不对劲，因为"如何"这词本身就意味着现实、思想以及诸如此类。那就创造一个奇迹吧！

博：那就是我们想要的。

克：你怎么才能在一个活在这种意识及其内容中的人身上创造奇迹呢？我在试着搞清楚，有没有一种行动将会消除这个整个意识？意识并非属于现实，它**就是**现实。我认为这就是区别所在。

博：让我们再试着说得更清楚一些。意识通常指反映现实的思想。但它**就是**现实。我们应该以某种方式说明意识是对事实的思考。例如，我们脑子里有桌子的现实，我们也可以看到它的实际影响。所以那个意

I say that the e1nptiness works in actuality fro1n truth, that the act of emptiness is actuality too?

K: Yes. But we are not in the state of the working of emptiness in actuality. One's mind is always occupied with desires, problems, sex, money, God, what people say—it's never empty.

Dr B: When we start from where we are, it will not be much use to discuss how the empty mind will act because, as you said, our mind is now occupied.

K: You see, after all, one is seeking complete security, that's what one wants, and one is seeking security in reality. Therefore one rejects any other security.

Dr B: Yes, I think there is a conviction that reality is all there is, and that this is the only place where you could find it.

K: Yes. And suppose you come along and say, "Look, in nothingness there is complete security".

Dr B: Yes, let's discuss that, because at first sight it may see1n very implausible.

K: Of course.

Dr B: One might ask how anything can come out of nothing.

K: Just a minute. I say to you, "In nothingness there is complete security and stability". You listen and you get an insight into it because you're attentive and there is a conversation going on between us. And you say, "That is so". But your mind, which is occupied, says, "What on earth does this mean? It's nonsense."

Dr B: Perhaps that would be the first reaction. But later it would be more like this: it sounds reasonable on one side, but on the other side you do have to take care of your real material needs.

识是现实和事实的某种特定组合，依我所见就是这样。

克：是的，我接受这一点。

博：我能不能换成这个说法：我们需要真理和事实？我能不能说空无通过真理在事实中运转，空无的行动也是事实？

克：可以。但我们并不处于"空无在事实中运转"这样的状态中。人的心总是被欲望、问题、性、金钱、上帝和别人说的话所占据——它从来不是空的。

博：当我们从我们的现状出发，讨论空无的心将会如何行动没什么意义，因为正如你所说，我们的心现在被占据着。

克：你知道，毕竟人在寻求彻底的安全，那就是他想要的，而他却在现实中寻找安全。因此他摒弃了其他所有的安全。

博：是的，我想人们确信现实就是所存在的一切，这里就是你能找到安全的唯一场所。

克：是的。假设你过来说："你瞧，空无中有彻底的安全。"

博：是的，让我们探讨一下这一点，因为乍一听来这似乎非常不合情理。

克：当然。

博：人们也许会问从空无一物中怎么可能产生任何东西。

克：等一下。我对你说："空无中有彻底的安全和稳定。"你听了然后对此有了洞察，因为你在全神贯注地听，于是你我之间就发生了一场对话。然后你说："是这样的。"但是你的心被占据着，它说："这究竟是什么意思？真是胡说八道。"

博：也许那是第一反应。但随后也许更可能是这样的：这一方面听起来有道理，但另一方面你确实不得不照顾你实际的物质需要。

K: That's understood.

Dr B: There arises a conflict because what you are proposing appears to be reasonable, but it doesn't seem to take care of your material needs. Without having taken care of these needs you're not secure.

K: Therefore they call the world of reality "maya".

Dr B: Why is that? How do you make the connection?

K: Because they say, to live in emptiness is necessary and if you live there you consider the world as maya.

Dr B: You could say all that stuff is illusion, but then you would find you were in real danger...

K: Of course.

Dr B: So you seem to be calling for a confidence that nothingness will take care of you, physically and in every way. In other words, from nothingness, you say, there is security.

K: No, in nothingness there is security.

Dr B: And this security must include physical security.

K: No, I say, psychological security...

Dr B: Yes, but the question almost immediately arises...

K: How am I to be secure in the world of reality?

Dr B: Yes, because one could say: I accept that it will remove my psychological problems, but I still have to be physically secure as well in the world of reality.

K: There is no psychological security in reality, but only complete security in nothingness. Then if that is so, to me, my whole activity in the world of reality is entirely different.

Dr B: I see that, but the question will always be raised: is it different enough to...

克：这点清楚了。

博：于是就产生了一种冲突，因为你所说的看起来是合理的，但似乎并没有照顾到你的物质需要。如果照顾不到这些需要，你就是不安全的。

克：所以他们把现实世界称为"幻境"。

博：为什么这么说？你是怎么把它们联系到一起的？

克：因为他们说，生活在空无中是必要的，如果你生活在那里，你就会认为这个世界是幻境。

博：你可以说所有那些东西都是幻觉，但然后你会发现自己处于真正的危险中……

克：当然。

博：所以你似乎是在呼吁这样一种信心：那种空无会从身体上以及从各方面照顾你。换句话说，你说的是，安全从空无中来。

克：不，空无中就有安全。

博：而这种安全必须包括身体上的安全。

克：不，我说的是心理上的安全……

博：是的，但问题几乎马上就出现了……

克：我要如何在现实世界中获得安全？

博：是的，因为一个人会说：我接受它会消除我心理上的问题，但在现实世界中我身体上也必须是安全的。

克：现实中没有心理上的安全，只有在空无中才有彻底的安全。如果是这样，那么对我来说，我在现实世界中的所有行为都会是完全不同的。

博：我明白这一点，但是问题始终会出现：那种不同是不是足够……

K: Oh yes, it would be totally different, because I'm not nationalistic, I'm not "English", I am nothing. Therefore our whole world is different. I don't divide...

Dr B: Let's bring back your example of one who understands and the one who wants to communicate to the other. Somehow what doesn't communicate is the assurance that it will take care of all that.

K: It won't take care of all that. I have to work here.

Dr B: Well, according to what you said, there is a certain implication that in nothingness we will be completely secure in every way.

K: That is so, absolutely.

Dr B: Yes, but we have to ask: what about the physical security?

K: Physical security in reality? At present there is no security. I am fighting all my life, battling economically, socially, religiously. If I am inwardly, psychologically, completely secure, then my activity in the world of reality is born of complete intelligence. This doesn't exist now, because that intelligence is the perception of the whole and so on. As long as I'm "English" or "something", I cannot have security. I must work to get rid of that.

Dr B: I can see you'd become more intelligent, you'd become more secure—of course. But when you say "complete security" there is always the question: is it complete?

K: Oh, it is complete, psychologically.

Dr B: But not necessarily physically.

K: That feeling of complete security, inwardly, makes me...

Dr B: It makes you do the right thing.

K: The right thing in the world of reality.

Dr B: Yes, I see that. You can be as secure as you can possibly be if you are completely intelligent, but you cannot guarantee that nothing is

克：噢是的，那会是完全不同的，因为我不再抱持民族主义，我不再是"英国人"，我什么也不是。因此我们的整个世界都不同了。我不划分……

博：让我们回来再看看你说的那个例子：有个人领悟了，他想跟别人沟通这件事情。不知怎的，没有得到沟通的部分是它会照顾一切的那种保证。

克：它不会照顾一切的。我必须在这里下功夫。

博：可是根据你的说法，似乎有某种暗示说：在空无中我们在各方面都是彻底安全的。

克：是这样的，绝对是。

博：是这样的，但我们不得不问：那身体上的安全呢？

克：现实中身体上的安全？现在是没有安全可言的。我毕生都在战斗，从经济上、社会上、宗教上不断斗争。如果我从内在、从心理上是彻底安全的，那么我在现实世界中的行为就产生于彻底的智慧。现在这并不存在，因为那种智慧是对整体等的洞察。只要我是"英国人"或者"什么人"，我就无法拥有安全。我必须下功夫除掉那些。

博：我可以看到，你变得越智慧，你就会越安全——当然了。但是当你说"彻底的安全"，就总是会有这个问题：它是彻底的吗？

克：噢，是彻底的，心理上的。

博：但不一定是身体上的。

克：那种内心彻底的安全感，让我……

博：让你做正确的事。

克：在现实世界中做正确的事。

博：是的，我明白这点。如果你是完全智慧的，你就能够得到最

going to happen to you.

K: No, of course not. My mind is rooted, or established, in nothingness, and it operates in the field of reality with intelligence. That intelligence says, "There you cannot have security unless you do these things".

Dr B: I've got to do everything right.

K: Everything right according to that intelligence, which is of truth, of nothingness.

Dr B: And yet, if something does happen to you, nevertheless you still are secure.

K: Of course—if my house burns down. But you see we are seeking security here, in the world of reality.

Dr B: Yes, I understand that.

K: Therefore there is no security.

Dr B: As long as one feels that the world of reality is all there is, you have to seek it there.

K: Yes.

Dr B: One can see that in the world of reality there is in fact no security. Everything depends on other things which are unknown, and so on. That's why there is this intense fear.

K: You mention fear. In nothingness there is complete security, therefore no fear. But that sense of no fear has a totally different kind of activity in the world of reality. I have no fear—I work. I won't be rich or poor—I work. I work, not as an Englishman, a German, an Arab—all the rest of that nonsense—I work there intelligently. Therefore I am creating security in the world of reality. You follow?

Dr B: Yes, you're making it as secure as it can possibly be. The more clear and intelligent you are, the more secure it is.

大程度的安全，但你无法保证你身上不会发生什么事情。

克：没错，当然不能。我的心扎根于、立足于空无，同时它带着智慧在现实领域中运转。那种智慧说："你在那里无法拥有安全，除非你做这些事情。"

博：我必须把所有事情都做对。

克：依据那种智慧，把所有事情都做对，那具有真理和空无的性质。

博：然而，即使你身上发生了什么事情，你依然是安全的。

克：当然了——如果我的房子烧毁了。但是你知道我们在这里，在现实世界中寻求安全。

博：是的，这点我明白。

克：因此根本没有安全。

博：只要你觉得现实世界就是所存在的一切，你就会在那里寻找安全。

克：是的。

博：你可以看到在现实世界中实际上是没有安全的。一切都取决于未知的其他事物，诸如此类。这就是为什么会有这种强烈的恐惧。

克：你提到了恐惧。空无中有彻底的安全，因而没有恐惧。但是那种无惧感在现实世界中会有一种截然不同的行动。我没有恐惧——我工作。我不会富有也不会贫穷——我就是工作而已。我工作，不是作为一个英国人、德国人、阿拉伯人——所有那些无稽之谈——我在那里智慧地工作。因此我在现实世界中创造着安全。你明白吗?

博：是的，你会把它变得尽可能安全。你越是清晰和智慧，那个世界就越安全。

K: Because inwardly I'm secure, I create security outwardly.

Dr B: On the other hand, if I feel that I depend inwardly on the world of reality, then I become disorganised inwardly.

K: Of course.

Dr B: Everybody does feel that he depends inwardly on the world of reality.

K: So the next thing is: you tell me this and I don't see it. I don't see the extraordinary beauty, the feeling, the depth of what you are saying about complete inward security. Therefore I say, "Look, how are you going to give the beauty of that to me?"

克：因为我内心是安全的，我就能创造外在的安全。

博：另一方面，如果我觉得自己内心依赖这个现实世界，那么我的内心就会变得混乱。

克：当然。

博：每个人都确实觉得自己的内心是依赖这个现实世界的。

克：所以接下来发生的事情就是：你告诉我这些，但我不明白。我看不到你关于彻底的内在安全所说的一切具有的那种非凡的美、感受和深度。于是我说："你瞧，你如何才能把那种美交给我呢？"

CHAPTER 3
第 3 章

THE SEED OF TRUTH

真理的种子

Krishnamurti: If a seed of truth is planted it must operate, it must grow, it must function, it has a life of its own.

Dr Bohm: Many millions of people may have read or heard what you say. It may seem that a large number of them haven't understood. Do you feel that they are all going eventually to see it?

K: No, but it's going on, they are worried about it, they ask, "What does he mean by this?" The seed is functioning, it's growing, it isn't dead. You can say something false and that also operates.

Dr B: Yes, but now we have a struggle between those two and we cannot foresee the outcome of this struggle; we can't be sure of the outcome.

K: You plant in me the seed that, "Truth is a pathless land". Also a seed is planted in my consciousness that says, "There is a way to truth, follow me". One is false, one is true. They are both embedded in my consciousness. So there is a struggle going on. The true and the false, both are operating, which causes more confusion, more misery and a great deal of suffering, if I am sensitive enough. If I don't escape from that suffering what takes place?

Dr B: If you don't escape, then it's clear what will take place. Then you will have the energy to see what is true.

K: That's right.

Dr B: But now let's take the people who do escape, who seem to be a

克里希那穆提：如果真理的种子被种下，它就必定会起作用，它必定会生长，它必定会运作，它有自己的生命。

博姆博士：数百万人也许读到过或者听到过你说的话，然而似乎他们中的大部分人并没有听懂。你觉得他们最终都会明白吗？

克：不会，但事情就在发生着，他们对此感到很焦急，他们问："他这么说是什么意思？"种子在起作用，在生长，它没有死。你也可以说些虚假的事情，那也会起作用。

博：是的，但现在我们在那两者之间有一场斗争，我们无法预见这场斗争的结果；我们无法确定结果会如何。

克：你在我内心种下了这颗种子："真理是无路之国。"同时另一颗种子也种在了我的意识中："有一条通往真理的道路，跟我来。"一个是虚假的，一个是真实的。它们都嵌入了我的意识，所以就发生了一场斗争。真实与虚假都在起作用，这导致了更多的混乱、更多的不幸和大量的痛苦，如果我足够敏感的话。如果我不逃避那种痛苦，那会怎么样？

博：如果你不逃避，那么会发生什么是很清楚的。然后你就会拥有看到真相的能量。

克：没错。

博：但现在让我们以确实会逃避的人为例，这样的人似乎非常多。

large number.

K: They are out, quite right, millions are out. But still, the struggle is going on.

Dr B: Yes, but it is creating confusion.

K: That is what they are all doing.

Dr B: Yes, but we don't know the outcome of that.

K: Oh yes, we do; dictatorship, deterioration.

Dr B: I know, it gets worse. But now we want to get it clear. In a few people who face the suffering, the energy comes to perceive the truth. And in a large number, who escape from suffering, things get worse.

K: And they rule the world.

Dr B: Now what is the way out of that?

K: They say there is no answer to that, get away from it.

Dr B: That also won't do.

K: They say you can't solve this problem, go away into the mountains or join a monastery, become a monk—but that doesn't solve anything. All one can do is to go on shouting.

Dr B: Yes, then we have to say we don't know the outcome of the shouting.

K: If you shout in order to get an outcome, it is not the right kind of shouting.

Dr B: Yes, that is the situation.

K: You talk, you point out. If nobody wants to pay attention it's their business, you just go on. Now I want to go further. You see, there is a mystery; thought cannot touch it. What is the point of it?

Dr B: Of the mystery? I think you could see it like this: that if you look into the field of thought and reason and so on, you finally see it has

克：他们逃离，没错，数百万人会逃离。但斗争依然在继续。

博：是的，但那造成了混乱。

克：那就是他们都在做的事情。

博：是的，但我们不知道这样做的后果。

克：噢不，我们知道后果：独裁、腐败。

博：我知道，情况会变得更糟。但现在我们想把这一点说清楚。在面对痛苦的几个人身上，洞察真理的能量出现了。而在大部分逃避痛苦的人身上，事情变得更糟了。

克：而且他们统治着世界。

博：那么摆脱这种状况的出路是什么？

克：他们说这个问题没有答案，逃开吧。

博：那也没用。

克：他们说你解决不了这个问题，遁入深山或者加入修道院，成为僧侣——但那解决不了任何事情。你所能做的只有继续大声疾呼。

博：是的，那么我们不得不说我们不知道大声疾呼会有什么结果。

克：如果你为了得到某个结果而呼吁，那就不是正确的呼吁。

博：是的，这就是现状。

克：你讲话，你指出。如果没人愿意关注，那是他们的事情，你就那样继续讲下去。现在我想说得更深入一些。你瞧，存在着一种奥秘，思想无法触及它。它有什么意义？

博：奥秘的意义？我想你可以这样来看：如果你探索思想的领域以及理性等，你最终会发现它没有明确的基础。于是你发现"现状"必定超越了那些。"现状"就是那个奥秘。

克：是的。

no clear foundation. Therefore you see that "what is" must be beyond that. "What is" is the mystery.

K: Yes.

Dr B: I mean, you cannot live in this field of reality and thought, because of all we said.

K: No, of course not. But I don't mind, I have no fears.

Dr B: You don't mind because you have psychological security. Even if something happens to you, it does not deeply affect you.

K: I live in the field of reality, that is my life. There I am consciously aware, and I struggle and keep going in that field. And I can never touch the other. I cannot say, "I can touch it; there is no "I" to touch it when you really touch it.

You say to me, "There is a mystery which passes all understanding". Because I am caught in this, I would like to get that. You say there is a mystery, because to you it is an actuality, not an invention, not a superstition, not self-deception. It is truth to you. And what you say makes a tremendous impression on me, because of your integrity. You point it out to me and I would like to get it. Somehow I must get it. What is your responsibility to me?

You understand the position? You say words cannot touch it, thought cannot touch it, no action can touch it, only the action of truth; perhaps it will give you a feeling of that. And I, because I am a miserable human being, would like to get some of that. But you say, "Truth is a pathless land, don't follow anybody"—and I am left.

I realize, I am consciously aware of the limitation of thought, of all the confusion, misery, and all the rest of it. Somehow I can't get out of it. Is your compassion going to help me? You are compassionate, because part

博：我是说，你无法生活在这个现实和思想的领域中，因为我们之前说过的一切。

克：没错，当然不能。但我不介意，我没有恐惧。

博：你不介意，因为你拥有心理上的安全。即使发生了什么事情，也不会深刻地影响你。

克：我活在现实领域中，这就是我的生活。在那里我有明确的意识，我在那个领域中斗争并且一直那样生活。我永远无法触及另一种东西。我不能说"我可以触碰它"；当你真正触及它时，并没有一个"我"在碰触它。

你对我说："有一种奥秘贯穿了所有领悟。"因为我困在这里，我希望得到那个。你说存在一种奥秘，因为对你来说它是一个事实，而不是一种臆想，不是一种迷信，也不是自欺。它对你来说是真的。而你说的话给我留下了极其深刻的印象，因为你的诚恳。你向我指出来，我想得到它。无论如何我必须得到它。此时你对我有什么责任？

你明白这种处境吗？你说语言无法触及它，思想无法触及它，没有行动能够触及它，除了真理的行动：也许那会让你体会到它。而我，因为我是一个不幸的人，我想得到一点儿那种东西。但是你说，"真理是无路之国，不要追随任何人"——然后我就离开了。

我认识到，我明确地意识到了思想的局限，意识到了所有的困惑、不幸以及诸如此类。不知怎的我就是无法脱离出来。你的慈悲要如何帮助我？你是慈悲的，因为那种非凡奥秘的一部分就是慈悲。你的慈悲会帮助我吗？——显然不会。

那么我该怎么办？我极其渴望得到它，而你说："不要有任何渴望，你无法拥有它，它不是你的私人财产。"你只对我说：为现实领域

of that extraordinary mystery is compassion. Will your compassion help me? - obviously not.

So what am I to do? I have a consuming desire for that, and you say, "Don't have any desire, you can't have that, it isn't your personal property". All you say to me is: put order into the field of reality.

Dr B: Yes, and do not escape suffering.

K: If you actually put order into the field of reality then something will take place. And also you say to me, it must be done instantly.

Is that mystery something everybody knows?—knows in the sense that there is something mysterious. Not the desire that creates mysteries, but that there is something mysterious in life apart from my suffering, apart from my death, from my jealousy, my anxiety. Apart from all that, there is a feeling that there is a great mystery in life. Is that it?—that there is a mystery which each one knows?

Dr B: I should think that in some sense everybody knows it. Probably one is born with that sense and it gradually gets dimmed through the conditioning.

K: And has he got the vitality, or the intensity, to put away all that? You see, that means "God is within you"—that is the danger of it.

Dr B: Not exactly, but there is some sort of intimation of this. I think probably children have it more strongly when they are young.

K: Do you think that modern children have that?

Dr B: I don't know about them, probably less. You see, living in a modern city must have a bad effect.

Dr B: There are many causes. One is lack of contact with nature; I think any contact with nature gives that sense of mystery.

K: Yes.

带来秩序。

博：是的，而且不要逃避痛苦。

克：如果你真的把秩序带入了现实领域，那么就会发生一些事情。而且你还对我说，这一点必须瞬间做到。

那个奥秘是每个人都知道的东西吗？——知道的意思是存在某种神秘的东西。不是创造奥秘的愿望，而是生活中存在着某种神秘的东西，它远离了我的痛苦、我的死亡、我的嫉妒、我的焦虑。它远离了那一切，感觉生活中有一种巨大的奥秘。是这样吗？——有一种每个人都知道的奥秘吗？

博：我认为从某种意义来说每个人都知道它。也许人生来就有那种感觉，只是后来因为受到制约，那种感觉渐渐变弱了。

克：而他有那种活力或者热情摒弃那一切吗？你知道，那就意味着"神就在你内心"——这就是危险所在。

博：未必是这样，而是对此有某种暗示。我想也许孩子小时候的感受要强烈一些。

克：你认为现代的孩子有那种感受吗？

博：我不了解他们，也许会少一些。你知道，生活在现代城市里必定会产生恶劣的影响。

克：当然。

博：这有很多原因。原因之一是缺乏与自然的接触；我想与自然的任何接触都会带来那种神奇感。

克：是的。

博：如果你看看夜空，比如说。

克：但是你知道科学家们在解释星辰。

Dr B: If you look at the sky at night, for example.

K: But you see the scientists are explaining the stars.

Dr B: Yes, I understand that.

K: Cousteau explains the ocean; everything is being explained.

Dr B: Yes, the feeling has been created that in principle we could know everything.

K: So knowledge is becoming the curse. You see, perception has nothing to do with knowledge. Truth and knowledge don't go together; knowledge cannot contain the immensity of mystery.

Dr B: Yes, I think if we start with a little child, he may place the mystery in some part that he doesn't know. He could put it at the bottom of the ocean, or somewhere else outside, far away from where he is, and then he learns that people have been everywhere. Therefore the whole thing is made to appear non-existent.

K: Yes. Everything becomes so superficial.

Dr B: That's the danger of our modern age, that it gives the appearance that we know more or less everything. At least that we have a general idea of the scheme, if not of the details.

K: The other night I was listening to Bronowski, "The Ascent of Man". He explains everything.

Dr B: The original impulse was to penetrate into this mystery, that was the impulse of science. And somehow it has gone astray. It gives the appearance of explaining it.

K: May I ask, do you as a trained scientist get the feeling of this mystery.

Dr B: I think so, yes. But I've always had some of that, you see.

K: But in talking now, do you get more of the intensity of it? Not

博：是的，我明白。

克：库斯托在解释海洋；一切都在被解释。

博：是的，这产生了一种感觉：总体说来我们可以知道一切。

克：所以知识变成了诅咒。你知道，洞察与知识无关。真理与知识不是并行的；知识无法包含无限的奥秘。

博：没错，我想如果我们从小孩子开始，他也许会把奥秘放在某个他不知道的地方。他也许把它放在海底或者外面的其他什么地方，远离他所在的地方，然后他发现人们已经无处不在了。所以这整件事情就被弄得好像不存在了。

克：是的。一切都变得如此肤浅。

博：这就是我们现代社会的危险，它制造了一种我们或多或少知道一切的表象。即使我们不知道细节，至少我们对框架有一个大致的概念。

克：有天晚上我在听布鲁诺夫斯基的"人的芬芳"，他解释了一切。

博：最初的冲动是想一探这奥秘的究竟，那就是科学的动力。但不知怎么走偏了，带来了在解释一切的表象。

克：我冒昧问一下，你作为一名受过良好训练的科学家有没有感受到这种奥秘？

博：我想是的，有。但我一直只感受到一些，你知道。

克：但是此刻在谈话的过程中，你有没有更强烈地感受到它？不是因为我感觉很强烈，那就完全是另一回事了，那就变成了影响之类的事情。而是在探讨某件事情的过程中，我们打开了一扇门。

博：是的。我想我所受的特殊制约在很大程度上让我抗拒这个奥

because I feel intense, that's a totally different thing, that then becomes influence and all that. But in talking about something we open a door.

Dr B: Yes. I think that my particular conditioning has a great deal in it to resist this notion of mystery, although I think that science is now going in a wrong direction.

K: But even the scientists admit that there is a mystery.

Dr B: Yes, to some extent. The general view is that it could be eventually cleared up.

K: Cleared up in the sense of explained away.

Dr B: My own feeling is that every particular scientific explanation will be a certain part of this field of reality, and therefore will not clear away the mystery.

K: No, but it clears it away because I listen to you explaining everything, and then I say, "There is nothing".

Dr B: That is the main point of distinguishing between truth and reality, because we could say, in the field of reality we may explain more and more broadly without limit.

K: That is what the present day Communists are doing.

Dr B: Not only the Communists.

K: Of course not, I'm taking that as an example.

Dr B: I think you could say, anything in the field of reality can be explained, we can penetrate more deeply and broadly, there is limitless progress possible. But the essence is not explained.

K: No, I am asking a different question, I'm asking you, in talking like this, do you have an intimation of that mystery. Being a scientist, a serious person, perhaps you had an intimation long ago. In talking now, do you feel it's no longer an intimation but a truth?

秘的概念，尽管我认为科学现在走错了方向。

克：但哪怕是科学家们也承认有某种奥秘存在。

博：是的，在一定程度上是这样的。通常的看法是它也许最终会得到澄清。

克：那种澄清的意思是用解释来应付。

博：我自己的感觉是每一种特定的科学解释都是这个现实领域的一部分，因而不会澄清那个奥秘。

克：不会，但是它把那个奥秘给清除了，因为我听你解释了一切，然后我说："什么也没有。"

博：这就是真理和现实的主要区别，因为我们可以说，在现实领域中我们解释的范围可以无限宽广。

克：这就是共产主义者们如今所做的事情。

博：不仅仅是共产主义者。

克：当然不是，我只是拿它举个例子。

博：我认为你可以说，现实领域中的一切都可以得到解释，我们可以探索得更深、更广，无限的进步是可能的。但本质并没有得到解释。

克：不，我问的是另一个问题，我在问你，在这样的谈话过程中，你有没有得到那种奥秘的一点暗示？作为一个科学家，一个认真的人，也许你很久以前就得到了一种暗示。而在此刻的探讨中，你有没有感觉到那不再是一种暗示而是一个真理？

博：是的，它是一个真理。

克：所以它不再是一种暗示了？

博：我想它成为真理到现在已经有些时间了。因为它就隐含在我

Dr B: Yes, it is a truth.

K: So it's no longer an intimation?

Dr B: I think it's been a truth for some time now. Because it's implied in what we have been doing here at Brockwood.

K: Yes. You see there is something interesting: the truth of that mystery makes the mind completely empty, doesn't it ? it's completely silent. Or because it is silent, the truth of that mystery is.

I don't know if I'm conveying anything. When the mind is completely silent, not in use, not meditated upon, and because it has put order in reality it is free from that confusion, there is a certain silence, the mind is just moving away from confusion. Realizing that is not silence, not moving away from that realization but staying with it, means negating that which order has produced.

Dr B: You say, first you produce order. Why is it necessary to produce the order first and then negate it?

K: To negate is silence.

Dr B: This is why it has to take place in that sequence.

K: Because when I remove disorder there is a certain mathematical order, and as a result of that order my mind is quiet.

Dr B: You say that is not a true silence.

K: No. Realizing that is not true silence I negate the false silence, for the moment. So in the negation of that silence I don't want any other silence. There is no movement towards greater silence. Then this total silence opens the door to that. That is, when the mind, with all the confusion, is nothing—not a thing—then perhaps there is the other.

们在布洛克伍德这里所做的事情中。

克：是的。你看这里有件有趣的事情：那个奥秘所包含的真理让头脑彻底清空了，不是吗？它完全安静了。或者说，因为它安静了，那个奥秘的真实性就出现了。

我不知道我有没有说清楚什么。当心灵完全安静下来，不是在使用中，也不是在对它进行冥想：因为它为现实带来了秩序就能摆脱那种混乱，某种安静就会出现，心灵就会远离混乱。领会到那并不是寂静，不离开那种领悟而是与它共处，就意味着否定秩序所产生的一切。

博：你说首先你建立秩序。为什么需要首先建立秩序然后再否定它？

克：否定就是寂静。

博：那就是为什么必须按那个顺序进行。

克：因为当我消除了失序，就会出现一种精确的秩序，这种秩序的结果就是我的心灵安静了。

博：你说那不是真正的寂静。

克：没错。认识到那不是真正的寂静，我就暂时否定了虚假的寂静。所以在对那种寂静的否定中，我不想要任何别样的寂静，并没有朝向更大寂静的运动。然后这种全然的寂静就打开了通往那奥秘的大门。也就是说，当混乱不堪的心灵一无所是——什么也不是——也许此时另一个事物就出现了。

PART 2
第二部分

Talks and Dialogues
演讲与对话

CHAPTER 4
第 4 章

RIGHT ACTION

正确的行动

We must all be very concerned with what is going on in the world. The disintegration, the violence, the brutality, the wars and the dishonesty in high political places. In the face of this disintegration what is correct action? What is one to do to survive in freedom and be totally religious? We are using the word "religious" not in the orthodox sense, which is not religious. The meaning of that word is: gathering together all energy to find out what is the place of thought and where are its limitations and to go beyond it. That is the true significance and the meaning of that world "religious".

So what is one to do in this disintegrating, corrupt, immoral world, as a human being—not an individual, because there is no such thing as the individual—we are human beings, we are collective, not individual, we are the result of various collective influences, forces, conditioning and so on. As human beings, whether we live in this country, or in America or in Russia or in India, which is going through terrible times, what is one to do? What is the correct, right action? To find this out, if one is at all serious— and I hope we are serious here, otherwise you wouldn't have come—what is one to do? Is there an action that is total, whole, not fragmented, that is both correct and accurate, that is compassionate, religious in the sense we are using that word? This has nothing whatsoever to do with belief, dogma, ritual, or the conditioning of a certain type of religious enquiry. What is a human being confronted with this problem to do?

　　我们一定都非常关心当今世界上正在发生的事情：分崩离析、暴力肆虐、残忍无情，还有战争和政界高层的欺骗。面对这种分崩离析的状况，正确的行动是什么？一个人要怎么做才能生活在自由中，并具有彻底的宗教精神？我们用"宗教"这个词指的并不是传统的含义，那不是宗教。这个词的意思是：把所有的能量都聚集到一起，以发现思想的位置是什么，它的局限在哪里，并超越它。这就是"宗教"这个词真正的意义和内涵。

　　所以，在这个正在崩塌、腐败和不道德的世界上，作为一个人，你该怎么办——不是作为一个个体，因为根本没有个体这回事——我们是人类，我们是一个集体而非个体，我们是各种集体影响、力量和制约等的产物。作为人类，无论我们生活在这个国家，还是生活在美国、俄罗斯或者印度——那里正经历着可怕的时期——我们该怎么办？正确的、恰当的行动是什么？若要搞清楚这一点，如果你真的认真的话——而我希望我们在这里是认真的，否则你就不会来了——我们该怎么办？有没有一种行动是完整的、圆满的、不破碎的，是既正确又恰当的，是慈悲的，并且具有我们所讲的那种意义上的宗教精神？这与信仰、教条、仪式或者某种特定的宗教探询所具有的制约毫无关系。面临着这个问题的一个人该怎么办？

To find an answer, not imaginary, fictitious or pretended, to find the true, the right answer one must enquire into the whole movement of thought. Because all our conditioning, all our activity, all our political, economic, social, moral and religious life is based on thought. Thought has been our chief instrument in all the fields of life, in all the areas, religious, moral, political, economic, social, and in personal relationships: I think that is fairly obvious. Please, if I may point out, we are talking this over together. We are enquiring into this together, sharing it, your responsibility is to share it, not just merely listen to a few ideas, agree or disagree, but to share it; which means you must give attention to it, you must care for it, this problem must be serious, this problem must be something that touches your mind, your heart, everything in life—otherwise there is no sharing, there is no communion, there is no communication except verbally or intellectually and that has very little value. So we are together enquiring into this question.

What is the responsibility of thought?—knowing its limitation, knowing that whatever it does is within a limited area; and in that limited area is it possible to have correct, accurate response and action? At what level does one find for oneself, as a human being, the right action? If it is imaginary, personal, according to an idea, a concept, or an ideal, it ceases to be correct action. I hope we are understanding each other. The ideal, the conclusion is still the movement of thought as time, as measure. And thought has created all our problems; in our personal relationships, economically, socially, morally, religiously, thought has not found an answer. And we are trying to find out if we can, this morning—and in the next two or three talks—what is the action which is whole, non-traditional, non-mechanistic, which is not a conclusion, a prejudice, a belief. That is, I want

若要找到答案，不是想象出来的、虚构的或假装得出的答案，而是找到真实的、正确的答案，你就必须探究思想的整个运动。因为我们所有的局限，我们所有的行为，我们在政治、经济、社会、道德和宗教等方面的一切生活都以思想为基础。思想一直是我们生活的各个领域、各方面——宗教、道德、政治、经济、社会以及人际关系等方面的主要工具：我想这一点是显而易见的。请注意，如果我可以指出的话，我们是在一起探讨这个问题。我们是在一起探询这个问题，分担它，你的责任是分担它，不是仅仅听取几个观点，然后表示同意或不同意，而是来分担它；也就是说你必须对它付出你的注意力，你必须关心它，这个问题必须是很重要的问题，必须是一件触动了你的头脑、你的内心、你生活中一切的事情——否则就不存在分享，不存在交流，也不存在沟通，除了言辞上或观念上的交换，而那意义甚微。所以说我们是在一起探究这个问题。

思想的责任是什么？——知道了它自身的局限，知道了它所做的一切都在一个有限的领域内；而在那个有限的领域内，有没有可能拥有正确的、恰当的回应和行动？作为一个人，你是在哪个层面上亲自去发现正确的行动？如果它是根据某个观点、某个概念或者某个理想想象出来的或者是个人化的，那么它就不再是正确的行动了。我希望我们互相理解了对方的意思。理想、结论依然是思想即时间和衡量的运动。而正是思想制造了我们所有的问题；在我们的个人关系中，无论是从经济上、社会上、道德上还是宗教上，思想都没有找到答案。而今天早上，如果可以的话，我们就要试着去发现完整的、非传统的、不机械的行动

to find out, if I am at all serious, how am I to act?

An action in which there is no pretension, an action that has no regrets, an action that does not breed further problems, an action that will be whole, complete and answer every issue, whether at the personal level, or at the most complex social level. I hope this is your problem. Unless we solve this problem very deeply, talking about meditation, about what is God, what is truth and all the rest of it, has very little meaning. One must lay the foundation, otherwise one cannot go very far. One must begin as close as possible to go very far, and the nearness is you, as a human being living in this monstrous, corrupt society. And one must find for oneself an action that is whole, non-fragmented, because the world is becoming more and more dangerous to live in, it is becoming a desert and each one of us has to be an oasis. To bring about that—not an isolated existence—but a total human existence, our enquiry is into the problem of action.

Can thought solve our problems, thought being the response of memory, experience and knowledge? Memory is a material process; thought is material and chemical—the scientists agree about this. And the things that thought has created in the world and in ourselves is the world of reality, the world of things. Reality means the thing that exists. And to find out what truth is one must be very clear where the limitations of reality are, and not let it flow into the world that is not real.

One observes in the world and in oneself, thought has created an extraordinary complex problem of existence. Thought has created the centre as the "me" and the "you". And from that centre we act. Please look at it, observe it, you will see it for yourself; you are not accepting something the speaker is talking about, don't accept anything. You know, when one begins to doubt everything, then from that doubt, from that uncertainty

是什么，而且它不是一个结论、一种偏见或者一个信念。也就是说，我想弄清楚，如果我真的认真的话，我要如何行动？

一种没有伪装的行动，一种没有遗憾的行动，一种不会进一步滋生问题的行动，一种完整、圆满并且能解答所有问题的行动，无论是个人层面上的，还是最复杂的社会层面上的问题。我希望这就是你的问题。除非我们非常深刻地解决了这个问题，否则谈论冥想、谈论何为神、何为真理以及诸如此类的一切，都没什么意义。你必须首先打下基础，否则你就无法走远。若要走得很远，你就必须尽可能从最近的地方开始，而近处就是你，你作为一个人生活在这个可怕的、腐败的社会上。你必须自己去发现一种完整的、不破碎的行动，因为生活在这个世界上正变得越来越危险，世界正变成一片荒漠，而我们每个人都必须成为一座绿洲。若要实现这一点——不是一种隔绝的生活，而是一种完整的人类生活——我们就要探询行动的问题。

思想就是记忆、经验和知识的反应，它能解决我们的问题吗？记忆是一个物质过程；思想是物质的和机械的——科学家们同意这一点。而思想在世界上和在我们身上所造的一切就是现实世界、物质世界。现实意味着存在的事物。而若要弄清楚真理是什么，你就必须非常清楚现实的局限在哪里，而不让它流入非现实的世界。

你从这个世界和你自己身上观察到，是思想造成了这个错综复杂的生存问题。思想制造了"我"和"你"这样的中心，而我们就从那个中心出发去行动。请看看这一点，观察这一点，你自己会发现的；你不是在接受讲话者说的内容，不要接受任何东西。你知道，当你开始怀疑

grows certainty, clarity; but if you start with imagination, belief, and live within that area you will end up always doubting. Here we are trying to investigate, enquire, look into things that are very close to us: which is our daily life, with all its misery, conflict, pain, suffering, love and anxiety, greed, envy, all that.

As we said, thought has created the "me", and so thought in itself being fragmentary makes the me into a fragment. When you say "I", "me", "I want, I don't want, I am this, I am not that", it is the result of thought. And thought itself being fragmentary, thought is never the whole, so what it has created becomes fragmentary. "My world", "my religion", "my belief", "my country", "my god" and yours, so it becomes fragmentary. Thought intrinsically is a process of time, measure, and therefore fragmentary. I wonder if you see this? If you see this once very clearly, then we will be able to find out what is action, a correct, accurate action in which there is no imagination, no pretension, nothing but the actual.

We are trying to find out what is action that is whole, that is not fragmentary, that is not caught in the movement of time, not traditional and therefore mechanical. One wants to live a life without conflict and live in a society that doesn't destroy freedom, and yet survive. As the societies and governments throughout the world are becoming more and more centralised, more and more bureaucratic, our freedom is getting less and less. Freedom is not what one likes to do, what one wants to do, that is not freedom. Freedom means something entirely different. it means freedom from this constant battle, constant anxiety, uncertainty, suffering, pain, all the things that thought has created in us.

Now is there an action which is not based on the mechanical process of memory, on a repetition of an experience and therefore a continuing in

一切，那么从那种怀疑，从那种不确定性中就会出现确定和清晰；但是如果你从想象和信仰开始并活在那个领域内，你最后就会一直怀疑下去。我们在这里试着去探索、探究、探讨离我们很近的事物：那就是我们的日常生活，以及它所有的不幸、冲突、痛苦、苦难、爱和焦虑、贪婪、嫉妒，那一切。

正如我们所说，思想制造了"我"，所以本身支离破碎的思想让我也变成了一个碎片。当你说"我""自己""我想要，我不想要，我是这个，我不是那个"，这就是思想的产物。而思想本身是支离破碎的，思想从来不是完整的，所以它一手造就的东西也是破碎的。"我的世界""我的宗教""我的信仰""我的国家""我的神"，还有你的这些，所以一切都变得支离破碎。思想本质上就是一个时间和衡量过程，所以它是支离破碎的。我不知道你有没有看到这一点？一旦你非常清楚地看到了这一点，那么我们就能够发现什么是行动，什么是正确、恰当的行动了，其中没有想象，没有假装，什么都没有，只有事实。

我们在试着发现什么是完整的、不破碎的行动，它没有困在时间的运动中，不是传统的因而也不机械。我们想过一种没有冲突的生活，想生活在一个不破坏自由的社会上，同时又能生存下去。由于全世界的社会和政府都变得越来越集权化，越来越官僚，我们的自由正变得越来越少。自由并不是你喜欢做什么，你想做什么，那不是自由。自由意味着一种截然不同的东西，它意味着从这种不停的斗争、不停的焦虑、不确定性、不幸和痛苦，从思想在我们身上制造的一切中解脱出来。

那么，有没有一种行动并非基于记忆机械的过程，并非基于经验

the movement of time as past, present and future? Is there an action that is not conditioned by environment? You know the Marxists say that if you control the environment then you will change man, and that has been tried and man has not changed. Man remains primitive, vulgar, cruel, brutal, violent and all the rest of it, though they are controlling the environment. And there are those who say don't bother about the environment, but believe in some divinity and that will guide you; and that divinity is the projection of thought. So we are back again in the same field. Realizing all this what is a human being to do?

Can thought, which is a material, a chemical process, a thing, which has created all this structure, can that very thought solve our problems? One must very carefully, dill - gently, find out what are the limitations of thought. And can thought itself realize its limitation and therefore not spill over into the realm which thought can never touch? Thought has created the technological world, and thought has also created the division between "you" and "me". Thought has created the image of you and the "me" and these images separate each one of us. Thought can only function in duality, in opposites, and therefore all reaction is a divisive process, a separative process.

And thought has created division between human beings, nationalities, religious beliefs, dogmas, political differences, opinions, conclusions, all that is the result of thought. Thought has also created the division between you and me as form and name; and thought has created the centre which is the "me" as opposed to you, therefore there is a division between you and me. Thought has created this whole structure of social behaviour, which is essentially based on tradition, which is mechanical. Thought has also created the religious world, the Christian, the Buddhist, the Hindu, the Muslim, with all the divisions, all the practices, all the innumerable gurus

的重复，进而不是延续过去、现在和未来这样的时间运动？有没有一种行动是不受制于环境的？你知道马克思主义者说，如果你控制了环境，你就能改变人类，而这已经被检验过了，但人类并没有改变。人类还是那么原始、粗俗、残酷、无情、暴力……诸如此类，尽管他们正在控制环境。还有一些人说，不要为环境费心了，去相信某个神明吧，它会指引你的；而那神明正是思想的投射。所以我们又回到了同一个领域内。认识到了这一切之后，一个人该怎么办？

思想是一个物质过程，一个化学过程，是一种建立了这整个架构的东西，那么思想本身能够解决我们的问题吗？我们必须非常小心、非常认真地去弄清楚思想的局限是什么。那么思想本身能够认识到自己的局限，进而不泛滥到思想所不能触及的领域吗？思想创造了技术世界，思想也制造了"你"和"我"之间的分别。思想建立了你的形象和"自我"，而这些形象离间了我们每一个人。思想只能在二元性中、在对立面中运作，进而所有的反应都是一个分裂过程、一个分离过程。

思想还造成了人类、国家、宗教信仰、教条、政治差异、观点和结论之间的分裂，这一切都是思想的产物。思想也制造了你我之间名与形的分别；思想造就了与你相对立的"我"这个中心，因而我和你之间就有了分别。思想建立了这整个社会行为的架构，这种架构本质上是以机械的传统为基础的。思想还建立了宗教世界，基督教、佛教、印度教、穆斯林，连同它们所有的派别、所有的训练，以及如雨后春笋般涌现的不计其数的古鲁。而且思想也树立了它所认为的爱是什么。慈悲是那种"爱"的结果吗，是思想的结果吗？这就是我们的问题，这些都是

that are springing up like mushrooms. And thought has created what it considers is love. Is compassion the result of "love", the result of thought? That is our problem, those are all our problems.

Yet we are trying to solve all these problems through thought. Can thought see itself as the mischief maker, see itself as a necessary instrument in the creation of a society which is not immoral? Can thought be aware of itself? Please do follow this. Can your thought become conscious of itself? And if it does, is that consciousness part of thought? One can be aware of the activities of thought, and one can choose between those activities as good and bad, worthwhile and not worthwhile, but the choice is still the result of thought. And therefore it is perpetuating conflict and duality. Can thought be attentive to its own movements? Or is there an entity outside the field of thought which directs thought? I can say I am aware of my thoughts, I know what I am thinking, but that entity which says, "I know what I am thinking", that "I" is the product of thought. And that entity then begins to control, subjugate, or rationalize thinking. So there is an entity, we say, which is different from thought: but it is essentially thought. What we are trying to explain is: thought is tremendously limited, it plays all kinds of tricks, it imagines, it creates it.

So our problem then is : can thought realize for itself where it is essential to operate, where it is accurate in its operation, and yet totally limited in every other direction? That means, one has to go into this question of human consciousness. This sounds very philosophical, very complicated, but it isn't. Philosophy means the love of truth, not love of words, not love of ideas, not love of speculations, but the love of truth. And that means you have to find out for yourself where reality is and that reality cannot become truth. You cannot go through reality to come to

我们的问题。

然而我们却试图借助思想去解决所有这些问题。思想能看到它自己就是不幸的制造者，同时看到自己是建立一个不堕落的社会所需的工具吗？思想能觉知自己吗？请务必理解这一点。你的思想能意识到它自己吗？如果它能，那么那个意识还是思想的一部分吗？你能觉察到思想的活动，你也能在那些或好或坏、或值得或不值得的活动中进行选择，但选择依然是思想的产物。因此它是在无休止地延续冲突和二元性。思想能关注它自身的活动吗？还是说，在思想的领域之外有某个实体在指引着思想？我可以说我觉察到了我的思想，我知道我在想什么，但是那个说"我知道我在想什么"的实体，那个"我"还是思想的产物。然后那个实体开始控制、压抑思想或者把它合理化。所以我们说有一个与思想不同的实体，但它实际上还是思想。在这里我们想说明的是：思想是极其有限的，它会玩儿各种把戏，它会想象，它自己制造自己。

所以我们接下来的问题就是：思想自己能不能意识到它在哪里的运作是必要的，它在哪里的运作是精确的，而在其他的任何方向上都完全是局限的？也就是说，你必须探究人类的意识这个问题。这听起来很哲学、很复杂，但实际上不是。哲学的含义是热爱真理，不是热爱词句，不是热爱观念，也不是热爱猜想，而是热爱真理。而这就意味着你必须亲自去弄清楚现实在哪里，而那现实无法成为真理。你无法经由现实到达真理，你必须了解现实的局限，也就是整个思想过程的局限。

你知道，当你审视自己，了解自己的意识，你为什么思考，你的动机是什么，你的目的是什么，你的信仰、你的意图、你的伪装、你的

truth. You must understand the limitations of reality, which is the whole process of thought.

You know, when you look into yourself, knowing your consciousness, why you think, what your motives are, what your purposes are, your beliefs, your intentions, your pretensions, what your imaginations are, all that is your consciousness; and that consciousness essentially is the consciousness of the world. Please do see this. Your consciousness is not radically different from the consciousness of a Muslim, a Hindu, or anybody else, because your consciousness is filled with anxiety, hope, fear, pleasure, suffering, greed, envy, competition; that is cons- ciousness. Your beliefs and your gods, everything is in that consciousness. The content of that makes up your consciousness, and the content of that is thought—thought that has filled consciousness with the things it has created. Look into yourself and you will see how extraordinary obvious it is.

And from this content, which is conditioned, which is the tradition, which is the result of thought, we are trying to find a way to act within that area—within that area of consciousness which thought has filled with the things of thought. And one asks: if thought cannot solve all our human problems—other than technological or mathematical problems— then how can it limit itself and not enter into the field of the psyche, into the field of the spirit?—we can use that word for the moment. As long as we function within that area we must always suffer, there must always be disorder, there must always be fear and anxiety. So my question is: can I, can a human being bring about order in the world of reality? And when thought has established order in the world of reality, then it will realize its own tremendous limitations. I wonder if you see this? We live in a world of disorder, not only outwardly but inwardly. And we have not been able to

想象是什么，这一切都是你的意识；而这个意识实际上就是全世界的意识。请务必看到这一点。你的意识与一个穆斯林、一个印度教徒或者其他任何人的意识并没有显著的不同，因为你的意识装满了焦虑、希望、恐惧、欢愉、痛苦、贪婪、嫉妒和竞争；那就是意识。你的信仰和你的神明，一切都在那个意识中。那些内容就构成了你的意识，而那些内容就是思想——思想用它制造的东西装满了意识。看看你自己，你就会发现这一点是多么显而易见。

而我们试图根据这些内容——这些内容是局限的，它们就是传统，就是思想的产物——在那个领域中找到一种行动方式——在那个思想已经用它制造的东西塞满的意识的领域中。于是我们问：如果思想不能解决我们所有的人类问题——而不是技术或数学问题——那么它怎么能约束自己不进入心灵的领域、精神的领域？——我们可以暂时用一下"精神"这个词。只要我们在那个领域中运转，我们就必然会一直受苦，就必然始终存在失序、恐惧和焦虑。所以我的问题是：我作为一个人，能不能在这个现实世界中带来秩序？而当思想在现实世界中建立起了秩序，它会发现自身所具有的巨大局限。我想知道你们明白这一点了吗？我们生活在一个外在和内在都失序的世界上，而我们一直没能解决这种失序。我们想尽了一切办法——冥想、药物、接受权威、拒绝权威、追求自由、拒绝自由——我们用尽了一切可能的办法来建立秩序——借助强制、借助恐惧——但我们依然活在失序中。一颗失序的心现在试图弄清楚有没有一种正确的行动——你明白吗？一颗失序的心正试图弄清楚有没有一种正确的、恰当的、精确的行动。然而它只会找到一种不正确

solve this disorder. We try everything—meditation, drugs, accepting authority, denying authority, pursuing freedom and denying freedom - we have done everything possible to bring about order—through compulsion, through fear—but we still live in disorder. And a disordered mind is now trying to find out if there is a correct action—you follow? A disordered mind is trying to find out if there is a right, accurate, correct action. And it will find an action which is incorrect, disorderly, not whole. Therefore in the world of reality in which we live we must bring about order. I wonder if you see this?

Order is not the acceptance of authority. Order is not what one wants to do. Order is not something according to a blueprint. Order must be something highly mathematical, the greatest mathematical order is the total denial of disorder, and so within oneself, within the human being. Can you look at your disorder, be aware of it, not choosing particular forms of disorder, accepting some and denying others, but see the whole disorder? Disorder implies conflict, self-centred activity, the acceptance of a conclusion and living according to that conclusion, the ideal and the pursuit of the ideal which denies the actual; can you totally deny all that? It is only when you deny totally all that, that there is order, the order that is not created by thought in the world of reality. You understand? We are separating reality and truth. We say reality is everything that thought has created; and in that area, in that field, there is total disorder, except in the world of technology. In that field human beings live in complete disorder and this disorder is brought about, as we have explained, by conflict, by the pursuit of pleasure, fear, suffering, all that. Can you become aware of all that and totally deny it—walk away from it? Out of that comes order in the world of reality.

In that world of reality behaviour is something entirely different. When you have denied all that, denied the "me", which is the product of

的、失序的、不完整的行动。因此，我们必须在我们所生活的这个现实世界中建立秩序。我想知道你们明白这一点了吗？

秩序并非对权威的接受，秩序不是你想做的事，秩序也不是根据蓝图而来的东西。秩序必须是某种高度精确的东西，最精确的秩序就是对失序的全然否定，在你的内心，在人类的内心也是如此。你能不能看着你的失序，觉察它，不选取某些特定形式的失序，接受一些同时拒绝一些，而是看到失序的整体？失序意味着冲突、自我中心的行为、对结论的接受并根据那个结论生活，还意味着理想以及对理想的追求，而这否定了事实；你能彻底否定那一切吗？只有当你彻底否定了那一切，才会出现秩序，那种并非由思想在现实世界中建立的秩序。你明白吗？我们把现实和真理区分开了。我们说现实是思想所造的一切；在那个领域中，在那个范畴里，存在的是彻底的失序，除了科技界之外。在那个领域中，人类生活在彻底的失序中，而这种失序，正如我们解释过的，是由冲突、对欢愉的追求、恐惧、苦难等那一切造成的。那么，你能觉察到这一切并彻底否定它——脱离它吗？现实世界的秩序从这里就出现了。

那个现实世界中的行为将是完全不同的，当你否定了那一切，否定了"我"——它是思想的产物，是思想造成了分裂，是思想造就了"我"和所谓的超级意识，所有的想象、假装、焦虑、接受和拒绝。这些内容是如此传统，否定那种传统就拥有了秩序。然后我们就能探究真理是什么这个问题了，而不是在之前；否则就会变得浮夸、虚伪、荒唐。在这里，我们必须了解整个恐惧的问题，人类是如何生活在恐惧中

thought, which creates the division, the thought that has created the "me" and the super-conscious, all the imaginations, the pretensions, the anxieties, the acceptance and the denial. That is the content which is so traditional; to deny that tradition is to have order. Then we can go into the question of what truth is, not before; otherwise it becomes pretentious, hypocritical, nonsensical. In that one has to understand the whole question of fear, how human beings live in fear, and that fear is now becoming more and more acute, because the world is becoming so dangerous a place, where tyrannies are increasing, political tyrannies, bureaucratic tyrannies, denying freedom for the mind to understand, to enquire.

So can we as human beings, living in this disorderly, disintegrating world, become actually, not in theory or imagination, an oasis in a world that is becoming a desert? This is really a very serious question. And can we human beings educate ourselves totally differently? We can do that only if we understand the nature and the movement of thought as time, which means really understanding oneself as a human being. To look at ourselves not according to some psychologist, but to look at ourselves actually as we are and discover how disorderly a life we lead—a life of uncertainty, a life of pain, living on conclusions, beliefs, memories. And becoming aware of it, that very awareness washes away all this.

For the rest of this morning can we talk over together, by question and enquiry, what we have talked about? Please, you are asking questions not of me, not of the speaker. We are asking questions of ourselves, saying it aloud so that we can all I share it because your problem is the problem of everybody share. Your problem is the problem of the world, you are the world. I don't think we realize that. You are actually in the world, in the very deepest essence—your manners, your dress, your name and your form

的，而那种恐惧正变得越来越强烈，因为这世界正在变成一个如此危险的地方，暴政在增长，政治暴政、官僚暴政，否定了心智去了解、去探询的自由。

所以，我们作为人类，活在这个失序、分崩离析的世界上，能不能实实在在地——而不是从理论上或想象中——成为这个正在变成荒漠的世界中的一块绿洲？这真的是一个非常严肃的问题。我们人类能不能以完全不同的方式来教育自己？只有当我们理解了思想即时间的本质和运动，也就是真正了解了作为人类一员的自己，我们才能做到这一点。不是参考某个心理学家来观察我们自己，而是如实地了解自己，并发现我们过着怎样一种混乱的生活———种不确定的生活，充满了痛苦的生活，依赖结论、信仰和记忆的生活。觉察到了这些，那种觉察本身就会将那一切涤荡一清。

今天上午剩下的时间，我们可以通过提问和探询的方式来谈谈我们刚刚讲过的内容吗？请注意，你们不是在向我、向讲话者提出问题。我们是在向自己提出问题，请大声说出来好让我们都能一起分担，因为你的问题就是每个人共有的问题。你的问题就是全世界的问题，你就是世界。我不知道我们有没有意识到这一点。在最深层的意义上，实际上你就是世界——你的举止，你的衣着，你的名字和你的外形也许不同——但从根本上，在内心深处，你就是世界，你建立了这个世界，这个世界就是你。所以，如果你提出一个问题，你就是在替全人类提问。我不知道你们有没有明白这一点？——这并不是说你不能提问，恰恰相反。提问于是就变成了一件极其严肃的事情，而不是一个轻率的问题和

may be different—but essentially, deep down, you are the world, you have created the world and the world is you. So if you ask a question you are asking it for the whole of mankind. I don't know if you see that?—which doesn't mean that you mustn't ask questions, on the contrary. Questioning then becomes a very serious matter, not a glib question and a glib answer, some momentary question and forget it till another day. If you ask, ask about a really human problem.

Questioner: Did you say that by walking away from the disorder of traditions we create order? Is that what you meant?

Krishnamurti: Yes, that is what I meant. Now just a minute, that needs a great deal of explanation of what you mean by tradition, what you mean by walking away, what you mean by order.

Q: In addition to that question, the seeing of this disorder already implies that the "see-er" has gone, that you have walked away.

K: There are three things involved in this: order, walking away, and the observation of disorder. Walking away from disorder, the very act of moving away from it, is order. Now first, how do you observe disorder? How do you observe disorder in yourself? Are you looking at it as an outsider looking in, as something separate and there is therefore a division, you and the thing which you are observing? Or are you looking at it, if I may ask, not as an outsider, without the outsider, without the observer who says, "I am disorderly"? Let us put it round the other way. When you look at something, those trees and that house, there is a space between you and that tree and that house. The space is the distance and you must have a certain distance to look, to observe. If you are too close you don't see the whole thing. So if you are an observer looking at disorder, there is a space between you and that disorder. Then the problem arises, how to cover that

一个轻率的答案，某个暂时的问题然后过几天就忘了。如果你提问，请提出一个真正的人类的问题。

提问者：你是不是说，通过脱离传统的失序，我们就能创造秩序？这是你的意思吗？

克里希那穆提：是的，那就是我的意思。但是请等一下，那需要详细解释你说的传统是什么，脱离意味着什么，秩序意味着什么。

问：除了这个问题以外，看到这种失序已经意味着"观者"已经不在了，你已经离开了。

克：这里涉及三件事情：秩序，脱离和对失序的观察。脱离失序，离它而去的行动本身就是秩序。那么首先，你要如何观察失序？你要如何观察自己身上的失序？你是作为一个分离在外的局外人在向内看着失序吗？于是你和你观察的事物之间就有了分裂。还是说你看着它，如果我可以问一下的话，不是作为一个局外者，没有一个局外者，没有一个观察者在说"我是失序的"？让我们换个说法来表达。当我们看着某样东西，看着那些树和那座房子，在你和树以及房子之间存在着一个空间。那个空间就是距离，你必须有一段距离用来看、用来观察。如果你离得太近，你就无法看到事物的全貌。所以，如果你是一个正在看着失序的观察者，你和失序之间就有一个空间。然后问题就产生了：如何跨越那个空间，如何控制那种失序，如何把失序合理化，如何抑制它或者无论你做什么。但是如果没有空间的话你就是失序。我想知道你看到这一点了吗？

问：我如何才能脱离它？

space, how to control that disorder, how to rationalize the disorder, how to suppress it, or whatever you do. But if there is no space you are that disorder. I wonder if you see that?

Q: How can I walk away from it?

K: I am going to show it to you; I am going to go into that. You understand my question?

When you observe your wife, your husband, a boy or a girl—nowadays they don't marry—or your friend, how do you observe him or her? Watch it please. Go into it, it is very simple. Do you observe directly, or do you observe that person through an image, through a screen, from a distance? Obviously, if you have lived with a person - it doesn't matter if it's for a day or ten years —there is an image, a distance. You are separate from her or him. And when you observe disorder you have an image of what order is; or an image which says, "this disorder is ugly". So you are looking at that disorder from a distance, which is time, which is tradition, which is the past. And is that distance created by thought? Or does this distance actually exist? When you say, "I am angry", is anger different from you? No, so you are anger. You are disorderly: not you separate from disorder. I think that is clear.

So you are that disorder. Any movement - please follow this—any movement of thought away from that disorder is still disorder. Because that disorder is created by thought. That disorder is the result of your self-centred activity, the centre that says, "I am different from somebody else" and so on. All that produces disorder. Now can you observe that disorder without the observer?

Q: Then you will find in yourself what you are criticizing in the other?

K: No, no. I am not talking about criticizing the others. That has very little meaning criticizing others.

克：我这就指给你看，我这就探讨这个问题。你明白我的问题吗？

当你观察你的妻子或丈夫、男朋友或女朋友——现在他们都不结婚了——或者你的朋友时，你是如何观察他或她的？请观察一下。探究一下，这很简单。你是直接观察呢，还是透过一个形象、一面屏障从一段距离之外去观察那个人呢？显然，如果你和那个人一起生活过——一天还是十年都无关紧要——就会有一个形象、一段距离，你与她或他就分开了。而当你观察失序时，你会抱有"什么是秩序"这样一个意象，或者有个意象说，"这种失序很丑陋"。所以你是从一段距离之外去看那种失序的，而那段距离就是时间，就是传统，就是过去。那段距离是不是思想制造的？还是说那段距离实际上是存在的？当你说"我很愤怒"时，愤怒和你是不同的吗？不，所以你**就是**愤怒。你就是失序，你与失序并不是分开的。我想这一点清楚了。

所以你就是那种失序。任何运动——请注意听——思想离开那种失序的任何运动都依然是失序，因为失序正是由思想所造。那种失序就是你自我中心行为的结果，那个中心说，"我和别人是不一样的"，等等。这些都造成了失序。那么，你能不能观察这种失序而不带着观察者？

问：然后你会发现自己身上也有你指责别人的那些地方？

克：不，不，我谈的不是指责别人。指责别人没什么意义。

问：不，你在别人身上发现的，你会发现自己身上也有。

克：不，女士。别人就是我；从本质上讲别人就是我。他有他的焦虑、他的恐惧、他的希望、他的绝望、他的不幸、他的痛苦、他的悲伤，他缺乏爱以及诸如此类；那个男人或女人就是我。如果明白了这一

Q: No, what you found in the other, you will find it in yourself.

K: No, madam. The other is me; essentially the other is me. He has his anxieties, his fears, his hopes, his despairs, his suffering, his pain, his loneliness, his misery, his lack of love and all the rest of it; that man or women is me. If that is clear, then I am not criticizing another, I am aware of myself in the other.

Q: That is what I meant.

K: Good. So is there an observation without the past, the past being the observer? Can you look at me, or look at another, without all the memories, all the chicanery, all the things that go on—just look? Can you look at your husband, wife and so on, without a single image? Can you look at another without the whole past springing up? You do, when there is an absolute crisis. When there is a tremendous challenge you do look that way. But we live such sloppy lives, we are not serious, we don't work.

Q: How can you live permanently at crisis pitch?

K: I'll answer that question, sir, after we have finished this.

So the walking away from it is to be totally involved in that which you observe. And when I observe this disorder without all the reactions, the memories, the things that crop up in one's mind, then in that total observation, that very total observation is order. I wonder if you see this? Which raises the question, have you ever looked at anything totally? Have you looked at your political leaders, your religious beliefs, your conclusions, the whole thing on which we live, which is thought, have you looked at it completely? And to look at it completely means no division between you and that which looks. I can look at a mountain and the beauty of it, the line of it, the shadows, the depth, the dignity, the marvellous isolation and beauty of it, and it is not a process of identification. I cannot become the mountain, thank God! That is a trick

点，我就不会指责别人，我能在别人身上看到自己。

问：这就是我的意思。

克：很好。那么有没有一种不带着过去也就是观察者的观察？你能不能看着我或者看着别人，不带着所有的记忆、所有的花招以及如今发生的一切——只是去看？你能看着你的丈夫、妻子等而不抱有丝毫形象吗？你能看着别人而不让整个过去跳出来吗？你可以，当发生重大危机时。当出现了巨大的危机，你确实会那样去看。但是我们过着一种如此懒散草率的生活，我们不认真，我们没有下功夫。

问：你怎么能永远活在危机那样的高度呢？

克：我会回答那个问题的，先生，让我们先把这个说完。

所以脱离失序就需要完全投入你所观察的事物。而当我观察这种失序时不带有任何反应、记忆以及脑子里涌现出来的一切，那么在那完整的观察中，那种完整的观察本身就是秩序。我不知道你有没有明白这一点？于是这个问题就出现了：你可曾完整地看过任何东西？你可曾看着你的政治领袖、你的宗教信仰、你的结论，我们所赖以生活的一切，也就是思想，你可曾完整地看过它？而完整地看就意味着你和所看的事物之间没有分裂。我可以看着一座山并欣赏它的美、它的线条，它的投影、深度、庄严，它神奇的独立与美，这不是一个认同过程。我不会变成那座山，感谢上天！那是想象力的一个伎俩。但是，当我不带着"山"这个词观察时，我发现就有了一种对那种美的全然洞察，激情就从中而来。那么，我能否观察另一个人，我的妻子、朋友、孩子，无论是谁，我能否完整地观察？也就是说，我能否观察而不带着观察者，也

of the imagination. But when I observe without the word "mountain", I see there is a perception of that beauty entirely. A passion comes out of that. And can I observe another, my wife, friend, child, whoever it is, can I observe totally? That means can I observe without the observer who is the past? Which means observation implies total perception. There is only perception, not the perceiver. Then there is order.

Q: If there is only perception and no perceiver, what is it that looks? If I see that I am disorder, what is it that sees it?

K: Now go into it, sir. Disorder is a large word, let us look at it. When you see that you are violent and that violence is not different from you, that you are that violence—what takes place? Let us look at it round the other way.

What takes place when you are not the violence? You say violence is different from "me", what happens then? In that there is division, in that there is trying to control violence, in that there is a projection of a state of non-violence, the ideal, and conformity to that ideal; therefore further conflict, and so on. So when there is a division between the observer and the observed, the sequence is a continuous conflict in different varieties and shapes; but when the observer is the observed, that is when the observer says, "I am violent, the violence is not separate from 'me'", then a totally different kind of activity takes place. There is no conflict, there is no rationalization, there is no suppression, control, there is no non-violence as an ideal: you are that. Then what takes place? I don't know if you have ever gone into this question.

Q: Then what is "you"? One cannot speak without "you".

K: No, madam, that is a way of speaking. Look, please. You see the difference between the observer and the observed. When there is a difference between the observer and the observed there must be conflict in

就是过去？也就是说观察意味着全然的感知。只有感知，而没有感知者。然后就有了秩序。

问：如果只有感知而没有感知者，那么是什么在看？如果我看到我就是失序，那又是什么看到了这一点？

克：现在就来探究一下，先生。失序是一个很大的范畴，让我们来看一下。当你看到了你很暴力，那暴力与你没有任何不同，你就是那暴力——这时会发生什么？让我们换一个角度来看这个问题。

当你不是暴力时会发生什么？你说暴力与"我"是不同的，然后会发生什么？其中就有分裂，其中就有控制暴力的努力，其中就有对非暴力状态的投射、理想以及对那个理想的追随；因而就有了进一步的冲突，等等。所以，当观察者和被观察之物之间有了分裂，其后果就是种类和形式各异的持续不断的冲突；然而，当观察者**就是**被观察之物，也就是当观察者说"我很暴力，暴力与'我'并无不同"，此时一种截然不同的行动就会发生。此时没有冲突，没有合理化，没有压抑、控制，也没有作为理想的非暴力：你就是暴力。然后会发生什么？我不知道你有没有探究过这个问题。

问：那么"你"是什么？如果没有"你"，一个人就无法讲话了。

克：不，女士，"你"只是一种表达方式。请看一下。你看到了观察者和被观察之物之间的差别。当观察者和被观察之物之间存在差别，就必然会有各种形式的冲突，因为存在着分裂。当政治上存在着分裂，当国家层面上存在着分裂，冲突就必然会产生，就像当今世界上所发生的那样。哪里有分裂，哪里就必然会有冲突，这是规律。然而，当

various forms because there is division. When there is a political division, when there is a national division there must be conflict; as is going on in the world. Where there is division there must be conflict; that is law. And when the observer is the observed, when violence is not separate from the observer, then a totally different action takes place. The word "violence" is already condemnatory; it is a word we use in order to strengthen violence, though we may not want to, we strengthen it by using that word, don't we? So the naming of that feeling is part of our tradition. If you don't name it then there is a totally different response. And because you don't name it, because there is no observer different from the observed, then the feeling that arises, which you call violence, is non-existent. You try it and you will see it. You can only act when you test it. But mere agreement is not testing it. You have to act and find out. The next question was about challenge. Must we always live with challenge?

Q: I said crisis.

K: Crisis, it is the same thing. Aren't you living in crisis? There is a political crisis in this country, an economic crisis, crisis with your wife or your husband; crisis means division, doesn't it? Which means crisis apparently becomes necessary for those people who live in darkness, who are asleep. If you had no crisis you would all go to sleep. And that is what we want—"For God's sake leave me alone!"—to wallow in my own little pond, or whatever it is. But crisis comes all the time.

Now a much deeper question is: is it possible to live without a single crisis and keep totally awake? You understand? Crisis, challenge, shock, disturbance exist when the mind is sluggish, traditional, repetitive, unclear. Can the mind become completely clear, and therefore to such a mind there is no challenge? Is that possible?

观察者就是被观察者，当暴力与观察者并不是分开的，此时一种截然不同的行动就会发生。"暴力"一词已经具有谴责意味了；它是一个我们用来强化暴力的词，尽管我们也许本意并非如此，然而我们通过使用那个词强化了暴力，不是吗？所以给那种感受命名是我们传统的一部分。如果你不给它命名，那么就会有一种完全不同的反应。因为你不给它命名，因为没有一个与被观察者不同的观察者，所以出现的那种你称为暴力的感受就不复存在了。你去试一试就会发现这一点的。只有当你检验它的时候你才能行动。但仅仅同意这个说法并不是检验，你得去行动并亲自弄清楚。接下来的问题是关于挑战的。我们必须一直和挑战生活在一起吗？

问：我说的是危机。

克：危机，那是一回事。你难道不正生活在危机当中吗？这个国家中有政治危机、经济危机，还有你和你妻子或你丈夫的危机；危机就意味着分裂，不是吗？也就是说，对那些生活在黑暗中、正在昏睡的人来说，危机显然就变得必要了。如果你们没有危机感，你们就都会睡去。而那就是我们想要的——"看在老天的分上，别管我！"——让我在自己的小水塘里打滚，或者无论怎样。但危机时时刻刻都在出现。

接下来一个更深层的问题是：有没有可能没有丝毫危机地活着，同时又彻底保持清醒？你明白吗？当心智怠惰、因循守旧、惯于重复以及不清晰时，危机、挑战、打击、干扰才会存在。心智能不能变得完全清晰，因而对这颗心来说挑战并不存在？这可能吗？

这意味着我们必须向更深层探究。我们依赖经验来改变我们的心

That means, we have to go deeper still. We live on experiences to change our minds, to further our minds, to enlarge our minds; experiences, we think will create, will open the door to clarity. And we think a man who has no experience is asleep, or dull or stupid. A man who has no experience, but is fully awake, has an innocent mind, therefore he sees clearly. Now is that possible? Don't say yes or no.

Q: When you say he has no experience, do you mean in the sense that he is ignorant of basic life?

K: No, no. Sir, look. We are conditioned by the society in which we live, by the food we eat, clothes, climate. We are conditioned by the culture, by the literature, by the newspapers, our mind is shaped by everything, consciously, or unconsciously. When you call yourself a Christian, a Buddhist, or whatever it is, that is your conditioning. And we move from one conditioning to another. I don't like Hinduism so I jump into Christianity, or into something else. If I don't like one guru I just follow another guru. So we are conditioned. Is it possible to uncondition the mind so that it is totally free? That means is it possible to be aware of your total conditioning—not choose which conditionings you like, but total conditioning, which is only possible when there is no choice and when there is no observer. To see the whole of that conditioning, which is at both the conscious level as well as at the unconscious level, the totality of it! And you can see the totality of something only when there is no distance between you and that—the distance created as movement of thought, time. Then you see the whole of it. And when there is a perception of the whole, then the unconditioning comes into being. But we don't want to work at that kind of thing. We want the easiest way with everything. That is why we like gurus. The priest, the politician, the authority, the specialist, they know,

智、发展我们的心智、扩张我们的心智；我们以为经验具有创造力，会开启通往清晰的大门。我们以为一个没有经验的人是昏睡着的，或者是迟钝的、愚蠢的。但一个没有经验但完全清醒的人，拥有一颗纯真的心，因而他能清晰地洞察。而这可能吗？不要说可能或不可能。

问：当你说他没有经验，你的意思是不是他不懂得最基本的生活常识？

克：不，不是的，先生，请看一下。我们被我们所处的社会、我们所吃的食物、所穿的衣服以及所处的气候所制约。我们被文化、被文学、被报纸所制约，我们的心智有意识或无意识地被一切塑造着。当你称自己为基督教徒、佛教徒或者无论什么，那就是你所受的制约。而且我们从一种制约换到另一种制约。我不喜欢印度教，所以我跳到了基督教或者别的什么。如果我不喜欢一个古鲁，我就去追随另一个古鲁好了。所以我们受到了制约。有没有可能解除心灵所受的制约于是它可以彻底地自由？也就是说，有没有可能觉察你所受的一切制约——不选择你喜欢的那些制约，而是觉察全部制约？只有当毫无选择，当观察者不存在时，这才有可能实现。看到制约的整体，既包括意识层面的也包括无意识层面的，看到它的全部！只有当你和你看的事物之间没有距离时，你才能看到它的整体——那距离由思想、时间的运动所造。此时你就看到了它的全部。而当你洞察了整体，制约的解除就发生了。但我们不想在这种事情上下功夫。关于一切我们都想要最简便的办法，那就是我们喜欢古鲁的原因。牧师、政客、权威、专家，他们知道，而我们不知道；他们会告诉我们该怎么办，这就是我们传统上对权威的接受。

but we don't know; they will tell us what to do, which is our traditional acceptance of authority.

Q: A question about true action. Actually, as we are, every action is a self-centred activity. So when you see that, you are afraid to act because everything has no significance. That is a reality, there is no choice or imagination. You are facing a terrible void and you...

K: I understand the question...

Q: Even material activity.

When there is an observation and you see you can't do anything, then you say there is a void. just hold on to that sentence, to that phrase. There is an observation, you realize you can't do anything and therefore there is a void. Is that so? When I see that I have been able to do something before, there was no void. You understand? I could do something about it, join the Liberal Party, become a neurotic or whatever it is—sorry! (Laughter). Before I could do something and I thought by doing something there was no void. Because I had filled the void by doing something, which is running away from that void, that loneliness, that extraordinary sense of isolation. And now when I see the falseness of this doing, a doing about something —which doesn't give a significance or an answer—then I say to myself, "I observe that I am the observer, and I am left naked, stark naked, void. I can't do anything. There is no significance to existence." Before, you gave significance to existence, which is the significance created by thought, by aU kinds of imaginings, hope and all the rest of it, and suddenly you realize that thought doesn't solve the problems and you see no meaning in life, no significance. So you want to give significance to life—you understand? You want to give it. (Laughter). No, don't laugh, this is what we are doing. Living itself has no meaning for most of us now. When we are young we

问：问个关于真正的行动的问题。事实上，我们现在的每个行动都是以自我为中心的行为。所以当你看到了这一点，你会害怕行动，因为一切都没有意义。这是一个现实，这里没有选择或者想象。你面对着一种可怕的空虚，而你……

克：我明白这个问题……

问：即使物质方面的行为也是如此。

克：当你有一种观察然后发现你什么都不能做，于是你说有一种空虚。现在就来看看这句话、这个表达。你有一种观察，然后你意识到你什么都不能做，因而就有一种空虚。是这样吗？当我发现我过去是能做些事情的，那时就没有空虚。你明白吗？我过去可以做些什么，加入自由党，变成一个神经病或者无论什么——抱歉！（笑声）之前我可以做点儿什么，我以为做点儿事情就不会有空虚了，因为我用做事把那种空虚填满了，而做事实际上是在逃避那种空虚、那种孤独、那种强烈的隔绝感。可现在我看到了这种做事、对某事要做点儿什么的错误——而这并没有带来任何意义或者答案——然后我对自己说："我观察到我就是观察者，我现在完全赤裸，一片空虚。我什么也不能做。生活没有了意义。"之前，你赋予了生活意义，而那是思想通过各种各样的想象、希望以及诸如此类的一切捏造出来的意义，然后你突然意识到思想解决不了问题，你看不到生活的意义和价值。所以你想赋予生活意义——你明白吗？你想给它个意义。（笑声）不，不要笑，这就是我们在做的事情。现在生活本身对我们大多数人来说都是没有意义的。年轻时我们说："哦，至少我会很快乐"——享受性以及诸如此类。随着年纪渐

say, "Well at least I'll be happy"—sex and all the rest of it. As we grow older we say, "My God, it is such an empty life", and you fill that emptiness with literature, with knowledge, with beliefs, dogmas, ritual, opinions, judgements, and you think that has tremendous significance. You have filled it with words, nothing else but words. Now when you strip yourself of words you say, "I am empty, void".

Q: These are still words.

K: Still words, that is what I am saying. Still words. So when you see that thought has created what you considered to be significance, now when you see the limitation of thought, and that what it has created has no significance, you are left empty, void, naked. Why? Aren't you still seeking something? Isn't thought still in operation? When you say, "I have no significance, there is no significance to life", it is thought that has made you say there is no significance, because you want significance. But when there is no movement of thought, life is full of significance. It has tremendous beauty. You don't know of this.

Q: Thought is afraid not to think.

K: So thought is afraid not to think. We will go into that tomorrow: the whole problem of thought creating fear and toying to give significance to life. If one actually examines one's life, there is very little meaning, is there? You have pleasant memories or unpleasant memories, which is in the past, dead, gone, but you hold on to them. There is all this fear of death. You have worked and worked and worked—God knows why—and there is that thing waiting for you. And you say, "Is that all?" So we have to go into this question of the movement of thought as time and measure.

长，我们说，"我的天，生活真是空虚"，然后你用文学、知识、信仰、教条、仪式、观点、评判来填补空虚，你认为那些东西具有巨大的意义。你用来填补空虚的只是言辞而已，只有言辞，别无其他。而现在当你扯掉了那些言辞，你说："我很空虚，空洞无比。"

问：这些依然是言辞。

依然是言辞，这就是我说的意思。依然是言辞。所以，当你看到是思想制造了你所谓的意义，现在你发现了思想的局限，思想所造的一切都没有意义，于是你只剩下一片空虚，赤裸空洞。为什么？你难道不是依然在寻求什么吗？思想难道不是依然在运转吗？当你说"我找不到意义，生活没有意义"时，正是思想让你说没有意义的，因为你想得到意义。但是，当思想的运动不存在时，生活就充满了意义。它有着浩瀚的美，而你不知道这些。

问：思想害怕不思考。

克：所以思想害怕不思考。我们明天会探讨这个问题：造成了恐惧并玩弄生活的意义的思想这整个问题。如果你真正去审视自己的生活，它确实意义甚微，不是吗？你拥有愉快或者不愉快的记忆，而那是过去的、僵死的，已经离去，但你抓住它们不放。还有对死亡的所有恐惧。你一直努力努力再努力——老天知道为什么——可那件事情还是在那里等着你。于是你说："就是这样了吗？"所以我们必须探究思想即时间和衡量的运动这个问题。

CHAPTER 5
第 5 章

THE PROBLEM OF FEAR
恐惧的问题

"If you can be totally free of fear, then heaven is with you."

We must be serious in facing what we have to do in life, with all the problems, miseries, confusion, violence and suffering. Only those live who are really ernest, but the others fritter their life away and waste their existence. We were going to consider this morning the whole complex problem of fear.

The human mind has lived so long, so many centuries upon centuries, putting up with fear, escaping from it, trying to rationalize it, trying to forget it, or completely identifying with something that is not fear—we have tried all these methods. And one asks if it is at all possible to be free totally, completely of fear, psychologically and from that physiologically. We are going to discuss this, talk it over together, and find out for ourselves if it is at all possible.

First, we must consider energy, the quality of energy, the types of energy, and the question of desire; and whether we have sufficient energy to delve deeply into this question. We know the energy and friction of thought; it has created most extraordinary things in the world technologically. But psychologically we don't seem to have that deep energy, drive, interest to penetrate profoundly into this question of fear.

We have to understand this question of thought bringing about its own energy and therefore a fragmentary energy, an energy through friction,

"如果你能彻底摆脱恐惧，那么天堂即与你同在。"

在面对我们在生活中需要做什么这个问题时，我们必须认真对待所有的难题、不幸、困惑、暴力和痛苦。只有那些真正认真的人才是活着的，而其他人则是在虚度着他们的生活，浪费着他们的生命。今天早上我们要一起来思考这整个复杂的恐惧问题。

人类已经存在了那么久，那么多个世纪以来一直在忍受恐惧、逃避恐惧，试图将它合理化，试图忘记它，或者完全与某种并非恐惧的事物相认同——这些方法我们都试过了。而我问的是，究竟有没有可能完全地、彻底地从心理上摆脱恐惧，进而从生理上摆脱恐惧。我们这就来探讨这个问题，一起来谈一谈，并且亲自去发现这究竟有没有可能。

首先，我们必须考虑一下能量，能量的品质、能量的类型以及欲望的问题，看看我们有没有充分的能量来深入探究这个问题。我们知道思想的能量和冲突；它在科技世界中创造了极为非凡的事物。但是在心理上，我们似乎并没有那种深刻的能量、动力和兴趣去深入地穿透恐惧这个问题。

我们必须了解思想这个问题，思想带来了它自身的能量，因而是一种破碎的能量，一种来自摩擦和冲突的能量。这就是我们所知道的一

through conflict. That is all we know: the energy of thought, the energy that comes through contradiction, through opposition in duality, the energy of friction. All that is in the world of reality, reality being the things with which we live daily, both psychologically and intellectually and so on.

I hope we can communicate with each other. Communication implies not only verbal understanding, but actually sharing what is being said, otherwise there is no communion. There is not only a verbal communication but a communion which is non-verbal. But to come to that non-verbal communion, one must understand very deeply whether it is possible to communicate with each other at a verbal level, which means that both of us share the meaning of the words, have the same interest, the same intensity, at the same level, so that we can proceed step by step. That requires energy. And that energy can come into being only when we understand the energy of thought and its friction, in which we are caught. If you investigate into yourself you will see that what we know, or experience, is the friction of thought in its achievement, in its desires, in its purposes—the striving, the struggle, the com. petition. All that is involved in the energy of thought.

Now we are asking if there is any other kind of energy, which is not mechanistic, not traditional, non-contradictory, and therefore without the tension that creates energy. To find that out, whether there is another kind of energy, not imagined, not fantastic, not superstitious, we have to go into the question of desire.

Desire is the want of something, isn't it? That is one fragment of desire. Then there is the longing for something, whether it be sexual longing or psychological longing, or so-called spiritual longing. And how does this desire arise? Desire is the want of something, the lack of something, missing something; then the longing for it, either imaginatively,

切：思想的能量，来自二元性的矛盾、对立的能量，冲突的能量。这一切都存在于这个现实世界中，而现实就是每天与我们生活在一起的事物，既包括心理方面的也包括智力等方面的事物。

我希望我们彼此能相互交流。交流不仅仅意味着语言上的理解，还包含着对所说的话实实在在的分享，否则就不存在交流。既有一种语言上的交流，还有一种非语言的交流。但若要实现那种非语言的交流，你就必须非常深刻地了解有没有可能在语言层面上和彼此交流，也就是说，我们双方共享词语的含义，拥有同样的兴趣、同样强烈的热情，处在同一个层面上，这样我们就可以一步步前进了。这需要能量。而只有当我们理解了思想的能量及其冲突——我们就困在其中——那种能量才能产生。如果你探索你自己，你就会发现我们所知道的一切或者经验，都是思想在它的成就、欲望和目的中产生的冲突——那种努力，那种挣扎，那种竞争。那一切都包含在思想的能量中。

现在我们问的是，有没有另一种能量，它不是机械的、传统的，它没有矛盾，因而也没有产生能量的紧张。若要弄清楚这一点：有没有另一种能量，它不是虚幻的，不是异想天开的，不是迷信的，我们就必须探究欲望的问题。

欲望就是想得到某种东西，不是吗？ 那是欲望的一个碎片。然后还有渴望某种东西，无论是性欲的渴望、心理上的渴望还是所谓灵性渴望。而这种欲望是如何产生的？欲望是想得到某种东西，缺乏某种东西，缺少某种东西；然后就有了对它的渴望，无论是虚幻的还是实际的需要，比如饥饿；然后还有欲望是如何在一个人身上产生的这个问题。

or actual want, like hunger; and there is the problem of how desire arises in one. Because, in coming face to face with fear, we have to understand desire —not the denial of desire, but insight into desire. Desire may be the root of fear. The religious monks throughout the world have denied desire, they have resisted desire, they have identified that desire with their gods, with their saviours, with their jesus, and so on. But it is still desire. And without the full penetration into that desire, without having an insight into it, one's mind cannot possibly be free from fear.

We need a different kind of energy, not the mechanistic energy of thought, because that has not solved any of our problems; on the contrary, it has made them much more complex, more vast, impossible to solve. So we must find a different kind of energy, whether that energy is related to thought or is independent of thought, and in enquiring into that one must go into the question of desire. You are following this?—not somebody else's desire, but your own desire. Now how does desire arise? One can see that this movement of desire takes place through perception, then sensation, contact and so desire. One sees something beautiful, the contact of it, visual and physical, sensory, then sensation, then from that the feeling of the lack of it. And from that desire. That is fairly clear.

Why does the mind, the whole sensory organism, lack? Why is there this feeling of lacking something, of wanting something? I hope you are giving sufficient attention to what is being said, because it is your life. You are not merely listening to words, or ideas, or formulas, but actually sharing in the investigating process so that we are together walking in the same direction, at the same speed, with the same intensity, at the same level. Otherwise we shan't meet each other. That is part of love also. Love is that communication with each other, at the same level, at the same time, with the same intensity.

因为当我们与恐惧面对面时，我们就必须了解欲望——不是否定欲望，而是洞察欲望。欲望也许就是恐惧的根源。全世界的宗教僧侣都否定欲望，他们抗拒欲望，或者把欲望与他们的神明、他们的救世主、他们的耶稣等相认同。但那依然是欲望。如果不彻底穿透那种欲望，没有对它的洞察，你的心灵是不可能摆脱恐惧的。

我们需要另一种能量，而不是思想机械的能量，因为那没有解决我们的任何问题；恰恰相反，它使问题变得更多、更复杂、更广泛、更不可能解决。所以我们必须找到另一种能量，看看那种能量是与思想有关的，还是独立于思想的，而在探询这个问题的过程中，你必须探究欲望的问题。你明白这一点吗？——不是别人的欲望，而是你自己的欲望。那么欲望是如何产生的？你可以看到这种欲望的活动是通过感官知觉发生的，然后有了感受、接触，进而有了欲望。你看到一件漂亮的东西，接触到了它，有了视觉和身体上的感知，然后有了感受，然后从这里就产生了缺乏感，然后就有了欲望。这是显而易见的。

为什么心智——这个整个感官有机体会有缺乏感？为什么会有这种缺乏某种东西、想得到某种东西的感觉？我希望你对我说的话给予了充分的关注，因为这是你的生活。你不是仅仅在听取言辞、观念或者公式，而是在探索过程中实实在在地共同分享，这样我们就能朝着同一个方向、以相同的速度、带着同样强烈的热情、在同一个层面上一起前进。否则我们就无法与彼此相遇。这也是爱的一部分。爱就是在同一个层面、在同一时间、以同样强烈的热情与彼此进行的那种交流。

那么人的内心为什么会有缺乏感或者需求感？我不知道你究竟有

So why is there the sense of lacking or wanting in oneself? I do not know if you have ever gone into this question at all? Why the human mind, or human beings, are always after something—apart from technological knowledge, apart from learning languages and so on and so on, why is there this sense of wanting, lacking, pursuing something all the time? —which is the movement of desire, which is also the movement of thought in time, as time and measure. All that is involved.

We are asking, why there is this sense of want. Why there is not a sense of complete self-sufficiency? Why is there this longing for something in order to fulfil or to cover up something? Is it because for most of us there is a sense of emptiness, loneliness, a sense of void? Physiologically we need food, clothes and shelter, that one must have. But that is denied when there is political, religious, economic division, nationalistic division, which is the curse of this world, which has been invented by the Western world, it did not exist in the Eastern world, this spirit of nationality; it has come recently into being there too, this poison. And when there is division between peoples, between nationalities and between beliefs, dogmas, security for everybody becomes almost impossible. The tyrannical world of dictatorship is trying to provide that, food for everybody, but it cannot achieve it. We know all that, we can move from that.

So what is it that we lack? Knowledge?—knowledge being the accumulation of experience, psychological, scientific and in other directions, which is knowledge in the past. Knowledge is the past. Is this what we want? Is this what we miss? Is this what we are educated for, to gather all the knowledge we can possibly have, to act skilfully in the technological world? Or is there a sense of lack, want, psychologically, inwardly? Which means you will try to fill that inward emptiness, that lack, through or with

没有探究过这个问题？为什么人类的心灵或者说人类，总是在追求某种东西——除了科技知识，除了学习语言等，为什么会有这种需要、缺乏、始终在追求什么的感觉？——也就是欲望的活动，也是作为时间和衡量的思想在时间中的活动。这一切都包含其中。

我们在问为什么会有这种需求感。为什么没有一种完全自足的感觉？为什么会为了实现或者掩盖某种东西而渴望得到某些东西？是不是因为对我们大多数人来说都有一种空虚感、孤独感，一种空洞感？生理上我们需要食物、衣服和栖身之所，那是人必须拥有的。然而这被否定了，因为存在政治、宗教、经济上的划分，还有民族划分——这是这个世界的诅咒，由西方世界所发明，这种民族主义精神在东方世界本不存在；但是这种毒药近来也开始在东方出现了。而当存在着人群、国家、信仰、教条之间的划分，对所有人来说的安全就变得几乎不可能了。独裁者的专制世界正试图提供这种安全，让每个人都有饭吃，但它无法做到。这些我们都知道，我们可以从这个事实出发。

那么我们缺乏的到底是什么？知识吗？——知识是积累的经验，心理方面的、科学方面的以及其他方面的，经验是过去的知识。知识就是过去。这就是我们想要的吗？这就是我们缺乏的吗？这就是我们受教育的目的吗？收集所有我们可能获得的知识，以便在技术世界里熟练地行动？或者是不是从内在、从心理上还有一种缺乏感、需求感？也就是说，你会通过或者借助经验，也就是积累起来的知识，努力去填满那种内在的空虚、那种缺乏。所以你试图用思想制造的东西去填满那种空洞，那种虚无，那种无边的孤独感。因此欲望来自这种填补空虚的渴

experience, which is the accumulated knowledge. So you are trying to fill that emptiness, that void, that sense of immense loneliness, with something which thought has created. Therefore desire arises from this urge to fill that emptiness. After all, when you are seeking enlightenment, or self-realization as the Hindus call it, it is a form of desire. This sense of ignorance will be wiped away, or put aside, or dissipated by acquiring tremendous knowledge, enlightenment. It is never the process of investigating "what is", but rather of acquiring; not actually looking at "what is", but inviting something which might be, or hopeful of a greater experience, greater knowledge. So we are always avoiding "what is". And the "what is" is created by thought. My loneliness, emptiness, sorrow, pain, suffering, anxiety, fear, that is actually "what is". And thought is incapable of facing it and tries to move away from it.

So in the understanding of desire—that is perception, seeing, contact, sensation, and the want of that which you have not, and so desire, the longing for it—that involves the whole process of time. I have not, but I will have. And when I do have it is measured by what you have. So desire is the movement of thought in time as measure. Please don't just agree with me. I am not interested in doing propaganda. I don't care if you are here or not here, if you listen or don't listen. But as it is your life, as it is so urgently important that we be deadly serious—the world is disintegrating— you have to understand this question of desire, energy, and the enquiry into a different kind of non-mechanical energy. And to come to that you must understand fear. That is, does desire create fear? We are going to enquire together into this question of fear, what is fear? You may say, "Well let's forget about energy and desire and please help me to get rid of my fear"— that is too silly, they are all related. You can't take one thing and approach it that way. You must take the whole packet.

望。毕竟，当你追求开悟或者自我实现——这是印度教徒的叫法——那就是欲望的一种形式。通过取得大量的知识或者开悟，那种无知感就会被抹去、摒弃或者消除。而这永远不是探索"现在如何"的过程，而只是一个求取过程；这不是真正去看"现在如何"，而只是在邀请某种也许是或希望是更非凡的经验、更多知识的东西。所以我们总是在逃避"现在如何"，而"现在如何"由思想所造。我的孤独、空虚、悲伤、痛苦、焦虑、恐惧，这就是实际的"现在如何"。而思想没有能力面对它，然后试图逃避它。

所以在对欲望的了解中——欲望就是感知、看到、接触、感受然后想得到你没有的东西，于是欲望、对它的渴望产生了——这涉及整个时间过程。我现在没有，但是我会拥有的。但是当我真的拥有了之后，又会拿你拥有的来衡量。所以欲望是思想在时间即衡量中的运动。请不要仅仅只是赞同我。我对宣传不感兴趣，我不在乎你来不来这里，或者你听不听。但因为这是你的生活，因为我们应该极其认真，这点真的非常重要——这个世界正在崩塌——你必须了解欲望和能量这些问题，并探索另外一种不机械的能量。若要邂逅那种能量，你就必须了解恐惧。也就是说，是不是欲望造成了恐惧？我们这就来一起探询恐惧这个问题，什么是恐惧？你也许会说，"哦，让我们忘掉能量和欲望吧，请帮我除掉我的恐惧"——那就太愚蠢了，它们都是相关的。你不能只选取其中一个然后就那样探究，你必须探究这个整体。

那么什么是恐惧，它是如何产生的？是不是某一个层面上存在恐惧而另一个层面上就没有？恐惧存在于意识层面还是无意识层面？还是

So what is fear, how does it arise? Is there a fear at one level and not at another level? Is there fear at the conscious level or at the unconscious level? Or is there a fear totally? Now how does fear arise? Why does it exist in human beings? And human beings have put up with it for generations upon generations, they live with it. Fear distorts action, distorts clear perceptive thinking, objective efficient thinking, which is necessary, logical sane healthy thinking. Fear darkens our lives. I do not know if you have noticed it? If there is the slightest fear there is a contraction of all our senses. And most of us live, in whatever relationship we have, in that peculiar form of fear.

Our question is, whether the mind and our whole being can ever be free completely of fear. Education, society, governments, religions have encouraged this fear; religions are based on fear. And fear also is cultivated through the worship of authority—the authority of a book, the authority of the priest, the authority of those who know and so on. We are carefully nurtured in fear. And we are asking whether it is at all possible to be totally free of it. So we have to find out what is fear. Is it the want of something? —which is desire, longing. Is it the uncertainty of tomorrow? Or the pain and the suffering of yesterday? Is it this division between you and me, in which there is no relationship at all? Is it that centre which thought has created as the "me" —the me being the form, the name, the attributes—fear of loosing that "me"? Is that one of the causes of fear? Or is it the remembrance of something past, pleasant, happy, and the fear of losing it? Or the fear of suffering, physiologically and psychologically? Is there a centre from which all fear springs? —like a tree, though it has got a hundred branches it has a solid trunk and roots, and it is no good merely pruning the branches. So we have to go to the very root of fear. Because if you can be totally free of fear, then heaven is with you.

说有一种整体上的恐惧？那么恐惧是如何产生的？人类身上为什么会存在恐惧？而人类对恐惧已经忍受了一代又一代，他们与恐惧生活在一起。恐惧扭曲了行动，扭曲了有洞察力的清晰思考、客观高效的思考，而这种思考是必要的、符合逻辑的、理智的、健康的思考。恐惧黯淡了我们的生活。我不知道你有没有注意到这一点？哪怕只有最轻微的恐惧，我们的所有感官都会收缩。而我们大多数人无论处于何种关系，都生活在那种特定形式的恐惧中。

我们的问题是，心灵或者我们的整个存在究竟能否彻底摆脱恐惧。教育、社会、政府和宗教助长了这种恐惧；宗教就基于恐惧之上。而恐惧也通过对权威的崇拜得到了培植——书本的权威，牧师的权威，那些知道的人具有的权威，等等。我们在恐惧中被精心地培养着。而现在我们问，究竟有没有可能彻底摆脱恐惧。所以我们必须弄清楚什么是恐惧。是想得到什么东西吗？——也就是欲望、渴望。是因为对明天的不确定吗？还是昨天的疼痛和苦难？是因为你我之间的这种划分吗？这种划分之中根本没有任何关系可言。是不是因为思想制造的"我"那个中心——"我"就是那个外形、名字和个性——害怕失去那个"我"？这是恐惧的根源之一吗？还是因为对过去有开心、快乐的记忆，因而害怕失去它？或者是因为害怕遭受心理或生理上的痛苦？是不是存在一个所有恐惧得以产生的中心？——就像一棵树，尽管它有千百根枝条，但主干和根部只有一个，单纯修剪枝叶没有任何用处。所以我们必须深入恐惧的根本。因为如果你能彻底摆脱恐惧，那么天堂就与你同在。

恐惧的根源是什么？是时间吗？请注意，我们是在一起探索、一

What is the root of it? Is it time? Please we are investigating, questioning, we are not theorizing, we are not coming to any conclusion, because there is nothing to conclude. The moment you see the root of it, actually, with your eyes, with your feeling, with your heart, with your mind—actually see it—then you can deal with it; that is if you are serious. We are asking: is it time?—time being not only chronological time by the watch, as yesterday, today and tomorrow, but also psychological time, the remembrance of yesterday, the pleasures of yesterday, and the pains, the grief, the anxieties of yesterday. We are asking whether the root of fear is time. Time to fulfil, time to become, time to achieve, time to realize God, or whatever you like to call it. Psychologically, what is time? Is there such a thing—please listen—as psychological time at all? Or have we invented psychological time? Psychologically is there tomorrow? If one says there is no time psychologically as tomorrow, it will be a great shock to you, won't it? Because you say, "Tomorrow I shall be happy; tomorrow I will achieve something; tomorrow I will become the executive of some business; tomorrow I will become the enlightened one; tomorrow the guru promises something and I'll achieve it". To us tomorrow is tremendously important. And is there a tomorrow psychologically? We have accepted it: that is our whole traditional education, that there is a tomorrow. And when you look psychologically, investigate into yourself, is there a tomorrow? Or has thought, being fragmentary in itself, projected the tomorrow? Please, we will go into this, it is very important to understand.

One suffers physically, there is a great deal of pain. And the remembrance of that pain is marked, is an experience which the brain contains and therefore there is the remembrance of that pain. And thought says, "I hope I never have that pain again: that is tomorrow. There has

起询问，我们不是在理论化，我们也不想得出任何结论，因为没什么好总结的。一旦你看到了它的根源，实实在在地看到，用你的眼睛，用你的感受，用你的内心，用你的头脑——真正看到它——那么你就可以处理它了；也就是说如果你认真的话。我们问的是：它的根源是时间吗？——时间不仅仅是钟表上的物理时间，比如，昨天、今天和明天，还包括心理上的时间，对昨天的记忆，昨天的欢愉，昨天的痛苦、悲伤和焦虑。我们问恐惧的根源是不是时间。用来达到什么的时间，用来成为什么的时间，用来成功的时间，用时间来领悟神或者无论你称之为什么。从心理上讲，时间是什么？究竟有没有——请注意听——心理时间这回事？或者是我们发明了心理时间？心理上存在明天吗？如果有人说心理上没有明天这样的时间，那对你来说将是一个巨大的震撼，不是吗？因为你说："明天我会很开心；明天我会实现某个目标；明天我会成为某家企业的主管；明天我会开悟；古鲁承诺了某样东西，明天我就会得到它。"对我们来说，明天太过重要了。然而心理上存在明天吗？我们已经接受了这一点：心理上存在明天，那就是我们的整个传统教育。而当你从心理层面上去看，当你审视你自己，时间存在吗？或者说，是不是本身支离破碎的思想投射出了明天？请注意，我们会探究这个问题，理解它非常重要。

一个人身体上遭受了痛苦，有巨大的疼痛。然后那种疼痛的记忆留下了，那是大脑装载的一个经验，因而就有了对那种疼痛的记忆。然后思想说，"我希望再也不要遭受那种痛苦了"，而这就是明天。昨天有过巨大的快乐，性快感或者人拥有的无论哪种欢愉，然后思想说，

been great pleasure yesterday, sexual or whatever kind of pleasure one has, and thought says, "Tomorrow I must have that pleasure again". You have a great experience—at least you think it is a great experience—and it has become a memory; and you realize it is a memory yet you pursue it tomorrow. So thought is movement in time. Is the root of fear time?—time as comcomparison with you, "me" more important than you, "me" that is going to achieve something, become something, get rid of something.

So thought as time, thought as becoming, is the root of fear. We have said that time is necessary to learn a language, time is necessary to learn any technique. And we think we can apply the same process to psychological existence. I need several weeks to learn a language, and I say in order to learn about myself, what I am, what I have to achieve, I need time. We are questioning the whole of that. Whether there is time at all psychologically, actually; or is it an invention of thought and therefore fear arises? That is our problem; and consciously we have divided consciousness into the conscious and the hidden. Again division by thought. And we say, "I may be able to get rid of conscious fears, but it is almost impossible to be free of the unconscious fears with their deep roots in the unconscious". We say that it is much more difficult to be free of unconscious fears, that is the racial fears, the family fears, the tribal fears, the fears that are deeply rooted, instinctive. We have divided consciousness into two levels and then we ask: how can a human being delve into the unconscious? Having divided it then we ask this question.

It is said it can be done through careful analysis of the various hidden fears, through dreams. That is the fashion. We never look into the whole process of analysis, whether it be self-introspective, or professional. In analysis is implied the analyser and the analysed. Who is the analyser?

"明天我必须再次拥有那种快乐"。你有了一次非凡的体验——至少你认为那是一次非凡的体验——而它变成了一段记忆；你意识到它是一段记忆，然而你明天还是要追求它。所以思想是时间中的运动。恐惧的根源是时间吗？——时间就是和你比较，"我"比你更重要，"我"要达成什么，成为什么，或者去除什么。

所以思想是时间，思想是成为什么，它就是恐惧的根源。我们说过，要学习一门语言，时间是必要的，学习一门技术，时间也是必要的。而我们认为同样的过程可以应用在心理存在上面。我需要几个星期学习一门语言，同时我说，为了了解我自己，了解我现在如何，我必须达成什么，我也需要时间。我们质疑这整个事情。心理上的时间究竟是不是真的存在；还是说，它是思想的发明，恐惧因而得以产生？这就是我们的问题；而我们有意识地把意识分成了意识和潜意识，这还是思想进行的分割。而我们说："我也许能够去除有意识的恐惧，但摆脱潜意识的恐惧及其深藏在潜意识中的根源，几乎是不可能的。"我们说，摆脱潜意识的恐惧，也就是种族的恐惧、家庭的恐惧、部落的恐惧、根深蒂固的本能的恐惧，要困难得多。我们把意识分成了两个层面，然后我们问：一个人要如何才能深入潜意识？在划分了意识之后，我们提出了这个问题。

有人说，通过仔细分析各种隐藏的恐惧、通过梦境就可以深入潜意识。我们从来没有审视过分析的整个过程，无论是自我内省式的还是专业的。分析就隐含了分析者和被分析之物。谁是分析者？他与被分析之物是不同的吗？抑或分析者就是被分析之物？因此分析是完全徒劳无

Is he different from the analysed, or is the analyser the analysed? And therefore it is utterly futile to analyse. I wonder if you see that? If the analyser is the analysed, then there is only observation, not analysis. But the analyser as different from the analysed—that is what you all accept, all the professionals, all the people who are trying to improve themselves—God forbid!—they all accept that there is a division between the analysed and the analyser. But the analyser is a fragment of thought which has created that thing to be analysed. I wonder if you follow this? So in analysis is implied a division and that division implies time. And you have to keep on analysing until you die.

So where analysis is totally false—I am using the word "false" in the sense of incorrect, having no value—then you are only concerned with observation. To observe!—we have to understand what is observation. You are following all this? We started out by enquiring if there is a different kind of energy. I am sorry we must go back so that it is in your mind—not in your memory, then you could read a book and repeat it to yourself, which is nothing. So we are concerned with, or enquiring into energy. We know the energy of thought which is mechanical, a process of friction, because thought in its very nature is fragmentary, thought is never the whole. And we have asked if there is a different kind of energy altogether and weare investigating that. And in enquiring into that we see the whole movement of desire. Desire is the state of wanting something, longing for something. And that desire is a movement of thought as time and measure: "I have had this, and I must have more".

And we said in the understanding of fear, the root of fear may be time as movement. If you go into it you will see that it is the root of it: that is the actual fact. Then, is it possible for the mind to be totally free of

益的。我想知道你明白这一点了吗？如果分析者就是被分析之物，那么就只有观察，没有分析。但分析者与被分析之物是不同的——这就是我们所有人都接受的，所有的专业人员，所有在努力改善自己的人——但愿不要这样！——他们都接受了分析者与被分析者之间存在着区分。但分析者是思想的一个碎片，是思想制造了被分析之物。我想知道你跟上了吗？所以分析中隐含着一种划分，而那种划分就意味着时间。你到死都得一直分析。

所以当分析是完全谬误的——我用"谬误"这个词指的是不正确、没有价值——那么你就只关心观察了。去观察！——我们得弄明白观察是什么。你明白这些吗？我们是从探询有没有另一种能量开始的。抱歉我们必须回顾一下，这样那个问题就能留在你心里——不是留在你记忆里，那样的话你可以去读本书然后重复给自己听，但那毫无意义。所以我们关注或者探究的是能量。我们知道思想的能量——思想是机械的，是一个冲突过程，因为思想的本质就是支离破碎的，思想从来不是完整的。而我们刚才问了有没有一种完全不同的能量，我们正在探究这个问题。在探询这个问题的过程中，我们看到了欲望的整个活动。欲望是想得到某种东西、渴望某种东西的状态。那种欲望是思想即时间和衡量的一种活动："我有了这个，而我必须拥有更多。"

正如我们在了解恐惧的过程中所说的，恐惧的根源也许是时间这种运动。如果你探究这个问题，你就会发现时间就是恐惧的根源：这是一个真切的事实。那么，心灵有没有可能彻底摆脱恐惧？对积累了知识的大脑来说，只有存在彻底的安全时，它才能高效地运转——但那种安

fear? For the brain, which has accumulated knowledge, can only function effectively when there is complete security—but that security may be in some neurotic activity, in some belief, in the belief that you are the great nation; and all belief is neurotic, obviously, because it is not actual. So the brain can only function effectively, sanely, rationally, when it feels completely secure, and fear does not give it security. To be free of that fear, we asked whether analysis is necessary. And we see that analysis does not solve fear. So when you have an insight into the process of analysis, you stop analysing. And then there is only the question of observation, seeing. If you don't analyse, what are you to do? You can only look. And it is very important to And out how to look.

What does it mean to look? What does it mean to look at this question of desire as movement in time and measure?

How do you see it? Do you see it as an idea, as a formula, because you have heard the speaker talking about it? Therefore you abstract what you hear into an idea and pursue that idea—which is still looking away from fear. So when you observe, it is very important to find out how you observe.

Can you observe your fear without the movement of escaping, suppressing, rationalizing, or giving it a name? That is, can you look at fear, your fear or not having a job tomorrow, of not being loved, a dozen forms of fear, can you look at it without naming, without the observer?—because the observer is the observed. I don't know if you follow this? So the observer is fear, not "he" is observing "fear".

Can you observe without the observer?—the observer being the past. Then is there fear? You follow? We have the energy to look at something as an observer. I look at you and say, "You are a Christian, a Hindu, Buddhist", whatever you are, or I look at you saying, "I don't like you",

全也许在某种神经质的行为中，在某个信仰中，在"你是一个伟大的民族"这个信仰中；而所有的信仰显然都是神经质的，因为它不属于事实。所以，只有当大脑感觉彻底安全时，它才能高效地运转，而恐惧无法给它这种安全。要摆脱那种恐惧，我们问分析是不是必要的。而我们发现分析解决不了恐惧。所以，当你对分析过程有了一种洞察，你就停止了分析。此时就只剩下观察和看到的问题了。如果你不分析，你会做什么？你只能去看。弄清楚如何去看，这非常重要。

"看"是什么意思？去看"欲望就是时间和衡量中的运动"这个问题，意味着什么？

你是怎么去看它的？你是不是把它当作一个理念、一个公式来看的，因为你听讲话者说过这方面的事情？所以你把你听到的抽象成了一个理念并追逐那个理念——这依旧是让眼光离开了恐惧。所以当你观察时，弄清楚你是如何观察的，这很重要。

你能不能观察你的恐惧，而没有逃避、压抑、合理化或者给它命名这些活动？也就是说，你能不能看着恐惧，看着你的恐惧，你或许明天没了工作、不被人爱，各种形式的恐惧，你能不能看着它而不命名，也没有观察者？——因为观察者就是被观察之物。我不知道你有没有明白这一点？所以观察者就是恐惧，而不是"他"在观察"恐惧"。

你能不带观察者地观察吗？——观察者就是过去。然后还有恐惧吗？你明白吗？我们拥有作为一个观察者去看事情的能量。我看着你，说"你是一个基督教徒、印度教徒、佛教徒"，无论你是什么，或者我看着你，说"我不喜欢你"或者"我喜欢你"。如果你跟我相信同样的

or "I like you". If you believe in the same thing as I believe in you are my friend; if I don't believe the same thing as you do, you are my enemy. So can you look at another without all those movements of thought, of remembrance, of hope, all that, just look? Look at that fear which is the root of time. Then is there fear at all? You understand? You will And this out only if you test it, if you work at it, not just play with it.

Then there is the other form of desire, which not only creates fear but also pleasure. Desire is a form of pleasure. Pleasure is different from joy. Pleasure you can cultivate, which the modem world is doing, sexually and in every form of cultural encouragement—pleasure, tremendous pleasure and the pursuit of pleasure. And in the very pursuit of pleasure there must be fear also, because they are the two sides of the same coin. joy you cannot invite; if it happens then thought takes charge of it and remembers it and pursues that joy which you had a year ago, or yesterday, and which becomes pleasure. And when there is enjoyment—seeing a beautiful sunset, a lovely tree, or the deep shadow of a lake—then that enjoyment is registered in the brain as memory and the pursuit of that memory is pleasure. There is fear, pleasure, joy. Is it possible - this is a much more complex problem—is it possible to observe a sunset, the beauty of a person, the lovely shape of an ancient tree in a solitary field, the enjoyment of it, the beauty of it—observe it without registering it in the brain, which then becomes memory, and the pursuit of that tomorrow? That is, to see something beautiful and end it, not carry it on.

There is another principle in man. Besides fear and pleasure, there is the principle of suffering. Is there an end to suffering? We want suffering to end physically, therefore we take drugs and do all kinds of yoga tricks and all that. But we have never been able to solve this question of suffering, human suffering, not only of a particular human being but the suffering of

事情，你就是我的朋友；如果我不跟你相信同样的事情，你就是我的敌人。所以，你能不能看着另一个人，没有所有这些思想、记忆、希望之类的活动，而只是看着？看看恐惧，它本身就是时间的根本。此时难道还有恐惧吗？你明白吗？你只有去检验这一点，在这上面下功夫，而不只是闹着玩儿，你才能把这一点搞清楚。

此外还有另一种形式的恐惧，它不仅仅制造了恐惧，还带来了欢愉。欲望是一种形式的欢愉。欢愉不同于喜悦。欢愉你可以培养，现代世界正在这么做，通过性以及各种文化上的鼓励——欢愉，巨大的欢愉以及对它的追求。而对欢愉的追求本身之中必定同时存在着恐惧，因为它们是同一个硬币的两面。你无法邀请喜悦，如果它发生了然后思想接管了它，记住了它，然后去追求你一年前或者昨天有过的那种喜悦，那就变成了欢愉。当你感受到了喜悦——看到一朵美丽的花、一棵漂亮的树或者湖面上深深的倒影——然后那种喜悦感被作为记忆记录在了脑子里，对那个记忆的追逐就是欢愉。所以这里有恐惧、欢愉和喜悦。有没有可能——这是一个复杂得多的问题——有没有可能观看一场日落、一个人的美、独处的一棵古树漂亮的轮廓，它的乐趣，它的美——观察它而不把它记录在脑子里？那会变成记忆，然后明天会去追求它。也就是说，看到美丽的东西然后就此打住，不把它带走。

人类身上还有另一个元素。除恐惧和欢愉之外，还有痛苦这个因素。痛苦可以终结吗？我们希望结束身体上的痛苦，于是我们服用药物，练习各种形式的瑜伽等诸如此类的把戏。但我们从来没能解决痛苦这个问题，人类的苦难，不只是某个人的痛苦，而是全人类的苦难。你

the whole of humanity. There is your suffering, and millions and millions of people in the world are suffering, through war, through starvation, through brutality, through violence, through bombs. And can that suffering in you as a human being end? Can it come to an end in you, because your consciousness is the consciousness of the world, is the consciousness of every other human being? You may have a different peripheral behaviour but basically, deeply, your consciousness is the consciousness of every other human being in the world. Suffering, pleasure, fear, ambition, all that is your consciousness. So you are the world. And if you are completely free of fear you affect the consciousness of the world. Do you understand how extraordinarily important it is that we human beings change, fundamentally, because that will affect the consciousness of every other human being? Hitler, Stalin affected all the consciousness of the world, what the priests have achieved in the name of somebody has affected the world. So if you as human beings radically transform, are free of fear, you will naturally affect the consciousness of the world.

Similarly, when there is freedom from suffering there is compassion, not before. You can talk about it, write books about it, discuss what compassion is, but the ending of sorrow is the beginning of compassion. The human mind has put up with suffering, endless suffering, having your children killed in wars, and willingness to accept further suffering by future wars. Suffering through education-modern education to achieve a certain technological knowledge and nothing else—that brings great sorrow. So compassion, which is love, can only come when you understand fully the depth of suffering and the ending of suffering. Can that suffering end, not in somebody else, but in you? The Christians have made a parody of suffering—sorry to use that word—but it is actually so. The Hindus have

有痛苦，世界上有千百万人也在受苦，因为战争，因为饥荒，因为兽行，因为暴力，因为炸弹。而作为一个人，你身上的痛苦能够结束吗？它能否在你身上终结？因为你的意识就是全世界的意识，就是每一个人的意识。你也许有一些表面上不同的行为，但从根本上，从内心深处，你的意识就是世界上其他每一个人的意识。痛苦、欢愉、恐惧、野心，这一切都是你的意识。所以你就是世界。如果你彻底摆脱了恐惧，你就会影响整个世界的意识。你明不明白，我们人类从根本上改变具有多么重大的意义，因为那将会影响其他每一个人的意识？希特勒、斯大林影响了全世界的意识，牧师们假某人之名所取得的一切，也影响了整个世界。所以，如果你作为一个人从根本上转变了，摆脱了恐惧，那么你自然就会影响全世界的意识。

同样，当你摆脱了痛苦，然后就拥有了慈悲，而不是之前。你可以对它高谈阔论、著书立说，讨论慈悲是什么，但悲伤的终结才是慈悲的开始。人类的心灵一直忍受着痛苦，无尽的痛苦，你们的孩子在战争中被杀害，你们还愿意接受未来的战争所带来的进一步的苦难。教育带来的苦难——现代教育就是获得某些科技知识，别无其他——带来了巨大的悲伤。所以，只有当你完全理解了痛苦的深度并终结了痛苦，慈悲，也就是爱，才会到来。那种痛苦能不能在你身上终结，而不是在别人身上？基督教徒把痛苦变成了一幕荒诞剧——抱歉使用这个词——但确实如此。印度教徒把它变成了一件智力游戏——你前世做了什么，你将会在此生付出代价，如果你现在行为端正，幸福就在未来等着你。但我们现在从来没有端正行为；所以他们抱着这个毫无意义的信仰一如既往地

made it into an intellectual affair: what you have done in a past life you are paying for it the present life, and in the future there will be happiness if you behave properly now. But they never behave properly now; so they carry on with this belief which is utterly meaningless. But a man who is serious is concerned with compassion and with what it means to love; because without that you can do what you like, build all the skyscrapers in the world, have marvellous economic conditions and social behaviour, but without it life becomes a desert.

So to understand what it means to live with compassion, you must understand what suffering is. There is suffering from physical pain, physical disease, physical accident, which generally affects the mind, distorts the mind—if you have had physical pain for some time it twists your mind; and to be so aware that the physical pain cannot touch the mind requires tremendous inward awareness. And apart from the physical, there is suffering of every kind, suffering in loneliness, suffering when you are not loved, the longing to be loved and never finding it satisfactory; because we make love into something to be satisfied, we want love to be gratified. There is suffering because of death; suffering because there is never a moment of complete wholeness, a complete sense of totality, but always living in fragmentation, which is contradiction, strife, confusion, misery. And to escape from that we go to temples, and to various forms of entertainment, religious and non-religious, take drugs, group therapy, and individual therapy. You know all those tricks we play upon ourselves and upon others—if you are clever enough to play tricks upon others. So there is this immense suffering brought by man against man. We bring suffering to the animals, we kill them, we eat them, we have destroyed species after species because our love is fragmented. We love God and kill human beings.

活着。但是一个认真的人，关心慈悲，关心爱意味着什么；因为如果没有爱，你可以做你喜欢的事情，在世界上建造无数的摩天大楼，拥有了不起的经济条件和社会行为，但如果没有爱，生活就会变成一片荒漠。

　　所以，若要了解慈悲地活着意味着什么，你就必须了解痛苦是什么。有来自身体上的疼痛、生理上的疾病、意外的痛苦，这通常会影响心灵、扭曲心灵——如果你在一段时间内一直遭受身体上的疼痛，那会扭曲你的心；若要对此完全觉知乃至身体上的疼痛不会沾染心灵，那就需要无比非凡的内在觉察。除了身体上的疼痛，还有各种各样的痛苦，孤独中的痛苦，当你不被人爱、渴望被爱但从没得到满足的时候，感受到的那种痛苦；因为我们把爱变成了得到满足，我们希望爱能得到满足。还有因为死亡导致的痛苦；痛苦是因为从来没有一刻是全然完满的，没有一刻有那种完整感，而是始终活在支离破碎中，也就是矛盾、挣扎、困惑和不幸中。为了逃避痛苦，我们光顾寺庙，从事各种各样宗教或非宗教的娱乐活动，服用药物，借助什么集体疗法和个人疗法。你知道我们在自己身上和别人身上玩的所有那些把戏——如果你足够聪明，会在别人身上玩把戏的话。所以人与人之间存在着这种因为相互对抗而导致的无尽的痛苦。我们也给动物带来了痛苦，我们屠杀它们，以它们为食，我们已经灭绝了一个又一个物种，因为我们的爱是支离破碎的。我们热爱上帝却屠杀人类。

　　这一切能够结束吗？痛苦能够彻底结束从而让完整而圆满的慈悲出现吗？因为痛苦意味着，这个词的词根义是拥有激情——不是基督教

Can that end? Can suffering totally end so that there is complete and whole compassion? Because suffering means, the root meaning of that word is to have passion—not the Christian passion, not lust, that is too cheap, easy, but to have compassion, which means passion for all, for all things, and that can only come when there is total freedom from suffering.

You know it is a very complex problem, like fear and pleasure, they are all interrelated. Can one go into it and see whether the mind and the brain can ever be free completely of all psychological suffering, inward suffering. If we don't understand that and are not free of it we will bring suffering to others, as we have done, though you believe in God, in Christ, in Buddha, in all kinds of beliefs—and you have killed men generation after generation. You understand what we do, what our politicians do in India and here. Why is it that human beings who think of themselves as extraordinarily alive and intelligent, why have they allowed themselves to suffer? There is suffering when there is jealousy; jealousy is a form of hate. And envy is part of our structure, part of our nature, which is to compare ourselves with somebody else; and can you live without comparison? We think that without comparison we shall not evolve, we shall not grow, we shall not be somebody. But have you ever tried—really, actually tried—to live without comparing yourself with anybody? You have read the lives of saints and if you are inclined that way, as you get older you want to become like that; not when you are young, you spit on all that. But as you are approaching the grave you wake up.

There are different forms of suffering. Can you look at it, observe it without trying to escape from it?—just remain solidly with that thing. When my wife—I am not married—runs away from me, or looks at another man—by law she belongs to me and I hold her—and when she runs away

的激情，也不是性欲，那太廉价、太容易了，而是拥有慈悲，也就是
对一切、对万物的激情，而只有当彻底从痛苦中解脱时，那种慈悲才
会到来。

　　你知道这是一个非常复杂的问题，就像恐惧和欢愉一样，它们都
是互相关联的。你能不能深入探究这个问题，看看心灵和头脑究竟能不
能彻底摆脱所有心理上的、内在的痛苦。如果我们不明白这一点，如果
我们没有摆脱痛苦，我们就会给他人带来痛苦，就像我们之前所做的那
样，尽管你们相信上帝、基督、佛陀以及各种信仰——但你们一代又一
代地杀害了无数人类。你明白我们做了些什么，我们的政客在印度和这
里都做了些什么。为什么认为自己无比有活力以及智慧的人类，允许他
们自己受苦？有嫉妒时也会有痛苦；嫉妒是一种仇恨。而羡妒是我们结
构的一部分，我们本性的一部分，也就是拿自己跟别人比较；那么你能
不比较地活着吗？我们以为不比较我们就不会进步，我们就不会成长，
我们就不会功成名就。但你究竟有没有试过——真正地、实际地尝试
过——活着但不拿自己跟任何人比较？你读过无数圣人的生平故事，如
果你倾向于像他们那样，当你年纪渐长时你就想要变成那样；你年轻的
时候不会那么做，你会唾弃那一切。但是当你越来越接近坟墓时，你似
乎就醒悟了。

　　有各种不同形式的痛苦。你能不能看着它、观察它而不试图逃避
它？——只是实实在在地和那件事情待在一起。当我妻子——我没结
婚——离我而去或者在看别的男人——依照法律她是属于我的，我拥有
她——当她离我而去，我就嫉妒；因为我要占有，在占有中我觉得满

from me I am jealous; because I possess, and in possession I feel satisfied, I feel safe; and also it is good to be possessed, that also gives satisfaction. And that jealousy, that envy, that hatred, can you look at it without any movement of thought and remain with it? You understand what I am saying? Jealousy is a reaction, a reaction which has been named through memory as jealousy, and I have been educated to run away from it, to rationalize it, or to indulge in it, and hate with anger and all the rest of it. But without doing any of that, can my mind solidly remain with it without any movement? You understand what I am saying? Do it and you will see what happens.

In the same way when you suffer, psychologically, remain with it completely without a single movement of thought. Then you will see out of that suffering comes that strange thing called passion. And if you have no passion of that kind you cannot be creative. Out of that suffering comes compassion. And that energy differs totally from the mechanistic energy of thought.

足，觉得安全；而且被占有也很好，那也能带来满足。而那种嫉妒、那种羡慕、那种仇恨，你能不带任何思想活动地看着它并与之共处吗？你明白我说的意思吗？嫉妒是一种反应，是通过记忆被命名为嫉妒的一种反应，而我所受的教育是要逃避它，把它合理化或者沉溺于它，还有报之以愤怒的仇恨，等等。但是，如果不做任何此类的事情，你的心能不能丝毫不动地、实实在在地和它待在一起？你明白我说的话吗？去这么做，然后你就会看到会发生什么。

同样，当你心理上遭受痛苦时，完全与它待在一起，没有丝毫思想活动。然后你就会发现，从那种痛苦中产生了一种叫作激情的奇特事物。如果你没有那种激情，你就不可能具有创造性。慈悲就从那种痛苦中而来，而那种能量与思想机械的能量完全不同。

CHAPTER 6
第 6 章

DIALOGUE I
对话一

"Nobody can put you psychologically into prison. You are already there!"

Krishnamurti: This is in the nature of a dialogue between two friends, talking over their problems, who are concerned not only with their own personal affairs, but also with what is happening in the world. Being serious, these two friends have the urge to transform themselves and see what they can do about the world and all the misery and confusion that is going on. So could we this morning spend some time together having a friendly conversation, not trying to be clever, nor opposing one opinion against another opinion or belief, and together examine earnestly and deeply some of the problems that we have? In this, communication becomes rather important; and any one question is not only personal but universal. So if that is understood, then what shall we talk over together this morning?

Questioner: The compilation of your biography has caused much confusion and quite a lot of questions. I have boiled them down to a few. May I at least hand them over to you.

K: Do you want to discuss the biography written by Mary Lutyens? Do you want to go into that?

Q: No.

K: Thank God! (laughter).

Q(1): Briefly and then finish with it.

Q(2): I would propose that you go into the question of correct and

"没人能从心理上把你投入牢笼。你已经身处其中了！"

克里希那穆提：两个朋友之间对话的本质就在于一起探讨他们的问题，他们不仅关心自己个人的事情，而且关心这个世界上所发生的一切。带着认真的态度，这两个朋友感到迫切需要转变自身，看看对于这个世界以及正在发生的所有不幸和混乱他们能做些什么。所以，今天早上我们能不能一起花些时间进行一场友好的对话，不是看谁聪明，也不是用一个观点去反对另一个观点或信仰，而是一起真诚地、深入地审视我们的某些问题？在这当中，交流就变得相当重要了；而且任何一个问题都不仅仅是个人的，也是全世界共有的。所以，如果这一点清楚了，那么我们今天早上要一起来谈点儿什么呢？

提问者：你个人传记的编纂引来了很多困惑和不少疑问。我已经把它们归结成了几个，请允许我冒昧地把它们递给你。

克：你们想讨论玛丽·勒琴斯写的传记吗？你们想探讨这个吗？

问：不想。

克：感谢上帝！（笑声）

问（1）：简单说说然后就结束。

问（2）：我提议你谈谈正确和不正确的思考这个问题：这是一个

incorrect thinking: that is a problem. Both kinds of thought, or thinking processes, are mechanical processes.

K: I see. Can we discuss this? Do you want to talk over the biography —have many of you read it? Some of you. I was just looking at it this morning (laughter). Most of it I have forgotten and if you want to talk over some of the questions that have been given me, shall we do that briefly?

Basically the question is: what is the relationship between the present K and the former K? (laughter). I should think very little. The basic question is, how was it that the boy who was found there, "discovered" as it was called, how was it that he was not conditioned at all from the beginning, though he was brought up in a very orthodox, traditional Brahmin family with its superstitions, arrogance and extraordinary religious sense of morality and so on? Why wasn't he conditioned then? And also later during those periods of the Masters, Initiations and so on—if you have read about it—why wasn't he conditioned? And what is the relationship between that person and the present person? Are you really interested in all this?

Audience: Yes.

K: I am not. The past is dead, buried and gone. I don't know how to tackle this. One of the questions is about the Masters, as they are explained not only in Theosophy but in the Hindu tradition and in the Tibetan tradition, which maintain that there is a Bodhisattva; and that he manifests himself and that is called in Sanskrit Avatar, which means manifestation. This boy was discovered and prepared for that manifestation. And he went through all kinds of things. And one question that may be asked is, must others go through the same process. Christopher Columbus discovered America with sailing boats in dangerous seas and so on, and must we go through all that to go to America? You understand my question? It is much

难题。这两种思想或者思考过程，都是机械的过程。

克：我明白了。我们可以讨论这个问题吗？你们想讨论传记吗？——你们有多少人读过？有一些。我今天早上才开始看（笑声）。其中的大部分内容我都忘了，而如果你们想探讨我刚刚收到的一些问题，我们可以简要地过一遍吗？

基本上就是这个问题：现在的克和以前的克有什么关系？（笑声）我会说没什么关系。主要的问题就是：那个被找到的男孩——当时的说法是"被发现"——他从一开始就没有受到制约，尽管他是在一个有着各种迷信、傲慢和极强的宗教道德感等的非常正统、非常传统的婆罗门家庭中长大的，这是怎么回事？他为什么当时没有受到局限？还有后来在有各种"大师""启迪"等的那些时期——如果你们读过的话——他为什么没有受到制约？那个人和现在的这个人又有什么关系？你们对这些感兴趣吗？

听众：感兴趣。

克：我不感兴趣。过去已经死了，被埋葬了，不见了。我不知道怎么解答这个问题。问题之一是关于"大师"的，不仅在通神学中，而且在印度教传统和西藏传统中对大师都有解释，那些传统认为存在着"菩萨"，他会显现自己，在梵语中被称为"阿瓦塔"，这个词的意思就是"示现"。这个男孩被发现，然后为了那种示现而准备。于是他经历了各种各样的事情。可能会被问到的一个问题是：其他人是不是也必须经历同样的过程。克里斯托弗·哥伦布乘着帆船险渡重洋发现了美洲大陆，我们也必须经历那一切才能到达美洲吗？你明白我的问题吗？坐

simpler to go by air! That is one question. How that boy was brought up is totally irrelevant; what is relevant is the present teaching and nothing else.

There is a very ancient tradition about the Bodhisattva that there is a state of consciousness, let me put it that way, which is the essence of compassion. And when the world is in chaos that essence of compassion manifests itself. That is the whole idea behind the Avatar and the Bodhisattva. And there are various gradations, initiations, various Masters and so on, and also there is the idea that when he manifests all the others keep quiet. You understand? And that essence of compassion has manifested at other times. What is important in all this, if one may talk about it briefly, is: can the mind passing through all kinds of experiences, either imagined or real—because truth has nothing to do with experience, one cannot possibly experience truth, it is there, you can't experience it—but going through all those various imagined, illusory, or real states, can the mind be left unconditioned? The question is, can the mind be unconditioned always, not only in childhood. I wonder if you understand this question? That is the underlying problem or issue in this.

So as we say, all that is irrelevant. I do not know if you know anything about the ancient tradition of India and Tibet and of China and Japan, about the awakening of certain energy, called Kundalini. There are now all over America, and in Europe, various groups trying to awaken their little energy called Kundalini. You have heard about all this, haven't you? And there are groups practising it. I saw one group on television where a man was teaching them how to awaken Kundalini, that energy, doing all kinds of tricks with all kinds of words and gestures—which all becomes so utterly meaningless and absurd. And there is apparently such an awakening, which I won't go into, because it is much too complex and probably it is not

飞机要简单多了！那是同一个问题。那个男孩是如何长大的，这完全无关紧要；重要的是现在的教诲，别无其他。

关于菩萨，有一种非常古老的传统认为，存在一种意识状态——先让我这样表达——它是慈悲的本质。当世界一片混乱，那种慈悲的本质就会显现自身。这就是阿瓦塔和菩萨背后的一整套观念。还有很多不同的等级、进阶，各种各样的大师等，还有一种观念认为，当他示现时，其他所有人都得保持安静。你明白吗？而那种慈悲的本质已经在别的时代示现过了。恕我简短直言，这里真正重要的是：心灵经历了各种各样的体验，无论是幻想的还是真实的——因为真理与经验毫无关系，你不可能体验真理，它就在那里，你无法体验它——而是心灵经历了所有那些各式各样想象出来的、虚幻的或者真实的状态，它能不能依然未受制约？问题是：心灵能不能一直不受制约，而不仅仅在童年时代。我想知道你们有没有明白这个问题？这就是这里隐含的问题或课题。

所以正如我们所说，这一切都无关紧要。我不知道你们是不是了解印度、西藏、中国和日本有一种古老的传统，是关于唤醒某种叫作"昆达里尼"的能量的。如今在美国和欧洲，到处都有各种各样的团体，试图唤醒他们那微不足道的"昆达里尼"能量。你们听说过这些，不是吗？有些团体在练习这个。我在电视上看到过一个团体，有个人在教他们如何唤醒昆达里尼，那种能量，用各式各样的词语和姿势做着各种各样的把戏，这些我就不深入讲了，因为那就太复杂了，而且也许根本不重要也不相关。所以我想我已经回答了这个问题，不是吗？

另一个问题是：有没有一种不机械的行为？有没有一种运动——

necessary or relevant. So I think I have answered this question, haven't I?

The other question asked was: Is there a non-mechanistic activity? is there a movement—movement means time—is there a state of mind, which is not only mechanical but not in the field of time? That is what the question raised involves. Do you want to discuss that, or something else? Somebody also sent a written question, "What does it mean to be aware? Is awareness different from attention? Is awareness to be practised systematically or does it come about naturally?" That is the question. Are there any other questions?

Q(1): Would you go into the question of what it means, finding one's true will?

Q(2): What is the difference between denial and suppression?

Q(3): When being together with another person I lose all my awareness; not when I am alone.

K: Can we discuss awareness, begin with that and explore the whole thing, including the will of one's own destiny?

Q: What about earnestness and effort?

K: Earnestness and effort, yes. We are now discussing awareness. Does choice indicate freedom? I choose to belong to this society or to that society, to that cult, to a particular religion or not, I choose a particular job —choice. Does choice indicate freedom? Or does freedom deny choice? Please let us talk this over together.

Q: Freedom means that no choice is needed.

K: But we choose, and we think because we have the capacity to choose that we have freedom. I choose between the Liberal Party and the Communist party. And in choosing I feel I am free. Or I choose one particular guru or another, and that gives me a feeling that I am free. So

运动意味着时间——有没有一种心灵状态，不是仅仅机械的，而且不在时间的领域内？这就是这个问题涉及的内容。你们想讨论这个吗，还是讨论别的？有人又送来了另一个问题："觉察是什么意思？觉察与关注有什么不同吗？觉察需要系统地练习吗？还是说它是自然而然发生的？"这就是问题。还有别的问题吗？

问（1）：你能不能讲一讲"找到自己真正的意愿"是什么意思？

问（2）：否定和压抑有什么不同？

问（3）：当我跟其他人在一起时，我就失掉了所有的觉察；我自己一个人的时候就不会这样。

克：我们能不能探讨觉察，从这里开始，然后探索所有的问题，包括一个人自身使命的意愿？

问：谈谈认真和努力怎么样？

克：认真和努力，好的。我们现在讨论的是觉察。选择意味着自由吗？我选择属于这个社团或者那个社团、那个派别、某个宗教，或者选择不属于它们，我选择某一个工作——选择。选择意味着自由吗？或者自由否定了选择？请让我们一起详细谈谈这个问题。

问：自由意味着不需要选择。

克：但是我们确实选择，而且我们认为，因为我们有选择的能力，所以我们拥有自由。我选择加入自由党还是共产党。在选择中我觉得自己是自由的。或者我选择某个特定的古鲁或者另一个，那给了我一种感觉：我是自由的。所以选择能导向觉察吗？

问：不能。

does choice lead to awareness?

Q: No.

K: Go slowly.

Q: Choice is the expression of conditioning, is it not?

K: That is what I want to find out.

Q: It seems to me that one either reacts out of habit, or one responds without thinking.

K: We will come to that. We will go into what it means to respond without choice. We are used to choosing; that is our conditioning.

Q: Like and dislike.

K: All that is implied in choice. I chose you as my friend, I deny my friendship to another. One wants to find out if awareness includes choice. Or is awareness a state of mind, a state of observation in which there is no choice whatsoever? Is that possible? One is educated from childhood to choose and that is our tradition, that is our habit, that is our mechanical, instinctive reaction. And we think, because we choose there is freedom. What does awareness mean: to be aware? It implies, doesn't it, not only physical sensitivity, but also sensitivity to the environment, to nature, sensitivity to other people's reactions and to my own reactions. Not, I am sensitive, but to other people I am not sensitive: that is not sensitivity.

So awareness implies, doesn't it, a total sensitivity: to colour, to nature, to all my reactions, how I respond to others, all that is implied in awareness, isn't it? I am aware of this tent, the shape of it and so on. One is aware of nature, the world of nature, the beauty of trees, the silence of the trees, the shape and beauty and the depth and the solitude of trees. And one is aware also of one's relationship to others, intimate and not intimate. In that awareness is there any kind of choice? —in a total awareness,

克：慢慢来。

问：选择是制约的表现，不是吗？

克：那就是我想弄清楚的。

问：在我看来，一个人要么出于习惯做出反应，要么不假思索地做出回应。

克：我们会讲到那一点的。我们会讲到毫无选择地回应是什么意思。我们习惯了选择，这就是我们所受的制约。

问：还有好恶。

克：这些都隐含在选择中。我选择你做我的朋友，我拒绝对别人友好。我想弄清楚觉察是不是包括选择。还是说，觉察是一种心灵状态，一种毫无选择的观察状态？而这可能吗？我们从小所受的教育就是要选择，这就是我们的传统，这就是我们的习惯，这就是我们机械、本能的反应。而且我们认为，因为我们可以选择，所以就有自由。而觉察，去觉知意味着什么？它意味着不仅仅有身体上的敏感性，还有对环境、对自然的敏感，对他人的反应和我自身反应的敏感，不是吗？而不是说，我自己很敏感，但对别人就不敏感了，那不是敏感。

所以觉察意味着一种完整的敏感：对色彩、对自然、对我所有的反应，我如何回应他人，这一切都包含在觉察中，不是吗？我觉察到这顶帐篷，它的形状，等等。你觉察到大自然、自然界，树的美，树的寂静，树的轮廓、美丽、深度以及独立。你也觉察到自己与他人的关系，无论亲密与否。在那种觉察中有任何选择吗？——在全然的觉察中，从神经上、身体上、心理上对你周围的一切，对所有的影响、声音等完全

neurologically, physically, psychologically, to everything around one, the influences, to all the noises and so on. Is one aware?—not only of one's own beliefs but those of others, the opinions, judgements, evaluations, the conclusions, all that is implied—otherwise one is not aware. And can you practise awareness by going to a school or college, or going to a guru who will teach you how to be aware? Is that awareness? Which means, is sensitivity to be cultivated through practice?

Q: That becomes selfishness, concentration on oneself.

K: Yes, that is, unless there is total sensitivity, awareness merely becomes concentration on oneself.

Q: Which excludes awareness.

K: Yes, that is right. But there are so many schools, so many gurus, so many ashramas, retreats, where this thing is practised.

Q: When it is practised it is just the old trick again.

K: This is so obvious. One goes to India or Japan to learn what it means to be aware - Zen practice, all that. Or is awareness a movement of constant observation? Not only what I feel, what I think, but what other people say about me - to listen, if they say it in front of me - and to be aware of nature, of what is going on in the world. That is total awareness. Obviously it can't be practised.

Q: It is a non-movement, isn't it?

K: No, it is movement in the sense of, "alive".

Q: It is a participation.

K: Participation implies action. If there is action through choice, that is one kind of action; if there is an action of total awareness, that is a totally different kind of action, "being aware"? You understand? To be aware of the people around one, the colour, their attitudes, their walk, the

觉知。你在觉察吗?——不仅觉察自己的信仰,还觉察他人的信仰、观点、评估、判断、结论,那一切都包含在内——否则你就没有觉察。然而你可以通过上学或者上大学去练习觉察吗,或者找一个古鲁教你如何觉察?那是觉察吗?也就是说,敏感能通过练习培养吗?

问:那就变成了自私,对自己的专注。

克:是的,就是这样,除非有了完整的敏感性,否则觉察就只会变成对自己的专注。

问:那就排除了觉察。

克:是的,没错。但实际上有那么多学校,那么多古鲁,那么多修习所、静修中心,人们就在那里练习这个。

问:如果练习它,那就还是老一套的把戏。

克:这是如此明显。你到印度或者日本去学习觉察是什么——禅宗的练习,诸如此类。还是说,觉察是一种不停的观察活动?不仅仅是我感受到什么,我在想什么,还有别人怎么说我——去聆听,如果他们当着我的面说的话——还有觉察自然,觉察世界上发生着什么。这就是全然觉察。显然它是无法练习的。

问:这是一种不动,不是吗?

克:不,这是一种"鲜活的"这个意义上的运动。

克:这是一种参与。

克:参与就意味着行动。如果有选择产生的行动,那是一种行动;如果有一种全然觉察的行动,那就是另一种完全不同的行动了,显然如此。你是如此觉察的吗?还是说,我们沉溺在"保持觉察"这些词当中

way they eat, the way they think—without indulging in judgement.

Q: Is it something to do with motive? If you have a motive...

K: Of course. Motive comes into being when there is choice; that is implied. When I have a motive then choice takes place. I chose you because I like you, or you flatter me, or you give me something or other; another doesn't, therefore there is choice and so on. So is this possible? —this sense of total awareness.

Q: Is there a degree of awareness?

K: That is, is awareness a process of time?

Q: Can one man be more aware than another?

K: Why should I enquire if you are more aware than I am? just a minute, let us go into it. Why this comparision? Is this not also part of our education, our social conditioning, which says we must compare to progress?—compare one musician with another, one painter with another and so on. And we think by comparing we begin to understand. Comparing means measurement, which implies time, thought, and is it possible to live without comparing at all? You understand? One is brought up, educated in schools, colleges and universities to compare oneself with "A", who is much cleverer than myself, and to try to reach his level—this constant measurement, this constant comparison, and therefore constant imitation, which is mechanical! So can we find out for ourselves whether it is possible to be totally sensitive and therefore aware?

Q: Can you know if you are totally aware or not? Can we be aware of our awareness?

K: No (laughter). Q: You can be aware when you are not aware.

K: Watch it in yourself; verbally it becomes speculative. When you are aware do you know you are aware?

了？你明白吗？觉察到你周围的人们，衣服的色彩，他们的态度，他们的步伐，他们吃什么，他们想什么——而不耽溺于评判中。

问：这与动机有关吗？如果你有个动机……

克：当然。当存在选择时动机就会出现；其中就隐含了这一点。当我有一个动机，那么选择就会发生。我选择你，是因为我喜欢你，或者你奉承我，或者你给了我这个或那个；另一个人没有这么做，所以就有了选择之类。那么这可能吗？——这种全然觉察的感觉。

问：觉察有程度之分吗？

克：也就是说，觉察是一个时间过程吗？

问：一个人会不会比另一个人更有觉察？

克：我为什么要问你是不是比我更觉察？等一下，让我们看看这个问题。为什么要有这种比较？这难道不也是我们教育的一部分，我们所受社会制约的一部分，说我们必须比较才能进步吗？——把一个音乐家和另一个音乐家比较，把一个画家和另一个画家比较，等等。而我们认为通过比较我们就开始理解了。比较意味着衡量，而衡量隐含着时间、思想，那么有没有可能根本不比较地活着？你明白吗？一个人在成长过程中，在学校、学院和大学里受到的教育是拿自己跟"某某"比较，他比我聪明多了，而我要努力到达他的水平——这种不停的衡量，这种不停的比较，因而会不停地模仿，而这是机械的！所以我们能不能亲自去发现有没有可能完全敏感进而全然觉察？

问: 你能知道你是不是在全然觉察吗？我们能觉察到我们的觉察吗？

克：不能。（笑声）

Q: No.

K: Find out. Test it, madam, test it. Do you know when you are happy? The moment you are aware that you are happy it is no longer happiness.

Q: You know when you have got a pain.

K: That is a different matter. When I have pain I am aware of it and I act, do something about it. That is one part of being aware, unless I am paralysed—most people are, in other directions!

So we are asking ourselves, not asking somebody else to tell us, but one is asking oneself if there is that quality of awareness? Does one watch the sky, the evening stars, the moon, the birds, people's reactions, the whole of it? And what is the difference between that awareness and attention? In awareness is there a centre from which you are aware? When I say, "I am aware", then I move from a centre, I respond to nature from a centre, I respond to my friends, to my wife, husband or whatever it is - that centre being my conditioning, my prejudices, my desires, my fears and all the rest of it. In that awareness there is a centre. In attention there is no centre at all. Now please listen to this for two minutes. You are now listening to what is being said and you are giving total attention. That means you are not comparing, you do not say, "I already know what you are going to say", or, "I have read what you have said etc. etc". All that has gone, you are completely attentive and therefore there is no centre and that attention has no border. I don't know if you have noticed?

So, by being aware one discovers that one responds from a centre, from a prejudice, from a conclusion, from a belief, from a conditioning, which is the centre. And from that centre you react, you respond. And when there is an awareness of that centre, that centre yields and in that

问：你能觉察到你不在觉察。

克：在你自己身上观察这一点；从口头上说会变成揣测。当你觉察时，你知道自己在觉察吗？

问：不知道。

克：去弄清楚。检验一下，女士，试一试。当你快乐的时候你知道吗？一旦你发觉你很快乐，快乐就不在了。

问：当你有疼痛的时候你是知道的。

克：那就是另一回事了。当我有疼痛，我觉察到了然后我行动，对它做点儿什么。那是觉察的一部分，除非我麻痹了——大部分人实际上就是麻痹的，在另一些方向上！

所以我们在问自己，不是让别人来告诉我们，而是你在问自己：有没有那种品质的觉察？你有没有观察天空，观察晚星、月亮、鸟儿以及人们的反应，观察这个整体？而觉察和关注之间的区别是什么？在觉察中，存在一个你据以觉察的中心吗？当我说，"我在觉察"，那么我就是从一个中心出发的，我从一个中心对自然做出反应，对我的朋友、我的妻子、丈夫或者无论什么人做出反应——那个中心就是我的局限、我的偏见、我的欲望、我的恐惧以及诸如此类的一切。在那种觉察中有一个中心，而关注中根本没有中心。现在请注意听两分钟。你现在正聆听我说的话，你付出了你全部的注意力。这意味着你没在比较，你不说，"我已经知道你要说什么了"，或者"我读过你说过的话了"，等等。那一切都不见了，你全神贯注，因而没有中心，那种关注没有边界。我不知道你注意到这一点没有？

there is a total attention. I wonder if you understand this? And this you cannot practise; it would be too childish, mechanical. So we go to the next question, which is: "Is there an activity which is not mechanistic?" That means, is there a part of the brain which is non-mechanical. Do you want to go into this? No, no, please, this isn't a game. First of all one has to go into the question of what is a mechanical mind.

Is the brain, which has evolved through millennia, is that totally mechanical? Or is there a part of the brain which is not mechanical, which has never been touched by the machine of evolution? I wonder if you see.

Q: What do you mean by mechanical?

K: We are going to discuss that, sir. Part of this mechanical process is functioning within the field of conditioning. That is, when I act according to a pattern—Catholic, Protestant, Communist, Hindu, whatever it is, a pattern set by society, by my reading, or other influences, and accept that pattern or belief—then that is part of the mechanical process. The other part of the mechanical process is, having had experiences of innumerable kinds which have left memories, to act according to those memories: that is mechanical. Like a computer, which is purely mechanical. Now they are trying to prove it is not so mechanical, but let's leave that alone for the moment.

Mechanical action is accepting tradition and following tradition. One of the aspects of that tradition is acceptance and obedience to a government, to priests. And the mechanical part of the brain is following consciously or unconsciously a line set by thought as the goal and purpose. All that and more is mechanical; and we live that way.

Q: Is thought of itself mechanical?

K: Of course, that is the whole point. One has to discover this for

所以，通过觉察你发现你是从一个中心做出反应的，从一种偏见、一个结论、一种信仰、一种局限做出反应的，那些就是中心。你根据那个中心做出反应，做出回应。而当觉察到了那个中心，那个中心就让位了，此时就有了一种全然的关注。我不知道你明白这一点了没有？而这种关注你无法练习，那就太幼稚、太机械了。所以我们可以来看下一个问题了，那就是："有没有一种行动不是机械的？"也就是说，大脑有没有一个部分是不机械的。你们想探讨这个问题吗？不，不，拜托，这不是一个游戏。首先你必须探索什么是机械的心智这个问题。

大脑经过了几千年的进化，它是完全机械的吗？还是说，大脑有一个部分是不机械的，它从未受到机械的进化过程的影响？我想知道你是不是明白了。

问：你说的机械是什么意思？

克：我们这就讨论这个问题，先生。这个机械过程的一部分就在制约的领域内运转。也就是说，当我根据一个模式来行动——天主教、新教、共产主义、印度教，无论什么模式，有社会、我读的书或者其他的影响设下的模式，并接受了那种模式或者信仰——那么这就是那个机械过程的一部分。那个机械过程的另一部分是，拥有留下了记忆的种类不计其数的经验，然后根据那些记忆去行动：这也是机械的。就像计算机一样，那纯粹是机械的。现在他们在试图证明那并没有那么机械，但是让我们暂且先不管那个问题。

机械的行动就是接受传统并遵循传统。那种传统的一方面就是对政府、牧师的接受和服从。而大脑机械的部分在有无有意地遵循思想设下的

oneself, not be told by others, then it becomes mechanical. If we discover for ourselves how mechanical our thinking, our feeling, our attitudes, our opinions are, if one is aware of that, it means thought is invariably mechanistic—thought being the response of memory, experience, knowledge, which is the past. And responding according to the pattern of the past is mechanical, which is thought.

Q: All thought?

K: All thought, of course. Whether noble, ignoble, sexual, or technological thought, it is all thought.

Q: Thought of the great genius also?

K: Absolutely. Wait, we must go into the question of what is a genius. No, we won't go into that yet.

If all thought is mechanical, the expression which you often use, "clear thinking", seems to be a contradiction.

K: No, no. Clear thinking is to see clearly, clear thinking is to think clearly, objectively, sanely, rationally, wholly.

Q: It is still thought.

K: It is still thought, of course it is.

Q: So what is the use of it? (laughter).

K: If there was clear thought I wouldn't belong to any political party! I might create a global party—that is another matter.

Q: Can we get back to your question as to whether there is a part of the brain which is untouched by conditioning?

K: That's right, sir; this requires very careful, hesitant, enquiry. Not saying, "Yes, there is", or, "No, there isn't". "I have experienced a state where there is no mechanicalness"—that is too silly. But to really enquire and find out, you need a great deal of subtlety, great attentive quality to go

路线，也就是目标和目的。所有这些都是机械的，而我们就那样生活着。

问：思想本身是机械的吗？

克：当然，这就是整个重点。你必须自己发现这一点，而不是由别人告诉你，那样会变得机械。如果我们自己发现了我们的思维、我们的感受、我们的态度、我们的观点有多么机械，如果你觉察到了这一点，那就意味着思想不可避免是机械的——思想就是记忆、经验、知识的反应，也就是过去的反应。根据过去的模式做出的反应是机械的，那就是思想。

问：所有思想吗？

克：所有思想，当然。无论高尚、卑微，无论是性还是技术方面的想法，那都是思想。

问：伟大天才的思想也是？

克：绝对是。等一下，我们必须探讨一下什么是天才这个问题。不，我们现在还不用探讨这个。

问：如果所有的思想都是机械的，那么你经常用的一个表达——"清晰的思考"，看起来就是一个矛盾。

克：不，不。清晰的思考是清晰地看到，清晰的思考是清晰地、客观地、健全地、理性地、完整地思考。

问：那还是思想。

克：那还是思想，当然是。

问：那它有什么用呢？（笑声）

克：如果能够清晰地思考，我就不会属于任何一个政党！我也许会建立一个全球党——那就是另一回事了。

step by step into it, not jump.

So we say most of our lives are mechanical. The pursuit of pleasure is mechanical—but we are pursuing pleasure. Now, how shall we find out if there is a part of the brain that is not conditioned? This a very serious question, it is not for sentimentalists, romantic people, or emotional people; this requires very clear thinking. When you think very clearly you see the limitation of thinking.

Q: Are we going to look very clearly at the barriers which interfere with an unconditioned mind?

K: No, we are trying to understand, or explore together, the mechanical mind first. Without understanding the totality of that you can't find out the other. We have asked the question: "Is there a part of the brain, part of our total mind—in which is included the brain, emotions, neurological responses—which is not completely mechanical?" When I put that question to myself I might imagine that it is not all mechanical because I want the other; therefore I deceive myself. I pretend that I have got the other. So I must completely understand the movement of desire. You follow this? Not suppress it, but under. stand it, have an insight into it—which me;ms fear, time, and all that we talked about the day before yesterday. So we are now enquiring whether our total activity is mechanistic? That means am I, are you, clinging to memories? The Hitlerian memories and all that, the memories of various pleasurable and painful experiences, the memories of sexual fulfilment and the pleasures and so on. That is: is one living in the past?

Q: Always, I am.

K: Of course! So all that you are is the past, which is mechanical. So knowledge is mechanical. I wonder if you see this?

问：我们能不能回到你的问题上去：大脑有没有一部分是未被制约影响的？

克：好的，先生；这需要非常小心、非常谨慎的探询。不能说"是的，有"，或者"不，没有"。"我体验过一种没有机械性的状态"——那就太愚蠢了。但是若要真正地探询并弄清真相，你就需要非常敏感，需要全神贯注的品质，一步步地深入探索，不能一蹴而就。

所以我们说，我们大部分人的生活都是机械的。对欢愉的追求是机械的——但我们就在追求欢愉。那么，我们要如何发现大脑有没有一个部分是不受制约的？这是一个非常严肃的问题，它不是为多愁善感、罗曼蒂克的人或者情绪化的人准备的；这需要非常清晰的思考。当你非常清晰地思考时，你就会看到思想的局限。

问：我们要非常清楚地看到干扰未受制约的心灵的那些障碍吗？

克：不，我们首先要试着了解或者一起探索机械的心智。如果不了解它的全部，你就无法弄清楚另一个。我们问了这个问题："大脑有没有一部分，心灵有没有一部分——其中包括了大脑、情感和神经反应——不是完全机械的？"当我向自己提出这个问题，我可能会想象它不是完全机械的，因为我想要另一个；所以我欺骗了自己。我假装我拥有了另一个。所以我必须彻底弄明白欲望的活动。这点你跟上了吗？不是压抑它，而是了解它，洞察它——它就是恐惧、时间，以及我们前天探讨过的一切。所以我们现在问的是，我们的全部行为都是机械的吗？也就是说，我，还有你，是在抓住记忆不放吗？希特勒式的记忆以及那一切，对各种快乐和痛苦经验的记忆，对性满足和各种快感的记忆，等

Q: Why is it so difficult to see this?

K: Because we are not aware of our inward responses, of what actually is going on within ourselves—not to imagine what is going on, or speculate about it, or repeat what we have been told by somebody else, but actually to be aware of what is going on.

Q: Aren't we guided to awareness by experience?

K: No. Now wait a minute. What do you mean by experience? The word itself means, "to go through" —to go through, finish, not retain. You have said something that hurts me, that has left a mark on the brain, and when I meet you that memory responds. Obviously. And is it possible when you hurt me, say something cruel, or justified, or violent, to observe it and not register it? Try it, sir; you try it, test it out.

Q: It is very difficult because the memory has already been hurt; we never forget it.

K: Do go into this. From childhood we are hurt, it happens to everybody, in school, at home, at college, in universities, the whole of society is a process of hurting others. One has been hurt and one lives in that consciously or unconsciously. So there are two problems involved: the past hurt retained in the brain, and not to be hurt; the memory of hurts, and never to be hurt; Now is that possible?

Q: If "you" are not there.

K: Go into it. You will discover it for yourself and find out. That is, you have been hurt.

Q: The image of myself...

K: Go into it slowly. What is hurt? The image that you have built about yourself, that has been hurt. Why do you have an image about yourself? Because that is the tradition, part of our education, part of our

等。也就是说：你是活在过去吗？

问：我一直是。

克：当然了！所以你就是过去，过去是机械的。所以知识是机械的。我想知道你看到这一点了吗？

问：为什么看到这一点这么难？

克：因为我们没有觉察到我们内在的反应，我们内心实际上发生着什么——不是想象或者猜测发生着什么，也不是重复别人告诉我们的话，而是实实在在地觉察发生着的事情。

问：难道我们不是在经验的指引下去觉察的吗？

克：不是的。现在请等一下。你说的经验是什么意思？这个词本身的意思是"穿过"——穿越、结束，而不是保留。你说了伤害我的话，那在我大脑上留下了痕迹，当我再见到你时，那个记忆就会做出反应。显然如此。然而，当你伤害了我，说了残忍、公正或者暴力的话，我有没有可能观察它但不记录它？试一试，先生；你去试一下，检验一下。

问：这很难，因为记忆已经受到了伤害，我们永远也忘不了。

克：请务必深入探究这个问题。我们从小就受到了伤害，这在每个人身上都发生过，在学校里，在家里，在学院里，在大学里，整个社会都是一个伤害别人的过程。一个人受到了伤害，然后就有意识或无意识地活在伤害中。所以这里涉及两个问题：过去的伤害留在了大脑中，和不再受伤；对伤害的记忆，和永远不再受伤。那么这可能吗？

问：如果"你"不在的话。

克：深入进去。你会亲自发现真相的。也就是说，你受到了伤害。

social reactions. There is an image about myself, and there is an image about you in relation to my image. So I have got half a dozen images and more. And that image about myself has been hurt. You call me a fool and I shrink: it has been hurt. Now, how am I to dissolve that hurt and not be hurt in the future, tomorrow, or the next moment? You follow the question? There are two problems involved in this. One, I have been hurt and that creates a great deal of neurotic activity, resistance, self protection, fear; all that is involved in the past hurt. Second, how not to be hurt any more.

Q: One has to be totally involved.

K: Look at it and you will see. You have been hurt, haven't you—I am not talking to you personally—and you resist, you are afraid of being hurt more. So you build a wall round yourself, isolate yourself, and the extreme form of that isolation is total withdrawal from all relationship. And you remain in that but you have to live, you have to act. So you are always acting from a centre that is hurt and therefore acting neurotically. You can see this happening in the world, in oneself. And how are those hurts to be totally dissolved and not leave a mark? Also in the future how not to be hurt at all? The question is clear, isn't it.

Now how do you approach this question? How to dissolve the hurts, or how not to be hurt at all? Which is the question you put to yourself, which do you want answered? Dissolve all the hurts, or no more hurts? Which is it that comes to you naturally?

Q: No more hurts.

K: So the question is: "Is it possible not to be hurt?" Which means is it possible not to have an image about yourself?

Q: If we see that image is false...

问：我自己的形象……

克：慢慢地探索。伤害是什么？你为自己建立起来的形象，它受到了伤害。你为什么要对自己抱有形象？因为那是传统，是我们教育的一部分，我们社会反应的一部分。既有我自己的形象，还有与我的形象有关的你的形象。所以我有半打意象或者更多。而我自己的形象受到了伤害。你叫我傻瓜，我就心下畏缩：它受伤了。那么，我要如何消除那个伤害，并且未来，明天或者下一刻不再受伤？你明白这个问题吗？这里面涉及了两个问题。一个是，我受过伤害，而那造成了大量神经质的行为，抗拒、自我保护和恐惧；这一切都包含在过去的伤害中。另一个是，如何不再受伤。

问：你必须完全投入进去。

克：去看一看，你就会发现的。你受了伤，不是吗——我不是在说你个人——于是你抗拒，你害怕再次受伤。所以你在自己周围建起一道围墙，隔绝自己，那种隔绝的极端形式就是彻底退出所有的关系。你退守墙后，但你必须生活，你必须行动。所以你总是从一个受伤的中心出发去行动，因而做出神经质的行为。你可以看到这种情况在世界上，在人的内心都发生着。而那些伤害要如何才能彻底消除，不留丝毫痕迹呢？而且未来要如何才能完全不再受伤呢？问题清楚了，不是吗？

那么你如何着手这个问题？如何消除伤害，或者如何完全不再受伤？哪一个是你问自己的问题，哪一个你想得到回答？消除所有伤害，还是不再受伤？自然地出现你面前的是哪个问题？

问：不再受伤。

K: Not false or true. Don't you see, you are already operating in the field of thought? Is it possible not to have an image at all about yourself, or about another, naturally? And if there is no image, isn't that true freedom? Ah, you don't see it.

Q: Sir, if what happens to you is of no importance to you, then it doesn't matter and it won't hurt you. If you have managed to get rid of your self-importance...

K: The gentleman says if you can get rid of your self-importance, your arrogance, your vanity, then you won't be hurt. But how am I to get rid of all that garbage which I have collected? (laughter).

Q: I think you can get rid of it by being entirely aware of the relationship between yourself and your physical body and your thinking. How you control your physical body and...

K: I don't want to control anything, my body, my mind, my emotions. That is the traditional, mechanistic response. Sorry! (laughter). Please go into this a little bit and you will see. First of all, the idea of getting rid of an image implies that there is an entity who is different from the image. Therefore he can kick the image. But is the image different from the entity who says, "I must get rid of it"? They are both the same, therefore there is no control. I wonder if you see that. When you see that you are no longer functioning mechanically.

Q: Surely by destroying one image we are immediately building another one?

K: We are going to find out if it is possible to be free of all images, not only the present ones but the future ones. Now why does the mind create an image about itself? I say I am a Christian, that is an image. I believe in the saviour, in Christ, in all the ritual, why? Because that is my

克：所以问题是："有没有可能不再受伤？"也就是说，有没有可能完全不抱有自我形象？

问：如果我们看到那个形象是错误的……

克：不是错误还是正确的问题。你难道没有发现你已经在思想的领域中运转了？有没有可能自然而然地对自己或者别人都完全不抱有形象？如果没有了形象，那不就是真正的自由吗？啊，你没有看到这一点。

问：先生，如果发生在你身上的事情对你来说不重要，那就没什么关系，它不会伤害你。如果你已经设法去除了你的自我重要感……

克：这位先生说，如果能去除你的自我重要感、你的傲慢、你的虚荣，那么你就不会受伤。可是我要如何才能除掉我收集起来的所有那些垃圾呢？（笑声）

问：我想你可以通过完全觉知你自己和你的身体、你的思想之间的关系来除掉它们。你如何控制你的身体和……

克：我不想控制任何东西，我的身体、我的头脑、我的感情。那是传统的、机械的反应。抱歉！（笑声）请稍微深入地探索一下，你会发现的。首先，除掉形象的想法意味着存在一个有异于形象的实体。所以他才能责怪那个形象。但那个形象跟说"我必须除掉它"的实体有什么不同吗？它们都是一回事，所以控制是不存在的。我想知道你有没有看到这一点。当你看到了这点，你就会不再机械地运转了。

问：毁掉了一个形象，我们肯定会立刻建立另外一个吗？

克：我们要搞清楚的是有没有可能摆脱所有的形象，不仅仅是现在的这些，还有未来的那些形象。那么心智为什么要为自身建立形象

conditioning. Go to India and they say, "What are you talking about, Christ? I have got my own gods, as good as yours, if not better" (laughter). So that is their conditioning. If I am born in Russia and educated there I say, "I believe in neither. The State is my god and Marx is the first prophet and so on and so on." So the image formation is brought about through propaganda, conditioning, tradition.

Q: Is that related to the fact that out of fear one behaves in a certain way which is not natural for one to behave; and therefore one is not being oneself? And that is making the image you are talking about.

K: The image is what we call ourself: "I must express myself", "I must fulfil myself". "Myself" is the image according to the environment and culture in which one has been born. I believe there was a tribe in America, among the Red Indians, where anybody who had an image about himself was killed (laughter), was liquidated, because it led to ambition and all the rest of it. I wonder what would happen if they did it to all of us. It would be a lovely world, wouldn't it? (laughter).

So is it possible not to create images at all? That is, I am aware that I have an image, brought about through culture, through propaganda, tradition, the family, the whole pressure.

Q: We cling to the known.

K: That is the known, tradition is the known. And my mind is afraid to let that known go, to let the image go, because the moment it lets it go it might lose a profitable position in society, might lose status, might lose a certain relationship; so it is frightened and holds on to that image. The image is merely words, it has no reality. It is a series of words, a sense of responses to those words, a series of beliefs which are words. I believe in Marx, in Christ, or in Krishna or whatever they believe in India. They are

呢？我说我是个基督教徒，这是一个形象。我相信救世主，相信基督，相信所有的仪式，为什么？因为那就是我受到的制约。到了印度，他们就会说，"你在说什么呢，基督？我有我自己的神明，跟你的一样好，如果不是更好的话"。（笑声）所以那就是他们的制约。如果我出生在俄国并在那里受教育，我就会说，"那些我都不相信。国家是我们的神，马克思是首位先知"，等等。所以形象是通过宣传、制约和传统得以形成的。

问：这是不是和这个事实有关：出于恐惧，人会以一种对他来说不太自然的方式来行动；所以人就不是他自己了？而那就建立了你所说的形象。

克：形象是我们对自己的称谓："我必须表达自己"，"我必须成就自己"。"我自己"就是根据一个人出生的环境和文化而来的。我相信美国以前有一个部落，在北美的印第安人中，如果谁抱有自我形象就会被处死（笑声）、被清除，因为那会导致野心以及诸如此类的一切。我好奇如果他们也这样对待我们所有人的话，那会怎么样。那将是一个美好的世界，不是吗？（笑声）

所以，有没有可能根本不建立形象？也就是说，我觉察到我有一个形象，是通过文化、宣传、传统、家庭这整个压力产生的。

问：我们抓住已知不放。

克：那是已知，传统就是已知。而我的心智害怕放开已知、放开形象，因为一旦放开，它也许会失去一个有利可图的社会地位，也许会丢掉身份，也许会失去某种关系；所以它感到害怕，于是死死抓住那个形象不放。那个形象仅仅是语言而已，它没有真实性。它是一系列的词语，

just words ideologically clothed. And if I am not a slave to words, then I begin to lose the image. I wonder if you see how significant deeply rooted words have become.

Q: If one is listening to what you say and realizes that one has an image about oneself, and that there is a large discrepancy between the image one has of oneself and the ideal of freedom...

K: It is not an ideal...

Q:... freedom itself... then knowing that there is a discrepancy, can one think of freedom, knowing that it is just an idea?

K: Is freedom an abstraction, a word, or a reality?

Q: It is being free of relationship, is it not?

K: No please, we are jumping from one thing to another. Let us go step by step. We began by asking whether there is any part of the brain, any part of the total entity, that is not conditioned? We said conditioning means image-forming. The image that gets hurt and the image that protects itself from being hurt. And we said there is only freedom—the actuality of that state, not the word, not the abstraction—when there is no image, which is freedom. When I am not a Hindu, Buddhist, Christian, Communist, Socialist, I have no label and therefore no label inside. Now is it possible not to have an image at all? And how does that come about?

Q: Isn't it all to do with the activity...

K: Look, we come to a point and go off after something else. One wants to find out whether it is possible to live in this world without a single image.

Q: When there is no observer there is nothing observed, and yet one comes across something in this silence...

K: Madam, is this an actual fact that there is no observer in your life—

是对那些词语的一种反应，是一系列本身就是词语的信仰。我相信马克思，相信基督，相信奎师那或者他们在印度相信的任何东西。它们都只是披上了意识形态外衣的言辞而已。而如果我不是词语的奴隶，我就会开始丢掉那个形象。我想知道你有没有发现词语已经变得多么根深蒂固。

问：如果一个人听了你说的话，然后意识到他抱有自我形象，而且他对自己抱有的形象和自由的理想之间存在着巨大的差异……

克：那不是一个理想……

问：……就是理想本身……然后知道存在着差异，那他能思考自由，同时知道那只是个概念吗？

克：自由是一个抽象的概念，是一个词，还是一个现实？

问：它就是摆脱所有的关系，不是吗？

克：不，拜托，我们在从一件事情跳到另一件事情上。让我们一步一步来。我们开始问的是，大脑有没有一个部分，这整个存在体有没有一个部分是未受制约的？我们说制约意味着建立形象——受伤的形象以及保护自己免于伤害的形象。而我们说，只有当没有形象时——这本身就是自由——自由才会出现，而且是那种实际的状态，不是词语，也不是抽象的概念。当我不再是一个印度教徒、佛教徒、基督教徒、共产主义者、社会主义者，我就没有了标签，因而内心也没有标签。那么有没有可能完全不抱有形象？而这如何才能发生？

问：这难道不是都关系到那种行为……

克：你看，我们到了一个点上然后就偏离到别的事情上去了。我们想搞清楚有没有可能不抱丝毫形象地活在这个世界上。

not only occasionally. Is it possible to be free of the image that society, the environment, culture, education has built in one? Because one is all that; you are the result of your environment, of your culture, of your knowledge, of your education, of your job, of your pleasure, you are all that.

Q: What happens to one's sense of orientation without a centre.

K: All that comes a little later, please.

Q: If you are aware of your conditioning does that free you?

K: Now, are you actually aware—not theoretically or in the abstract—actually aware that you are conditioned this way, and therefore you have got an image?

Q: If you don't have the image then you don't know what your place is.

K: "If you have no image then you do not know what your place is." Listen to that carefully. If you have no image, you have no place in the world. Which means if you have no image you are insecure. Go step by step. Now are you, having a place in the world, secure?

Q: No.

K: Be actual.

Q: When you see that the image that you have built, which you are attached to, when you see that it is just a load of words...

K: You are finding security in a word: and it is not security at all. We have lived in words and made those words something fantastically · real. So if you are seeking security, it is not in an image; it is not in your environment, in your culture. One must have security, that is essential, food, clothes, and shelter; one must have it otherwise one can't function. Now that is denied totally when I belong to a small group. When I say I am a German, or a Russian, or an Englishman, I deny complete security. I deny

问：当没有观察者时就没有被观察之物，然而在这种寂静中我遇到了些事情……

克：女士，你的生活中没有观察者，这是不是一个实实在在的事实——不只是偶尔？有没有可能摆脱社会、环境、文化和教育在你身上建立的形象？因为你就是那一切；你就是你的环境、你的文化、你的知识、你的教育、你的工作、你的欢愉的产物，你就是那一切。

问：如果没有中心的话，那一个人的方向感会怎么样？

克：那些稍后才涉及，拜托。

问：如果你觉察到了自己的制约，那会解放你吗？

克：现在，你真的在觉察吗——不是从理论上或者抽象地说——而是实实在在地觉察到你就是受到了这样的被制约，所以你抱有形象？

问：如果你没有形象，那么你就不知道你的位置在哪里。

克："如果你没有形象，那么你就不知道你的位置在哪里。"仔细听听这句话。如果你没有形象，那么你在这个世界上就没有位置。也就是说，如果你没有形象，你就不安全。一步一步来。现在你在世界上有个位置，可是你安全吗？

问：不安全。

克：实际一点儿。

问：当你看到你执着于自己建立的形象，当你看到它只是一堆词语……

克：你从词语中找到了安全，而那根本不是安全。我们活在词语中，并且把那些词语变成了无比真实的东西。所以如果你在寻找安全，它不在形象中；它也不在你的环境、你的文化中。人必须拥有安全，那

security because the words, the labels have become important, not security. This is what is actually happening, the Arabs and the Israelis both want security, and both are accepting words and all the rest of it.

Now we come to the point. Is it possible to live in this world, not to go off into some fantastic realm of illusion, or to some monastery, and to live in this world without a single image and be totally secure.

Q: How can we be secure in a sick society?

K: I am going to go into this, madam, I'll show it to you.

Q: It is competitive, it is vicious.

K: Please go with me. I'll show you that there is complete security, absolute security, not in images.

Q: To be totally aware every moment, then your conditioning does not exist.

K: Not if you are aware. Are you aware that you have an image and that image has been formed by the culture, the society? Are you aware of that image? You discover that image in relationship, don't you? Now we are asking ourselves whether it is possible to be free of images. That means, when you say something to me that is vulgar, hurting, at the moment to be totally aware of what you are saying and how I am responding. Totally aware, not partially, but to be totally aware of both the pleasurable image and the displeasurable image. To be aware totally at the moment of the reaction to your insult or praise. Then at that moment you don't form an image. There is no recording in the brain of the hurt, the insult or the flattery, therefore there is no image. That requires tremendous attention at the moment, which demands a great inward perception, which is only possible when you have looked at it, watched it, when you have worked. Don't just say, "Well, tell me all about it; I want to be comfortable".

是必不可少的，食物、衣服和住所；人必须拥有这些，否则他就无法正常生活。然而，当我属于一个小团体，那种安全就被彻底否定了。当我说我是一个德国人，或者俄国人、英国人，我就否定了彻底的安全。我否定了安全，因为词语、标签变得重要了，而不是安全。这就是实际发生的事情，阿拉伯人和以色列人都想得到安全，然而他们都接受了词语以及诸如此类的一切。

现在我们来到了重点。有没有可能活在这个世界上，不逃避到某个异想天开的虚幻国度或者某个修道院，而是活在这个世界上，没有丝毫形象同时又彻底安全？

问：在这个病态的社会上我们怎么可能安全呢？

克：我会讲到这一点的，女士，我会解释给你听的。

问：这个社会争强好胜，它是邪恶的。

克：请和我一起往前走。我会跟你说明确实存在着彻底的安全、绝对的安全，但不是在形象中。

问：每时每刻都完全觉察，那么你的制约就不存在了。

克：不是如果你觉察。你觉察到你抱有形象，而那个形象是由文化、社会形成的吗？你觉察到那个形象了吗？你在关系中发现了那个形象，不是吗？现在我们问自己有没有可能摆脱形象。也就是说，当你对我说了些粗俗、伤害的话，在那一刻完全觉知你说了些什么，而我又是如何回应的。完全觉察，不是一部分，而是对令人愉快的形象和令人不快的形象都完全觉察。在对你的侮辱或赞扬产生反应的那一刻即全然觉察。在那一刻你就不会产生形象。大脑里没有对那个伤害、侮辱或奉承

Q: Who watches all this?

K: Now, who watches all this? If there is a watcher, then the image is continuous. If there is no watcher there is no image. In that state of attention the hurt and the flattery are both observed, not reacted to. You can only observe when there is no observer, who is the past. It is the past observer that gets hurt. Where there is only observation when there is flattery or insult, then it is finished. And that is real freedom.

Now follow it. In this world, if I have no image, you say I shall not be secure. One has found security in things, in a house, in property, in a bank account, that is what we call security. And one has also found security in belief. If I am a Catholic living in Italy, I believe that; it is much safer to believe what ten thousand people believe. There I have a place. And when my belief is questioned I resist.

Now can there be a total awareness of all this? The mind becomes tremendously active, you understand? Not just saying, "I must be aware", "I must learn how to be attentive". You are tremendously active, the brain is alive. Then we can move from that to find out if there is in the brain a part that has not been conditioned at all, a part of the brain which is non-mechanistic. I am putting a false question, I don't know if you see that. Do see it quickly, do see it. Please just listen for two minutes, I am on fire!

If there is no image, which is mechanical, and there is freedom from the image, then there is no part of the brain that has been conditioned. Full stop! Then my whole brain is unconditioned.

Q: It is on fire!

K: Yes, therefore it is non-mechanistic and that has a totally different kind of energy; not the mechanistic energy. I wonder if you see this. Please don't make an abstraction of it because then it becomes words. But to

的记录，因而没有形象。这需要在那一刻有极大的关注，这需要非凡的内在洞察，而只有当你看过、观察过，当你下过功夫之后，那才可能发生。不要只是说："哦，你来告诉我吧；我想舒舒服服的。"

问：是谁在看着这一切？

克：那么，是谁在看着这一切？如果有一个观察者，那么形象就会继续存在下去。如果没有观察者，就没有形象。在那种关注状态下，伤害和奉承都被观察到了，但不会对它们做出反应。只有当观察者也就是过去不存在时，你才能观察。正是过去的观察者受到了伤害。如果奉承或者侮辱出现时存在只有观察，那么它们就结束了。而这就是真正的自由。

请跟上这一点。在这个世界上，如果我没有形象，你说我就会不安全。人在外物中，在房子、财产、银行账户中找到了保障，这就是我们所谓的安全。而且人也在信仰中找到了安全。如果我是一个住在意大利的天主教徒，我就会抱有信仰；相信千千万万人都相信的东西要安全多了。我在那里找到了一个位置。当我的信仰遭到质疑时，我就会抵抗。

那么，对这一切能不能有一种全然的觉察？心于是变得极其有活力，你明白吗？而不只是说，"我必须觉察"，"我必须学习如何关注"。此时你具有非凡的活动，大脑生机勃勃。然后你就可以从那里上路去发现真相了，去弄清楚大脑有没有一部分是完全没有受到制约的，大脑是不是有一部分是不机械的。我提出的是一个虚假的问题，我不知道你有没有发现这一点。请务必快快看到，务必明白这一点。请暂且听上两分钟，我着火了！

如果没有机械的形象，从形象中解脱了出来，那么大脑就没有任

see this, that your brain has been conditioned through centuries, saying survival is only possible if you have an image, which is created by the circle in which you live and that circle gives you complete security. We have accepted that as tradition and we live in that way. I am an Englishman, I am better than anybody else, or a Frenchman, or whatever it is. Now my brain is conditioned, I don't know whether it is the whole or part, I only know that it is conditioned. There can be no enquiry into the unconditioned state until the conditioning is non-existent. So my whole enquiry is to find out whether the mind can be unconditioned, not to jump into the other, because that is too silly. So I am conditioned by belief, by education, by the culture in which I have lived, by everything, and to be totally aware of that, not discard it, not suppress it, not control it, but to be totally aware of it. Then you will find if you have gone that far there is security only in being nothing.

Q: What about images in racial prejudices? Do you belong to a community? I quite agree with you. You don't want any psychological image but you must have a physical image for your physical survival... even if you want to drop it everyone forces it on you.

K: Sir, if one wants to survive physically, what is preventing it? All the psychological barriers which man has created. So remove all those psychological barriers and you have complete security.

Q: No, because the other one involves you in it, not yourself.

K: Nobody can put you into prison.

Q: They kill you.

K: Then they kill you, all right (laughter). Then you will find out how to meet death (laughter). Not imagine what you are going to feel when you die—which is another image. Oh, I don't know if you see all this.

何一个部分受到了制约。结束了！然后我的整个大脑就解除了制约。

问：它着火了！

克：是的，因此它不再机械，于是就有了一种截然不同的能量，而不是机械的能量。我不知道你有没有看到这一点。请不要把这变成一个抽象的概念，因为那样它就变成了词语。而是看到这一点：你的大脑被制约了千百年，它说你只有抱有形象才有可能活下去，而那个形象是你生活的圈子制造出来的，那个圈子给了你彻底的安全感。我们把那些当作传统接受了下来，然后就那样活着。我是个英国人，我比其他人或者法国人，比无论什么人都好。而我的大脑受到了制约，我不知道是整个大脑还是只有一部分，我只知道它受到了制约。我无法探询那种毫无制约的状态，除非制约已经不复存在。所以我的全部探索就是要去搞清楚心智能不能解除制约，而不是跳到另一个，因为那就太愚蠢了。所以说，我被信仰、被教育、被我所处的文化、被一切所制约，完全觉察到这些，不抛弃，不压抑，不控制，而是完全觉察制约。如果你已经走了那么远，然后你就会发现，安全只存在于一无所是中。

问：在种族偏见中的形象呢？你有没有属于一个团体？我非常赞同你。你不想要任何心理上的形象，但你肯定对你身体上的生存有一个身体上的形象……即使你想把它丢下，但所有人都把它强加给你。

克：先生，如果人想在身体上生存下来，是什么在妨碍这一点？正是人类建立的心理上的障碍。所以除掉所有那些心理上的障碍，你就拥有了彻底的安全。

问：不是这样的，因为其他人会把你卷进去的，不是你自己。

So nobody can put you psychologically into prison. You are already there (laughter). We are pointing out that it is possible a to be totally free of images, which is the result of our conditioning. And one of the questions about the biography is about that very point. How was that young boy, whatever he was, how was he not conditioned right through? I won't go into that because it is a very complex problem. If one is aware of one's own conditioning then the whole thing becomes very simple. Then genius is something entirely different. And that leaves the question: What is creation?

克：没人能把你投进牢笼。

问：他们会杀了你的。

克：那他们就杀了你，好吧。（笑声）然后你就会发现该如何面对死亡。（笑声）不是想象当你死去时你会有什么感受——那是另一个意象。噢，我不知道你有没有明白这些。

所以说没人能从心理上把你投入牢笼，你已经在里面了。（笑声）我们指出的是有没有可能完全摆脱形象，也就是我们所受制约的产物。而有关传记的问题之一就是关于这一点的。那个小男孩，无论他是谁，他是如何从始至终都没有被制约的？我不会讲这个问题了，因为它非常复杂。如果你觉察到了自己的制约，那么整件事情就会变得非常简单。然后天才就是一件完全不同的事情了。而这就留下了这个问题：什么是创造？

CHAPTER 7
第 7 章

DIALOGUE II
对话二

"Are you facing in yourself what actually is gong on? And can you observe another without the past—without all the accumulated memories, insults, hurts—so that you can look at another with clear eyes? "

Questioner (1): You were going to speak on what is creation; could you say something about creative intelligence 1.

Q(2): Is there any reality in the belief in reincarnation? And what is the nature and quality of the meditative mind?

Q(3): What is the difference between denial and suppression of habits?

Q(4): You were saying that for the mind to function sanely one must have great security, food and shelter. This seems logical. But it seems that in order to try and find a way to having this security one encounters the horrors and the difficulties which make things so hard and impossible sometimes. What is the right action in this connection?

Krishnamurti: I don't quite follow this.

Q: How are we to live to have this basic security without taking part in all the horrors that are involved in it.

K: You are asking, what is correct action in a world that is chaotic, where there is no security and yet one must have security. What is one to do? Is that the question?

Q(5): I have a question which, when I ask it of myself, I always come

"你正面对着自己内心实际发生着的事情吗？同时你能不能观察别人而不带着过去——不带着积累起来的所有记忆、侮辱、伤害——于是你就可以用清澈的双眼看着别人？"

提问者（1）：你打算今天谈一谈创造是什么；你能不能讲一讲创造性的智慧？

问（2）：对转世的信仰有任何真实性吗？冥想的心具有怎样的特性和品质？

问（3）：对习惯的否定和压抑有什么不同？

问（4）：我们说过，心智若要健全地运转，人就必须拥有巨大的安全，拥有食物和住所。这看起来是符合逻辑的。然而，为了努力找到拥有这种安全的途径，人似乎遇到了很多可怕的事和困难，使得事情变得非常艰难，有时候甚至变得不可能。在这个过程中正确的行动是什么？

克里希那穆提：我不太明白你的意思。

问：我们要如何在生活中拥有这种基本的安全，却无须参与涉及的所有那些可怕的事情？

克：你问的是，在这个混乱的世界上，正确的行动是什么？世界上没有安全而人又必须拥有安全，那人该怎么办？是这个问题吗？

问（5）：我有一个问题，当我问自己这个问题时，我总是碰壁。

up against a wall. I say, "I am the observer, and I would like to see the whole of the observer. I cannot see the whole of the observer because I can only see in fragments. So how is the observer to see the whole of the observer unless there is no observer? How can the observer see the observer with no observer?"

K: How can one see the whole of the observer and can the observer watch himself as the observer. Is that the question?

Q(6) This is about the state of mind in observation. Now when a situation occurs, what holds one to the observation that the observer is not different from what is observed? There seems a lack of attention at the moment, at that point; but that attention requires a tremendous vitality that we don't have.

K: Have I understood the question rightly? We do not have enough energy to observe wholly. Is that it?

Q: Yes.

K: Now which of these questions shall we talk over together?

Q(7): May I ask a question? Can an act of willpower—I think you call it an act of friction - can this generate the vitality or the passion?

K: Can will generate sufficient energy to see clearly? Would that be right?

Q: Yes.

Q(8): What happens to the brain and the process of thought during hypnosis? For medical reasons we use hypnosis. What is the process of thought in that particular case?

K: We have got so many questions. What shall we begin with? The observer?

Q: Yes.

我说："我是观察者，而我想看看观察者的全貌。我无法看到观察者的全貌，因为我只能从片段中去看。所以，除非没有观察者，否则观察者要如何才能看到观察者的全貌？可是如果没有观察者，观察者又如何能看到观察者？"

克：人如何才能看到观察者的全貌，观察者能不能看着作为观察者的自己。是这个问题吗？

问（6）：这个问题是关于观察中的心智状态的。当有情况发生时，是什么让人保持在观察者与被观察者并无不同的那种观察中的？在那一刻，在那个点上，关注似乎是缺乏的；但那种关注需要一份我们所没有的巨大活力。

克：我正确地理解了这个问题吗？我们没有足够的能量进行完整的观察。是这个问题吗？

问：是的。

克：现在我们想探讨这些问题中的哪一个？

问（7）：我可以问一个问题吗？意志力的行为能否——我想你把它叫作冲突的行为——它能否产生活力或者激情？

克：意志能否产生看清所需要的充足能量？对吗？

问：对。

问（8）：催眠时大脑和思想过程发生了什么？出于医学原因我们会使用催眠。在那种特殊情况下的思想过程是怎样的？

克：我们有太多问题了。我们该从哪个开始？观察者那个？

问：好的。

克：看到观察者的全貌需要能量，而那种能量要如何才能产生？如何才能获得那种能量？而那种能量会不会揭示出观察者全部的本质和

K: To see the whole of the observer one needs energy and how is that energy to be derived? How is that energy to be acquired? And will that energy reveal the totality of the nature and structure of the observer? Should we discuss that? And what is the quality of the mind that has this meditative process? How is one to observe the whole of something, psychologically? How is one to be aware of oneself totally? Can we begin with that?

Q: Surely one can only be aware of the totality if one loses oneself.

K: Yes, sir. Is it possible to see the totality of one's reactions, the motives, the fears, the anxieties, the sorrows, the pain, the totality of all that? Or must one see it in fragments, in layers? Shall we discuss that? How is one to be aware of the content of one's consciousness?

What is consciousness? What do you think is consciousness—under hypnosis, as well as when one is not hypnotized? Most of us are hypnotised —by words, by propaganda, by tradition, by all the things that we believe in. We are hypnotized not only by external influence, but also we have our own peculiar process of hypnotizing ourselves into believing something, or not believing and so on. Can one see the totality of one's consciousness? Let us enquire into this.

Q: The observer cannot see it.

K: Don't let us say one can, one cannot, it is so, it is not so. Let's enquire.

Q: One has the feeling one has got to begin!

K: We are going to begin, sir (laughter). How shall I begin, from where shall I begin? To be aware of myself, myself being all the beliefs, the dogmas, conclusions, the fears, the anxieties, the pain, the sorrow, the fear of death, the whole of that—where shall we begin to find out the content of this?

结构？我们要讨论这个吗？拥有这种冥想过程的心具有怎样的品质？人要如何从心理上观察某件事情的整体？人要如何完全觉察自己？我们可以从这个问题开始吗？

问：毫无疑问，只有当一个人失去了自我时，他才能觉察到整体。

克：是的，先生。有没有可能看到自己所有的反应、动机、恐惧、焦虑、悲伤和痛苦，看到这一切的整体？还是说，人必须通过各个碎片、通过各个层次去看？我们可以讨论这个吗？人要如何觉察自身意识的内容？

什么是意识？你认为意识是什么——在催眠的状态下，以及没有被催眠的时候？我们大部分人都被催眠了——被言语、被宣传、被传统、被我们相信的所有东西催眠了。我们不仅被外在的影响所催眠，而且我们还有自己特殊的自我催眠过程，催眠自己去相信什么或者不相信什么，等等。人能看到自身意识的整体吗？让我们来探究这个问题。

问：观察者看不到。

克：我们先别说能还是不能，是这样，或者不是这样。让我们来探究。

问：我觉得我们必须得开始才行！

克：我们这就开始，先生。（笑声）我要如何开始，我要从哪里开始呢？觉察我自己，我自己就是所有的教条、结论、恐惧、焦虑、痛苦、悲伤和对死亡的恐惧，那一切——我们该从哪里开始搞清楚这个内容？

问：你刚刚问过意识是什么。

克：我们正在探讨这个问题。

Q: You just asked what consciousness was.

K: We are going into that.

Q: If one is going to observe, is it true that one has to stand outside the things that one is observing?

K: Madam, I am asking, if I may, how shall I begin to enquire into the whole structure of myself. If I am interested, if I am serious, where shall I begin?

Q: Is the question, "Who am I?"

K: That becomes intellectual, verbal. I begin to know myself in my relationship to others—do let's face that fact. I cannot know myself in abstraction. Whereas if I could observe what my reactions are in relationship to another, then I begin to enquire. That is much closer, more accurate and revealing. Can we do that? That is, in my relationship to nature, to the neighbour and so on, I discover the nature of myself. So how do I observe my reactions in my relationship with another?

Q: Each time I see something about myself in a reaction it becomes knowledge, it becomes something retainable.

K: I wonder if we are aware what takes place in our relationship with another. You all seem to be so vague about this matter.

Q: When I am very interested in some relationship I notice that I can't really observe. When I am angry in my relationship I see immediately that I really can't observe what is going on.

K: What do we mean by relationship?

Q: When we seem to want something...

K: Look at the word first, the meaning of the word.

Q: I like to compare myself with the other person.

K: We are asking the meaning of the word itself, relationship.

问：如果一个人要去观察，是不是他就必须置身于他所观察的事物之外？

克：女士，我问的是，如果可以的话，我要如何开始探究我自己的整个结构。如果我感兴趣的话，如果我认真的话，我要从哪里开始？

问：问题是"我是谁"吗？

克：那就变成智力上、语言上的事情了。我开始在我与他人的关系中了解自己——我们务必要面对这个事实。我无法抽象地了解自己。然而，如果我能够观察自己在与别人的关系中有什么反应，那么我就开始了探询。这要更进一步，更准确，也更有启发性。我们能这么做吗？也就是说，在我与自然、与邻居等的关系中，我探索我自己的本质。那么，我要如何在与别人的关系中观察自己的反应？

问：每次有关我自己的反应我发现了什么，它就会变成知识，变成某种可以保留的东西。

克：我想知道我们有没有觉察到在我们与别人的关系中发生了什么。你们看起来对这件事情都很模糊。

问：当我对某份关系非常感兴趣时，我注意到我就无法真正去观察了。当我在关系中生气时，我立刻发现我真的无法观察正在发生的事情了。

克：我们说的关系是什么意思？

问：当我们似乎想得到什么……

克：先看看这个词，这个词的含义。

问：我喜欢把自己跟另一个人比较。

克：我们问的是"关系"这个词本身的意思。

问（1）：交流。

Q(1): Communication.

Q(2): It means you are relating to that person.

K: When I say I am related to my wife, or to my husband, father, son, neighbour, what does that mean?

Q(1): I care for the person.

Q(2): The whole human race is one's brother.

Q(3): I'd rather you told us.

K: Ah! (laughter). Relationship means—I am enquiring please, I am not stating it—doesn't relationship mean to respond accurately. To be related, the meaning in the dictionary is, to respond—relationship comes from that word. Now how do I respond in my relationship to you, or to my wife, husband and all the rest of it? Am I responding according to the image I have about you? Or are we both free of the images and therefore responding accurately?

Q: Isn't it largely subconscious?

K: First let us see what the word in itself means.

Q: What do you mean by accurate?

K: Accurate means care—the word accurate means to have great care. If you care for something you act accurately. If you care for your motor you must be very well acquainted with it, you must know all the mechanical processes of it. Accurate means infinite care; we are using that word in that sense. When there is a relationship with another, either intimate, or distant, the response depends on the image you have about the other, or the image the other has about you. And when we act or respond according to that image, it is inaccurate, it is not with complete care.

Q: What is a love and hate relationship?

K: We will come to that. I have an image about you and you have an

问（2）：它的意思是你和那个人有关联。

克：当我说我和我妻子或者我丈夫、父亲、儿子、邻居有关系，那是什么意思？

问（1）：我关心那个人。

问（2）：整个人类是你的兄弟。

问（3）：还是你告诉我们吧。

克：啊！（笑声）关系意味着——我也在探询，我不是在下定义——关系难道不意味着恰当地回应吗？有关联，在词典里的意思是，回应——关系从那个词而来。那么，在我与你、与我的妻子、丈夫等人之间的关系中，我是如何回应的？我是根据我对你抱有的形象来回应的吗？还是说我们都摆脱了形象，因而是在恰当地做出回应？

问：回应难道不是基本上都是下意识做出的吗？

克：首先让我们来看看这个词本身的含义。

问：你说的恰当是什么意思？

克：恰当意味着关怀——"恰当"这个词意味着拥有巨大的关怀。如果你关心什么你就会恰当地行动。如果你关心你的汽车，你就必然会对它十分熟悉，你必然知道它所有的机械过程。恰当意味着无尽的关怀；我们用这个词指的是这个意思。当你与别人有关系，无论是亲密还是疏远，你们之间的回应就取决于你对另一个人抱有的形象，或者另一个人对你抱有的形象。而当我们根据那个形象去行动或回应时，那就是不恰当的，就没有带着完全的关怀。

问：又爱又恨的关系是什么？

克：我们会讲到那一点的。我对你抱有形象，你对我也抱有形象。那个形象是由欢愉、恐惧、唠叨、控制、占有、各种伤害和不耐烦等拼

image about me. That image has been put together through pleasure, fear, nagging, domination, possession, various hurts, impatience and so on. Now when we act or respond according to that image, then that action, being incomplete, is inaccurate, or without care, which we generally call love. Are you aware that you have an image about another? And having that image you respond according to the past, because the image has been put together and has become the past.

Q: And also it is according to one's selfish desires.

K: I said that, fear, desire, selfishness.

Q: You can't think of another person without an image; how can you write a letter without an image?

K: How quickly you want to resolve everything, don't you? First of all, can we be aware that we have an image, not only about ourselves but about another?

Q: The two images are in relation, images of the other are in relation with the image of yourself.

K: You see what you are saying—there is a thing different from the image.

Q: The image of the other is made from the image of yourself.

K: That is what we said.

Q: Would anything practical help?

K: This is the most practical thing if you listen to this. The practical thing is to observe clearly what we are and act from there. Is one aware that one has an image about another? And is one aware that one has an image about oneself? Are you aware of that? This is a simple thing. I injure you, I hurt you, and you naturally have an image about me. I give you pleasure and you have an image about me. And according to that hurt or pleasure you

凑而来的。那么，当我们根据那个形象去行动或回应时，那个行动因为是不完整的，所以是不恰当的或者缺乏关怀，这种关怀我们通常称之为爱。你觉察到你对别人抱有形象了吗？怀着那个形象，你是根据过去做出回应的，因为那个形象是拼凑起来的，并且变成了过去。

问：而且它也是通过人自私的欲望产生的。

克：这点我说过了，有恐惧、欲望和自私。

问：你想到别人的时候没办法不带着一个形象；如果心里没有一个形象你怎么写信？

克：你这么快就想解决所有的问题了，不是吗？首先，我们能不能觉察到我们抱有形象，不光是对自己，而且对别人也一样？

问：两个形象是相关的，别人的形象和你自己的形象是联系在一起的。

克：你看看你说的话——有一种东西与形象是不同的。

问：别人的形象是从你自己的形象中产生的。

克：这就是我们刚才说的。

问：有什么实用的做法可以帮上忙吗？

克：如果你听听我说的这些话，这就是最实用的事情。最实用的事情是清晰地观察我们现在如何，然后从那里去行动。你有没有觉察到你对别人抱有形象？你有没有觉察到你对自己也抱有形象？你发觉这一点了吗？这是一件很简单的事情。我弄伤了你，我伤害了你，于是你自然就对我产生了一个印象。我给了你快乐，你就对我产生了一个印象。然后你根据那个伤害或者快乐做出反应，而那个反应由于是支离破碎的，所以必定是不恰当的、不完整的。这很简单。我们可以从那里继续吗？

react, and that reaction, being fragmentary, must be inaccurate, not whole. This is simple. Can we go on from there.

Now what do you do with the image you have built about another? I am aware that I have an image about myself and I have an image about you, so I have got two images. Am I conscious of this? Now if I have an image, why has this image been put together? And who is it that has put the image together? You understand the question?

Q(1): Is it fear that creates the image?

Q(2): Is experience a necessary imaginative process?

Q(3): Previous images.

Q(4): Lack of attention.

K: How does it come? Not through lack of something, but how does it come? You say through experience, through various incidents, through words...

Q: Retaining it all as memory.

K: Which is all the movement of thought, isn't it? So thought as movement, which is time, put this image together, created this image. It does it because it wants to protect itself. Am I inventing, or fabricating this, or is this actual?

Q: Actual.

K: That means "what is". Actuality means "what is". (Sorry, I am not teaching you English!)

Q: It means that it then can see itself.

K: No, no. You have an image about me, haven't you?

Q: Well, it is changing. K: Wait, go slow (laughter). You have an image about me, haven't you, if you are honest, look into yourself, you see you have an image. How has that image been brought about? You have read

那么你该拿你对别人建立起来的形象怎么办？我觉察到我对自己、对你都抱有形象，所以我有了两个形象。我意识到这一点了吗？如果我抱有形象，那么这个形象为什么会建立起来？而建造形象的又是谁？你明白这个问题吗？

问（1）：是恐惧建立了形象吗？

问（2）：经验是一个必要的想象过程吗？

问（3）：是因为之前的形象。

问（4）：是因为缺乏关注。

克：它是如何产生的？不是缺少什么，而是它是如何产生的？你说是通过经验、时间、语言……

问：把它们都作为记忆保存了下来。

克：那都是思想的运动，不是吗？所以思想作为运动，也就是时间，造就了这个形象，建立了这个形象。它这么做是因为它想保护自己。我是在虚构或者捏造这些吗，还是说这就是事实？

问：是事实。

克：这意味着"现在如何"。事实意味着"现在如何"。（抱歉，我不是在教你英语！）

问：也就是说于是它能看到自己。

克：不，不是。你对我抱有一个印象，不是吗？

问：哦，它也在变化。

克：等一下，慢慢来。（笑声）你对我抱有一个印象，不是吗，如果你诚实的话，看看你自己的内心，你会看到你抱有一个形象。这个形象是如何产生的？你读过一些东西，你听过一些东西，我有些名声，有很多讲话，报纸上还有些文章，等等。所以这一切都影响了思想，从

something, you have listened to something, there is a reputation, a lot of talk about it, some articles in the papers and so on. So all this has influenced thought and out of that you have created an image. And you have an image, not only about yourself but about the other. So when you respond according to an image about the speaker you are responding inaccurately; in that there is no care. We said care implies attention, affection, accuracy. That means to act according to "what is". Now let's move from there.

Q: Is not an image a thought form?

K: We said that, a thought.

Q: Thought has created images and it seems to imply that thought has created thought so...

K: Wait, we will get very far if we go slowly. So thought has built this image through time. It may be one day or fifty years. And I see in my relationship to another this image plays a tremendous part. If I become conscious, if I don't act mechanically, I become aware and see how extraordinarily vital this image is. Then my next question is: is it possible to be free of the image? I have an image as a Communist, believing in all kinds of ideas, or as a Catholic—you follow. This whole cultural economic, social background has built this image also. And I react according to that, there is a reaction according to that image. I think this is clear.

Now is one aware of it? Then one asks: is it necessary? If it is necessary one should keep it, one should have the image. If it is not necessary how is one to be free of it? Now, is it necessary?

Q: Images form the whole chaos in the world where we live, so it is not necessary.

K: He says this whole image-making is bringing about chaos in the world.

中你就建立了一个形象。而且你抱有的形象不光是关于你自己的，还有对别人的。所以，当你根据对讲话者的形象做出回应时，你就是在不恰当地回应；其中没有关怀。我们说过关怀意味着关注、慈爱和恰当，那意味着根据"现在如何"去行动。现在让我们从这里出发。

问：形象是思想的一种形式吗？

克：这我们说过了，是思想。

问：思想建立了形象，而这似乎意味着思想建立了思想……

克：等一下，如果我们慢慢走，我们就会走得很远。所以思想通过时间建立了这个形象，可能是一天也可能是 50 年建立起来的。而我发现在我与别人的关系中，这个形象起到了非常重大的作用。如果我变得有意识，如果我不机械地行动，我就会变得觉知，进而能看到这个形象有多么重要。然后我的下一个问题就是：有没有可能摆脱形象？我抱有作为一个共产主义者的形象，相信各种理念，或者作为一个天主教徒的形象——你明白吗？这整个文化、经济和社会背景也建立了这个形象。而我根据它做出反应，有了根据那个形象做出的反应。我想这一点很清楚。

那么你觉察到形象了吗？然后你问：它有必要吗？如果有必要，你就应该留着它，你就应该抱有意象。如果没必要，那么你如何才能摆脱它？那么，它有必要吗？

问：形象造成了我们所生活的这个世界的所有混乱，所以它是不必要的。

克：他说这整个形象制造的过程带来了世界上的混乱。

问：我们这不是在下很多评判吗？

克：我们是在下很多评判吗？

Q: Aren't we making a lot of judgements?

K: Are we making a lot of judgements?

Q: In making an image there is a lot of judgement.

K: Yes, but we are asking a little more. We are asking whether it is necessary to have these images?

Q: No, we can be free of it.

K: Is it necessary? First let us see that.

Q: No.

K: Then if it is not necessary why do we keep it? (laughter).

Q: I have a feeling, being what we are, we can hardly help it.

K: We are going to find out whether it is possible to be free of this image, and whether it is worth while to be free of this image, and what does it mean to be free of the image.

Q: What is the relation with the chaos? Is it judging that is wrong?

K: No, no, sir. Look, I have an image about myself as a Communist and I believe in Marx, his economic principles, I am strongly committed to that. And I reject everything else. But you think differently and you are committed to that. So there is a division between you and me, and that division invariably brings conflict I believe that I am Indian and I am committed to Indian nationalism, and you are a committed Muslim and there is division and conflict. So thought has created this division, thought has created these images, these labels, these beliefs and so there is contradiction and division, which brings conflict and therefore chaos. That is a fact. So you think life is a process of infinite conflicts, neverending conflicts, then you must keep these images. I don't say it is, we are asking. I believe there have been more than five thousand wars within the last two thousand years and we have accepted that. To have our sons killed because we have these images. And if we see that is not necessary, that it is really a tremendous danger to survival, then I must

问：建立形象的过程中就存在大量的评判。

克：是的，但我们问的还要更深入一点儿。我们问的是我们需要抱有这些形象吗？

问：不需要，我们能摆脱它。

克：形象是不是必要的？我们首先来看看这个问题。

问：它不是必要的。

克：如果不是必要的，那你为什么还要留着它？（笑声）

问：我有一种感觉，我们就是现在的样子，这一点我们几乎无能为力。

克：我们这就来弄清楚有没有可能摆脱这个形象，是不是值得摆脱这个形象，还有摆脱形象是什么意思。

问：这和如今的混乱有什么关系？这是在评判它是错的吗？

克：不，不，先生。比如说，我对自己抱有一个共产主义者的形象，我相信马克思，相信他的经济原理，对此我十分坚定。于是你和我之间就有了分裂，而那种分裂不可避免地会带来冲突。我相信我是个印度人，我忠诚于印度的民族主义，而你是一个坚定的穆斯林，于是就有了分裂和冲突。所以思想制造了这种分裂，思想建立了这些形象、这些标签、这些信仰，于是就产生了矛盾和分裂，这会带来冲突，进而带来混乱。这是一个事实。所以你认为生活是一个有着无尽的冲突、没完没了的冲突的过程，于是你必须保有这些形象。我没有说就是这样，我们在询问。我相信过去两千年来发生了超过五千场战争，而我们接受了这些。让我们的儿子被杀害，就因为我们抱有这些形象。而如果我们看到那是完全没必要的，那对于生存真的是一种巨大的危险，那么我就必须搞清楚如何才能摆脱形象。

find out how to be free of the images.

Q: I think something else is involved in this, because you say we always react from the past, but what difference does it make—the past is a cyclic phenomenon that repeats so you can't prevent yourself, you know it is a fact that you will repeat it in the same way all the time.

K: We are talking about the necessity...

Q: (interrupting) You are pitting yourself against necessity...

K:... of having an image, or not having an image. If we are clear that these images are a real danger, really a destructive process, then we want to get rid of them. But if you say: I keep my little image and you keep your little image, then we are at each other's throat. So if we can see very clearly that these images, labels, words, are destroying human beings...

Q: Krishnamurti, doesn't spiritual commitment give us the penetration or energy? I mean if I am a committed Buddhist and I channel my energy in that direction, it doesn't necessarily mean that I am in conflict with those who aren't Buddhists.

K: Just examine that please. If I am a committed human being, committed to Buddhism, and another is committed to the Christian dogma, and another to Communism...

Q: That is not my concern.

K: Isn't this what is happening in life? Don't say it is not my business if you are a Communist. It is my business to see if we can live in security, in peace in the world, we are human beings, supposed to be intelligent. Why should I be committed to anything?

Q: Because it gives energy, the power of penetration.

K: No, no.

Q: The danger is that we are moving away from the central fact.

问：我想这里面还涉及其他的事情，因为你说我们是根据过去做出反应的，但是那又能带来什么不同呢——过去是一种不断重复的循环现象，所以你无法阻止自己那么做，你知道事实上你就是会一直用同样的方式重复它。

克：我们在说的是必要性……

问：（打断）你是在让自己对抗必要性……

克：……抱有形象或者不抱有形象的必要性。如果我们清楚了这些意象是一种真正的危险，实际上是一个破坏性的过程，那么我们就想要去除它们。但是如果你说：我要留着我的小形象，你也留着你的小形象，那么我们就拼个你死我活吧。所以，如果我们能够非常清楚地看到这些形象、标签、词语正在摧毁人类……

问：克里希那穆提，灵性上的献身精神难道不会给我们洞察力或者能量吗？我的意思是说，如果我是一个坚定的佛教徒，我就会把自己的精力集中在那个方向上，但那并不意味着我与不是佛教徒的人必然会发生冲突。

克：拜托来审视一下这个问题。如果我是一个有坚定信仰的人，信仰佛教，而另一个人信仰基督教的律条，还有一个人信仰共产主义……

问：我不关心那些。

克：这不就是生活中发生着的事情吗？不要说：如果你是一个共产主义者那不关我的事。看看我们在这个世界上能不能活在安全中、和平中，这是我的事情，我们是人类，应该是有智慧的。我为什么要坚定地信仰任何事情？

问：因为那会带来能量，洞察的力量。

克：不，不是的。

K: Yes, we are always moving away from the central fact.

Q: We are doing that right now: the image is not necessary.

K: People think it is necessary to be an Englishman, a German, a Hindu, a Catholic, they think it is important. They don't see the danger of it.

Q:1: Some people think it is not necessary.

Q:2: Why don't we see the danger?

K: Because we are so heavily conditioned, it is so profitable. My job depends on it. I might not be able to marry my son to somebody who is a Catholic. All that stuff. So the point is: if one sees the danger of these images, how can the mind free itself from them?

Q: Can "I" be there when no image is formed?

K: Images, whether they are old or new, are the same images.

Q: Yes, but when an image is formed can I be aware?

K: We are first of all going to go into that. How is an image formed? Is it formed through inattention? You get angry with me and if at that moment I am totally attentive to what you say there is no anger. I wonder if you realize this?

Q: So the image and the image-former must be the same in that case.

K: Keep it very simple. I say something that doesn't give you pleasure. You have an image instantly, haven't you? Now at that moment, if you are completely aware, is there an image?

Q: If you don't have that new image, all the other images are gone.

K: Yes, that is the whole point. Can one be attentive at the moment of listening? You are listening now, can you be totally attentive? And when someone called you by an unpleasant name, or gives you pleasure, at that moment, at that precise moment, can you be totally aware? Have you ever tried this? You can test it out, because that is the only way to find out, not

问：危险在于我们正在偏离那个核心的事实。

克：是的，我们一直在偏离核心的事实。

问：我们现在就在偏离：形象是不必要的。

克：人们认为有必要做一个英国人、德国人、印度教徒、天主教徒，他们认为那很重要。他们没有看到形象的危险。

问（1）：也有些人认为没必要有形象。

问（2）：我们为什么看不到这个危险？

克：因为我们受到了沉重的制约。形象显得太有利可图了，我的工作依赖它。我也许没办法让我儿子娶一个身为天主教徒的人，以及所有那类事情。所以重点在于：如果你看到了这些形象的危险，那么心灵能让自己摆脱它们吗？

问：当没有形象产生时，"我"还能存在吗？

克：形象无论新旧，都同样是形象。

问：是的，但是当形象产生时，我能觉察到吗？

克：我们首先就要来探讨一下这个问题。形象是如何产生的？它是因为漫不经心产生的吗？你对我很生气，而如果我在那一刻能全然关注你说的话，你就不会产生愤怒。我想知道你认识到这一点了吗？

问：所以在那种情况下，形象和形象制造者必定是一回事。

克：说得简单点儿。我说了些不让你开心的话，你立刻就有了一个印象，不是吗？那么在那一刻，如果你全然觉察，还有形象吗？

问：如果你没有那个新形象，那么其他所有的形象就都消失了。

克：是的，这就是整个重点。你能在聆听的那一刻全神贯注吗？你此刻就在听，那么你能全神贯注吗？而当有人给了你一个令人不愉快的称呼，或者给了你快乐，在那一刻，就在那一刻，你能全然觉察吗？

accept the speaker's words. You can test it out. Then if there is no image-forming, and therefore no image, then what is the relationship between the two. You have no image about me, but I have an image about you; then what is your relationship to me? You have no image because you see the danger of it, but I don't see the danger of it, I have my images and you are related to me, as wife, husband, father, whatever it is. I have the image and you have not. Then what is your relationship to me? And what is my relationship to you?

Q: There is a barrier somewhere.

K: Of course there is a barrier, but we are asking what is that relationship. You are my wife; and I am very ambitious, greedy, envious, I want to succeed in this world, make a lot of money, position, prestige, and you say, "How absurd all that is, don't be like that, don't be silly, don't be traditional, don't be mechanical, that is just the old pattern being repeated". What happens between you and me?

Q: Division.

K: And we talk together about love. I go off to the office here I am brutal, ambitious, ruthless, and I come home and am very pleasant to you—because I want to sleep with you. What is the relationship?

Q(1): No good.

Q(2): No relationship.

K: No relationship at all. At last ! And yet this is what we call love

So what is the relationship between you and me when I have an image and you have no image? Either you leave me, or we live in conflict. You don't create conflict but I create conflict because I have an image. So is it possible in our relationship with each other to help each other to be free of images? You understand my question? I am related to you by some

你可曾试过这么做？你可以检验一下，因为那是发现真相的唯一途径，而不是接受讲话者说的话。你可以检验一下。如果没有产生形象，进而没有形象，那么两个人之间的关系是什么？你对我没有意象，但我对你抱有意象，那么你与我的关系是什么？你没有形象，因为你看到了它的危险，而我没有看到，我有自己的各种形象，而你与我是有关系的，作为妻子、丈夫、父亲，无论什么人。那么我与你的关系是什么？

问：有某种障碍存在。

克：当然有障碍，但我们问的是那种关系是什么。你是我的妻子，而我非常野心勃勃、贪婪、嫉妒，我想在这个世界上取得成功，谋求大量的金钱、地位、威望，而你说："那些都太荒唐了，不要那样，不要犯傻，不要依循传统，不要那么机械，那只是重复着的旧模式。"那么你我之间会发生什么？

问：分裂。

克：我们还会一起探讨爱。我去办公室上班，在那里我残忍无情、野心勃勃，而回到家我让你很开心——因为我想和你上床。那么这里的关系是什么？

问（1）：没什么好处。

问（2）：没有关系。

克：根本没有关系。原来是这样！而这就是我们所谓的"爱"。

所以，当我有形象而你没有形象时，你和我之间的关系是什么？你要么离开我，要么我们生活在冲突中。你不制造冲突，但我会制造冲突，因为我有形象。所以，在我们彼此的关系中，我们有没有可能互相帮助对方摆脱形象？你明白我的问题吗？由于某种不幸的原因、性需求……之类，我和你有了关系。我与你有关，你摆脱了形象而我没有，

misfortune, sexual demands and so on and so on. I am related to you and you are free of the images and I am not, and therefore you care infinitely. I wonder if you see that? To you it is tremendously important to be free of images—and I am your father, wife, husband or whatever it is. Then will you abandon me?

Q: No.

K: Don't say "no" so easily. You care, you have affection, you feel totally differently. So what will you do with me?

Q: There is nothing you can do.

K: Why can't you do something with me? Do go into it, don't theorize about it. You are all in that position. Life is this.

Q(1): It depends if this person has the capacity to see what the truth of the matter is.

Q(2): See through it all and don't take any notice of it (laughter).

K: When I am nagging you all the time? You people just play with words. You don't take actuality and look at it.

Q: Surely if you have no image in yourself and you look at another person, you won't see their image either.

K: If I have no image I see very clearly that you have an image. This is happening in the world, this is happening in every family, in every situation in relationship—you have something free and I have not and the battle is between us.

Q: I think that situation is in everything.

K: That is what I am saying. What do you do? just drop it and disappear and become a monk? Form a community? Go off in meditation and all the rest of it? Here is a tremendous problem.

Q(1): I tell you how I feel, first of all.

所以你拥有无尽的关怀。我想知道你明白这一点了吗？对你来说，摆脱形象无比重要——而我是你的父亲、妻子、丈夫或者无论是谁。那么你会抛弃我吗？

问：不会。

克：不要那么轻易就说"不会"。你关心我，你有爱，你的感受完全不同。那么你会对我做什么？

问：你什么也做不了。

克：为什么你对我什么也做不了？请务必深入探索这个问题，不要把它理论化。你们都在那种处境下，生活就是这样的。

问（1）：那取决于这个人有没有能力看到事情的真相是什么。

问（2）：完全看穿它，但又完全不在意它。（笑声）

克：在我一直烦扰你的时候？你们这些人只是在玩弄词语。你们不肯拿起事实来看一看。

问：毫无疑问，如果你自己没有形象，当你看其他人的时候，你也不会看到他们的形象。

克：如果我没有形象，我会非常清楚地看到你有形象。这种事情在世界上发生着，在每个家庭里、在每一种关系里都发生着——你有了某种自由，而我没有，于是我们之间就有了斗争。

问：我认为一切事情中都有这种情况发生。

克：那就是我说的意思。那么你会怎么办？就那样抛下一切，消失掉然后变成一个僧人吗？成立一个社团吗？跑去冥想以及诸如此类吗？这里有一个巨大的问题。

问（1）：首先我会告诉你我的感受。

问（2）：但显然这是虚构的情况，因为我们在努力去想象会怎

Q(2): But surely this is fictitious, because we are trying to imagine.

K: I have said that if you have an image and I have an image, then we live very peacefully because we are both blind and we don't care.

Q: That situation you have created for us because you want us to be free of images!

K: Of course, of course, I want you to be free of images because otherwise we are going to destroy the world.

Q: I see that.

K: The situation is not being created for you: it is there. Look at it.

Q: I have an image about you, and I have had it for a long time. And there are different kinds of images. I have been trying to get rid of those images because I have read that they have created problems for me. Now every time I try to work it out with you; and yet it hasn't helped.

K: I'll show you how to get rid of it, how to be free of images.

Q: I don't believe you, sir.

K: Then don't believe me (laughter).

Q: All the time you are just sitting there talking. Abstractions and abstractions. Me having an image about you means you are sitting up on the platform being an enlightened person I am here as a listener, let's say a disciple or a pupil. Now I feel very strongly that is not actuality or reality because we are two human beings. But still you are the king of gurus, you are the one who knows and... (laughter).

K: Please don't laugh, sirs, be quiet, he is telling you some thing, please listen. May I show you something?

If that image of the guru has not created a problem you would live with that guru happily, wouldn't you? But it has created a problem, whether it is the guru, the wife, or the husband—it is the same thing. You have got

么样。

克：我说过，如果你有形象我也有形象，那么我们就可以和平共处了，因为我们两个人都是盲目的，我们不关心这些。

问：你为我们虚构了那种情形，因为你想让我们摆脱形象！

克：当然，当然，我想让你们摆脱形象，因为否则我们就会毁掉这个世界。

问：我明白这一点。

克：这种情形不是为你们虚构出来的：它就在那儿，去看一看。

问：我对你抱有一个形象，这个形象我有了好长一段时间了。另外还有各种各样其他的形象。我一直试图去除那些形象，因为我读到书上说它们给我制造了很多问题。每一次我都试图和你一起解决这个问题，但依然没有帮助。

克：如何除掉它们，如何摆脱形象，我会展示给你看的。

问：我不相信你，先生。

克：那就不要相信我好了。（笑声）

问：你一直坐在那里讲啊讲，讲的是一段又一段抽象的说法。我对你抱有一个形象，意思是说，你作为一个开悟的人高高地坐在讲台上，而我在这里是一个聆听者，就让我们说是一个弟子或者一个学生。现在我有一种非常强烈的感觉，那不是事实或者现实，因为我们是两个人。但你依然是古鲁之王，你是那个知道的人而且……（笑声）

克：请不要笑，先生们，请安静，他在告诉你一件事，请注意听。我可以指给你看一件事吗？

如果那个古鲁的形象没有造成问题，你就会快乐地和那个古鲁生活在一起，不是吗？但是它造成了问题，无论是古鲁、妻子还是丈夫的

the image about the speaker as the supreme guru (Krishnamurti and others laugh)—the word means, one who dispels ignorance, one who dispels the ignorance of another. But generally the gurus impose their ignorance on you. You have an image about me as the guru, or you have an image about another as a Christian and so on. If that pleases you, if that gives you satisfactIon you will hold on to it—won't you? That is simple enough. If it causes trouble then you say, "It is terrible to have this" and you move away, form another relationship which is pleasant; but it is the same image-making. So one asks: is it possible to be free of images. The speaker sits on the platform because it is convenient, so you can all see; I can equally sit on the ground but you will have the same image. So the height doesn't make any difference. The question is, whether the mind—the mind being part of thought, and thought has created these images—can thought dispel these images? Thought has created it and thought can dispel it because it is unsatisfactory and create another image which will be satisfactory. This is what we do. I don't like that guru for various reasons and I go to another because he praises me, gives me garlands and says, "My dear chap, you are the best disciple I have". So thought has created this image. Can thought undo the image?

Q: Not if you are looking at it intellectually. But looking at it intellectually, you are not using your senses.

K: I am asking that first. Look at it. Can the intellect, reasoning, dispel the image?

Q: No.

K: Then what will?

Q: The thing that stands in the way is merely self, the "I". If you overcome this...

K: I know; but I don't want to go into the much more complex

形象——那都是一回事。你对讲话者抱有的形象是一个超级古鲁（克里希那穆提和其他人都笑了）——古鲁这个词的含义是消除无知的人，消除他人的无知的人。但通常的情况是古鲁把他们的无知强加在你身上。你对我抱有的形象是一个古鲁，或者你对另一个人抱有的形象是一个基督教徒，等等。如果那让你高兴，如果那让你满意，你就会抓住它不放——不是吗？这非常简单。如果它给你带来了麻烦，你就会说，"抱有这种形象太糟糕了"，然后你离开，去建立另一份愉快的关系；但这同样是制造意象的过程。于是你问：有没有可能摆脱形象？讲话者坐在讲台上是为了方便，这样你们就都能看到；我可以和你们一样坐在地上，但你还会有同样的形象。所以高度不会带来任何区别。问题是，心智能否——心智是思想的一部分，而思想建立了这些形象——思想能否消除这些形象？思想建立了它，思想可以因为它令人不满而消除它，然后建立另一个令人满意的形象。这就是我们做的事情。我因为各种原因不喜欢那个古鲁，然后我去找另一个古鲁，因为他称赞我，给了我荣誉并且说："我亲爱的小伙，你是我最好的弟子。"所以思想建立了这个形象。思想能消除这个形象吗？

问：如果你用智力去看就不能。但是用智力去看，你就没有使用你的感官。

克：我首先问的就是这个问题。看一看。智力、理性能够消除形象吗？

问：不能。

克：那么什么能消除形象？

问：挡在路上的东西就是自我、"我"而已。如果你克服了这个……

克：我知道；但是我们不想探讨"我"这个要复杂得多的问题。

problem of the "I".

Q: You say the image is what he means by the "I", but what do you mean by the "I"?

K: Of course, of course. How does thought get rid of the image without creating another image?

Q: If the guru causes trouble and it feels uncomfortable with the image, if one can see the trouble then perhaps that guru can help?

K: You are not going into it at all, you are just scratching on the surface.

Q: Thought cannot get rid of the image.

K: If that is so, then what will?

Q: Understanding.

K: Don't use words like understanding. What do you mean by understanding?

Q: Getting rid of the thoughts.

K: Now who is going to get rid of thought?

Q: Is it a question of time? Could it be that our energies are all in the past, and we need to think now?

K: All the images are in the past. Why can't I drop all that and live in the now?

Q: That is what I meant.

K: Yes. How can I? With the burden of the past, how to get rid of the past burden? It comes to the same thing.

Q: if one lives in the present, do the past images still come through?

K: Can you live in the present? Do you know what it means to live in the present? That means not a single memory, except technological memories, not a single breath of the past. Therefore you have to

问：你说形象就是他说的"我"，但是你说的"我"是什么意思？

克：当然，当然。思想要如何消除这个形象而不制造另一个形象？

问：如果古鲁导致了麻烦，那个形象让人觉得不舒服，如果你可以看到这个麻烦，然后也许那个古鲁就能帮上忙了？

克：你根本就没有深入探究，你只触及了表面。

问：思想无法消除形象。

克：如果是这样，那什么能消除？

问：了解。

克：不要用"了解"之类的词。你说的"了解"是什么意思？

问：消除思想。

克：那又是谁要消除思想？

问：这是一个时间问题吗？会不会是因为我们的能量都在过去，而我们现在需要思考？

克：所有的形象都在过去。我为什么就不能抛下那一切然后活在此刻？

问：这就是我的意思。

克：是的。我怎么才能做到？带着过去的负担，如何丢掉过去的负担？这归结到了同一件事情上。

问：如果一个人活在此刻，过去的形象还会出现吗？

克：你能活在此刻吗？你知道活在此刻意味着什么吗？那意味着没有一丝记忆，除了技术层面的记忆，没有一丝一毫的过去。所以你必须了解过去的整体，也就是所有这些记忆、经验、知识、想象和意象。你从一件事情跳到另一件事情上，你没有坚定地把一件事情追究到底。

问（1）：请继续讨论"一个人没有形象而另一个人抱有形象"那

understand the totality of the past, which is all this memory, experience, knowledge, imagination, images. You go from one thing to another, you don't pursue one thing steadily.

Q(1): Please keep going with one having no image and the other having an image.

Q(2): Yes, but we don't answer it.

K: I'll answer it, all right. You have no image and I have an image. What happens? Aren't we eternally at war with each other?

Q: What am I going to do with you?

K: We are living on the same earth, in the same house, meeting often, living in the same community, what will you do with me?

Q: I would try to explain to him what I've learned.

K: Yes, you have explained it to me, but I like my image (laughter).

Q: Sir, we cannot know because we have these images of urselves.

K: That is all I am saying! You are living in images and you don't know how to be free of them. These are all speculative questions.

So let's begin again. Are you aware that you have images? If you have images that are pleasant and you cling to them, and discard those which are unpleasant, you still have images. The question really is, can you be free of them?

Q: Go and listen to some music.

K: The moment that music stops you are back to those images. This is all so childish. Take drugs, that also creates various images.

Q: Isn't there division between wanting to hold on to the images and wanting to let them go.

K: What is the line, the division? The division is desire, isn't it? Listen, sir. I don't like that image, I am going to let it go. But I like this image, I am going to hold on to it. So it is desire, isn't it?

个问题。

问（2）：是的，但我们还没有回答它。

克：我会回答的，好吧。你没有形象，而我有形象。会发生什么事情？我们难道不是会永远彼此交战吗？

问：我该拿你怎么办？

克：我们生活在同一个地球上，同一所房子里，经常见面，生活在同一个社区里，你要拿我怎么办？

问：我要试着向他解释我所了解到的事情。

克：是的，你已经跟我解释过了，但是我喜欢我的形象。（笑声）

问：先生，我们无法知道怎么办，因为我们对别人抱有这些形象。

克：那就是我说的意思！你生活在形象中，你不知道如何摆脱它们。这些都是猜测性的问题。

所以让我们重新开始。你觉察到了你有形象吗？如果你有令人愉快的形象，你就会抓住它们不放，然后扔掉那些令人不快的形象，可你还是抱有形象。

问：去听听音乐。

克：一旦音乐停止，你就又回到了那些形象中。这都太幼稚了。服用药物，那也会制造出各种景象。

问：想抓住形象不放和想要抛开它们，这之间难道不存在划分吗？

克：那条分界线、那种划分是什么？划分本身就是欲望，不是吗？请注意听，先生。我不喜欢那个形象，我要丢掉它。但是我喜欢这个形象，我想抱着它不放。所以这就是欲望，不是吗？

问：我觉得追求快乐的动机甚至存在于……

克：当然了。你没有紧扣一件事情，先生。

Q: I feel there is a pleasure-motive even in...

K: Of course. You don't stick to one thing, sir.

Q: If I have no image, then the other has no image at all.

K: How inaccurate that is. Because I am blind therefore you are also blind! This is so illogical; do think clearly. What should I do so that there is no image-forming at all? Let us think together.

Q: I think most people—I am sorry—I think most people here are looking for consolation in your words, rather than anything else...

K: I am aware that I have images, I know. There is no question of it, I know I have images. I have an image about myself and I have an image about you—that is very clear. If I am satisfied with you and we have the same images, then we are both satisfied. That is, if you think as I think —you like to be ambitious, I like to be ambitious—then we are both in the same boat, we don't quarrel, we accept it, and we live together, work together, are both ruthlessly ambitious. But if you are free of the image of ambition and I am not, the trouble begins. What then will you do, who are free of that image, with me? You can't just say, "Well it is not my business" - because we are living together, we are in the same world, in the same community, in the same group and so on. What will you do with me? Please just listen to this. Will you discard me, will you turn your back on me, will you run away from me, will you join a monastery, learn how to meditate? Do all kinds of things in order to avoid me? Or will you say, "Yes, he is here in my house". What will you do with regard to me, who has an image?

Q: First I would ask you politely to listen.

K: But I won't listen. Haven't you lived with people who are adamant in their beliefs. You are like that.

Q: It is best not to waste one's time.

问：如果我没有形象，那么另一个人也完全不会有形象。

克：这样说太不准确了。因为我瞎了所以你也瞎了！这太不符合逻辑了；请务必清晰地思考。我们该怎么办，才能根本不形成意象？让我们一起来思考。

问：我认为大多数人——抱歉这么说——我认为这里的大多数人是在从你说的话里找安慰，而不是别的……

克：我觉察到我有形象，我知道。这一点毫无疑问，我知道我抱着形象。我对自己抱有形象，我对你也抱有形象——这一点很清楚。如果我对你很满意，我们就有同样的形象，于是我们双方都很满意。也就是说，如果你和我想的一样——你喜欢野心勃勃，我也喜欢野心勃勃——那么我们都在同一条船上，我们不会争吵，我们接受了这一点，然后我们在一起生活，一起工作，两个人都极其有野心。但是如果你摆脱了野心的形象而我没有，麻烦就开始了。然后你，这个摆脱了那个形象的人，会拿我怎么办？你不能只是说，"哦，那不关我的事"——因为我们生活在一起，我们在同一个世界上，在同一个社区里，在同一个组织里，等等。你会拿我怎么办？请注意听一下这个问题。你会丢下我不管吗？你会背弃我吗？你会离开我吗？你会加入修道院，去学习如何冥想吗？你会为了避开我去做各种各样的事情吗？还是你会说，"好吧，他就在我的房子里"。对于我，这个抱有形象的人，你会做什么？

问：首先我会礼貌地请你听我说。

克：但我不会听的。你难道没有和对自己的信仰很坚定的人一起生活过吗？你就是那样的。

问：那就最好还是不要浪费自己的时间了。

我们这就来弄清楚，先生。你知道这实际上是一个虚构的问题，

K: We are going to find out, sir. You see this is really a hypothetical question because you have got images and you live in those images, and the other person lives in images. That is our difficulty. Suppose I have no images, and I haven't, I have worked at this for fifty years, so I have no image about myself, or about you. What is our relationship? I say please listen to me, but you won't. I say please pay attention, which means care, to attend means infinite care. Will you listen to me that way? That means you really want to learn—not from me, but learn about yourself. That means you must infinitely care and watch yourself, not selfishly, but care to learn about yourself—not according to me, or to Freud, or Jung, or to the latest psychologist, but learn about yourself. That means, watch yourself; and you can only do that in your relationship with each other. You say, "You are sitting on that platform and you have gradually assumed, at least in my eyes, a position of authority, you have become my guru". And I say to you, "My friend just listen. I am not your guru. I won't be a guru to anybody." It is monstrous to be a guru. Are you listening when I say this? Or do you say, "I can't listen to you because my mind is wandering'. So when you listen, listen with care, with affection, with attention, then you begin to learn about yourself, actually as you are. Then, from there we can move, we can go forward; but if you don't do that, but keep on repeating, "Oh I have got my image, I don't know how to get rid of it" and so on, then we don't move any further.

Now you have an image with regard to sex, that you must have a girl or a boy. We are so conditioned in this. I say to you please listen, are you aware that you are conditioned - don't choose parts of the conditioning: be totally aware of your whole conditioning. We are conditioned much more at the deeper levels than at the superficial levels—is that clear? One is conditioned very deeply, and superficially less so. listening with your heart, not with your little mind, with your heart, with the whole of your being, is

因为你有形象，你就生活在这些形象里，而另一个人也活在形象里。这就是我们的困难。假设我没有形象，我确实没有，我为此下了50年的功夫，所以我对自己或者对你都不抱有形象。那么我们的关系是怎样的？我说请你听我说，但你不肯。我说请你付出注意力，也就是关怀，关注就意味着无尽的关怀。你会那样聆听我吗？那意味着你真的想学习——不是向我学习，而是了解你自己。那意味着你必须无限地关心、观察你自己，不是以自私的方式，而是关心了解自己——不是按我说的，或者弗洛伊德、荣格或者最新的心理学家说的，而是了解你自己。也就是说，观察你自己，而只有在与别人的关系中你才能观察自己。你说："你坐在那个讲台上，你慢慢占据了——至少在我看来——一个权威的地位，你变成了我的古鲁。"做一个古鲁真是太可怕了。当我说这些的时候，你在听吗？还是你说，"我无法聆听你，因为我的脑子在走神。"所以当你聆听时，带着关怀、带着爱、带着关注去聆听，然后你就开始如实地了解自己了。然后从这里我们就能前进了，我们就能继续往前走了；但是，如果你不这么做，而是一直反复地说，"噢，我有我的形象，我不知道如何除掉它"等，那么我们就无法前进了。

关于性，现在你们抱有一个意象，那就是你必须有个女朋友或者男朋友。我们太受制于这一点了。我在跟你说，请注意听：你有没有觉察到自己受到了制约——不要只选取制约的一部分，而是完全觉察你所受的全部制约。在更深的层面上我们受到的制约比表面的制约更多——这一点清楚了吗？人在非常深的层面上受到了制约，而浅层的制约要少一些。用你的心去聆听，不是用你的小头脑，而是用你的心、你的整个存在去聆听：有没有可能完全觉察这一切，觉察意识的全部内容？全然觉察意味着没有观察者。观察者就是过去，所以当他观察时，他就造成

it possible to be totally aware of all this, the whole of consciousness? To be totally aware implies no observer. The observer is the past and therefore when he observes he brings about fragmentation. When I observe from the past, what I observe brings about a frag- mentary outlook. I only see parts, I don't see the whole. This is simple. So I have an insight that says, "Don't look from the past". That means, don't have an observer who is all the time judging, evaluating, saying, "This right, this is wrong", "I am a Christian, I am a Communist" —all that is the past, Now can you listen to that, which is a fact, which is actual, which is not theoretical? You are facing actually what is. Are you facing in yourself what actually is going on? And can you observe another without the past—without all the accumulated memories, insults, hurts - so that you can look at another with clear eyes? If you say, "I don't know how to do it", then we can go into that.

As we said, any form of authority in this matter is the reaction of submission to somebody who says he knows. That is your image. The professor, the teacher knows mathematics, geography, I don't, so I learn from him, and gradually he becomes my authority. He knows, I don't know. But here, psychologically, I think I don't know how to approach myself, how to learn about it, therefore I look to another—the same process. But the other is equally ignorant as me, because he doesn't know himself. He is tradition-bound, he accepts obedience, he becomes the authority, he says he knows and you don't know: "You become my disciple and I will tell you". The same process. But it is not the same process psychologically. Psychologically the guru is "me". I wonder if you see that? He is as ignorant as myself. He has got a lot of Sanskrit words, a lot of ideas, a lot of superstitions; and I am so gullible I accept him. Here we say there is no authority, no guru, you have to learn about yourself. And to learn about

了分裂。当我根据过去观察时，我所观察的就带来了一个支离破碎的视角。我只看到了局部，没有看到整体。这点很简单。于是我有了一个洞察，说"不要根据过去来观察"。也就是说，不要有一个观察者一直在评估、判断，说"这对了，那错了"，"我是一个基督教徒，我是一个共产主义者"——那一切都是过去。现在你能不能聆听这一点？这是一个事实，是实实在在的，不是理论上的。你正实实在在地面对着现状。你正面对着自己内心实际发生着的事情吗？同时你能不能观察别人而不带着过去——不带着积累起来的所有记忆、侮辱、伤害——于是你就可以用清澈的双眼看着别人？如果你说，"我不知道如何做到"，那么我们可以探讨这个问题。

正如我们所说，在这件事情上任何形式的权威都是一种反应——臣服于某个说他知道的人。这就是你抱有的形象。教授、老师懂数学、地理，我不懂，所以我向他学习，于是他逐渐变成了我的权威。他知道，我不知道。但是在这里，在心理上，我认为我不知道如何了解自己，所以我求助于别人——这是同样的过程。但是另一个人跟我一样无知，因为他也不了解自己。他受到了传统的束缚，你接受了服从，他变成了权威，他说他知道而你不知道："你成了我的门徒我就会告诉你的。"这是同样的过程。但在心理上并不是同样的过程。心理上的古鲁就是"我"。我想知道你看到这一点了吗？他跟我自己一样无知。他掌握了一大堆梵文的词句，一大堆概念和迷信，而我太容易上当受骗了，我接受了他。而我们说没有古鲁、没有权威，你必须去了解你自己。而要了解你自己，你就需要观察自己，你如何与他人相处，你如何走路。然后你就会发现你对自己抱有形象，一个巨大的形象。而且你发现这些形象造成了巨大的伤害，它们割裂了这个世界——奎师那意识派、超验

yourself, watch yourself, how you behave with another, how you walk. Then you find that you have an image about yourself, a tremendous image. And you see these images create great harm, they break up the world— the Krishna-conscious group, the Transcendental group, or some other group. And your own group; you have your own ideas, you must have sex, you must have a girl, you must have a boy, and all the rest of it, change the girl, change the boy, every week. You live like that and you don't see the tremendous danger and wastage of life.

Now we come to the point: how am I to be free of all image-making? That is the real question. Is it possible? I will not say it is, or it is not, I am going to find out. I am going to find out by carefully watching why images are made. I realize images are made when the mind is not giving its attention at the moment. At the moment something is said that gives pleasure, or something that brings about displeasure, to be aware at that moment, not afterwards. But we become aware afterwards and say, "My god, I must pay attention, terrible, I see it is important to be attentive and I don't know how to be attentive; I lose it and when the thing takes place it is so quick; and I say to myself I must be attentive". So I beat myself into being attentive - I wonder if you see this - and therefore I am never attentive. So I say to myself, "I am not attentive at the moment something is said which gives pleasure or pain", I see that I am inattentive. I have found that my whole mind, make-up, is inattentive, to the birds, to nature, to everything, I am inattentive - when I walk, when I eat, when I speak, I am inattentive. So I say to myself, I am not going to be concerned with attention, but inattention". Do you get this?

Q: Yes.

K: I am not going to be concerned with being attentive, but I am

派，还有其他的派别。还有你自己这一派：你有自己的想法，你必须有性行为，你必须有个女朋友，你必须有个男朋友，以及诸如此类，每个礼拜换个女朋友，换个男朋友。你就这样生活着，你没有发现其中有着巨大的危险以及这是浪费生命。

那么我们就来到了这一点：我要如何摆脱所有的形象制造过程？这是真正的问题。这可能吗？我不会说可能还是不可能，我要弄清楚。我要通过仔细观察形象为什么会产生来发现真相。我意识到，当心智在那一刻没有付出注意力时，意象就被制造了出来。在带来愉快或者带来不快的话说出来的那一刻就觉察到，而不是事后。但我们事后才觉察，然后说："我的天，我必须注意，太糟糕了，我发现全神贯注很重要，但我不知道该如何关注；我失去了关注，当事情发生时，一切都太快了；于是我对自己说我必须全神贯注。"所以我努力控制自己要全神贯注——我想知道这点你是不是明白了——因而我永远无法全神贯注。所以我对自己说，"当有人说了一句带来快乐或者痛苦的话，那一刻我没有注意"，我发现自己是漫不经心的。我发现我的整个心智、整个结构都是漫不经心的，对鸟儿、对自然、对一切，我都漫不经心——当我走路时，当我吃东西时，当我说话时，我都是漫不经心的。所以我对自己说，"我不关心关注，而是漫不经心"。这点你明白了吗？

问：是的。

我不关心全神贯注，而是要看看漫不经心是什么。我在观察漫不经心，而且我发现我多数时间都是漫不经心的。所以我要一次关注一件事情，也就是说，当我走路时，当我吃东西时，我要带着关注去走路、吃东西。我不会同时想着别的事情，而是我要关注每一件小事情。所以曾经的漫不经心变成了关注。我想知道你有没有明白这一点？所以我现

going to see what is inattention. I am watching inattention, and I see I am inattentive most of the time. So I am going to pay attention to one thing at a time, that is, when I walk, when I eat, I am going to walk, eat, with attention. I am not going to think about something else, but I am going to pay attention to every little thing. So what has been inattention becomes attention. I wonder if you see that? So I am now watching inattention. That is, I am watching that I am not attentive. I look at a bird and never look at it, my thoughts are all over the place—I am now going to look at that bird; it may take me a second but I am going to look at it. When I walk I am going to watch it. So that out of inattention, without any effort, there is total attention. When there is total attention, then when you say something pleasant or unpleasant there is no image-forming because I am totally there. My whole mind, heart, brain, all the responses are completely awake and attentive.

Aren't you very attentive when you are pursuing pleasure? You don't have to talk about attention, you want that pleasure. Sexually, when you want it, you are tremendously attentive, aren't you? Attention implies a mind that is completely awake, which means it doesn't demand challenge. It is only when we have images that challenges come. I wonder if you see this. Because of those images challenges come and you respond to the challenge inadequately. Therefore there is a constant battle between challenge and response, which means the increase of images; and the more it increases the more challenges come, and so there is always the strengthening of images. I wonder if you see this? Haven't you noticed people when they are challenged about their Catholicism or whatever it is, how they become more strong in their opinions? So by being completely attentive there is no image formation, which means conditioning disappears.

在看着漫不经心。也就是说，我现在观察到自己没有留心注意。我看到一只鸟，却从来没有看着它，我的思绪散乱不堪——我现在要看看那只鸟；也许我只花一秒钟，但是我要去看看它。当我走路时，我也要观察，于是从漫不经心中，全然的关注就毫不费力地到来了。当有了全然的关注，当你再说些令人愉快或令人不快的话，就不会形成印象了，因为我整个人都在那儿。我的整个心智、内心、大脑，所有的反应都是彻底清醒和留心关注的。

当你追逐欢愉的时候你难道不是非常用心吗？你都不用谈论关注，你想得到那种欢愉。在性方面，当你想得到欢愉的时候，你会全神贯注，不是吗？关注意味着一颗全然觉醒的心，也就是说它不需要挑战。只有当我们抱有意象时，挑战才会出现。我不知道你有没有明白这点。因为有那些意象，挑战于是到来，然后你对挑战做出不恰当的反应。因此挑战和反应之间就有一种不停的斗争，而这会增加意象；意象增加的越多，挑战就越多，所以意象一直在得到加强。我想知道你看到这一点了吗？你难道没有注意到，当人们的天主教信仰或者无论什么受到挑战时，他们抱有的观念是如何变得更坚定的？所以，通过全然的关注，意象就不会产生，而那意味着制约消失了。

CHAPTER 8
第 8 章

SUFFERING; THE MEANING OF DEATH

痛苦；死亡的意义

"The mutation in consciousness is the ending of time, which is the ending of the'me' which has been produced through time. Can this take place? Or is it just a theory like any other?"

May we go on with what we were discussing the other day? We were saying that the crisis in the world is not outward but the crisis is in consciousness. And that consciousness is its content: all the things that man has accumulated through centuries, his fears, his dogmas, his superstitions, his beliefs, his conclusions, and all the suffering, pain and anxiety. We said unless there is a radical mutation in that consciousness, outward activities will bring about more mischief, more sorrow, more confusion. And to bring about that mutation in consciousness a totally different kind of energy is required; not the mechanical energy of thought, of time and measure. When we were investigating into that we said there are three active principles in human beings: fear, pleasure and suffering. We talked about fear at some length. And we also went into the question of pleasure, which is entirely different from joy, enjoyment, and the delight of seeing something beautiful and so on. And we also touched upon suffering.

I think we ought this morning to go into that question of suffering. It is a nice morning and I am sorry to go into such a dark subject. As we said, when there is suffering there can be no compassion and we asked whether it is at all possible for human minds, for human beings right throughout the

"意识的突变就是时间的终结，也就是经由时间产生的'我'的终结。这能够发生吗？还是说这只是像其他所有理论一样的另一个理论？"

我们可以继续我们前几天讨论的内容吗？我们说世界上的危机并不是外在的，而是危机就在意识中。而那个意识就是它自身的内容：人类千百年来积累起来的一切，他的恐惧，他的教条，他的迷信，他的信仰，他的结论，以及所有的苦难、痛苦和焦虑。我们说过，除非那个意识中发生一次彻底的突变，否则外在的行为会带来更多的不幸、更多的悲伤、更多的混乱。而若要带来那种意识的突变，就需要一种截然不同的能量；而不是思想、时间和衡量的机械能量。当我们探究这个问题时，我们说过人类身上有三个活跃的因素：恐惧、欢愉和痛苦。我们已经相当详尽地探讨过恐惧了。我们也探究了欢愉的问题，它完全不同于喜悦、欢乐以及看到美丽事物的那种欣喜，等等。我们也稍稍触及了痛苦的问题。

我想我们今天早上应该探讨痛苦这个问题。这是一个怡人的早晨，我很抱歉要探讨这样一个灰暗的话题。正如我们所说，痛苦存在时就不可能有慈悲，我们也问过，人类的心灵，全世界的人类究竟有没有可能

world, to put an end to suffering. For without that ending to suffering we live in darkness, we accept all kinds of beliefs, dogmas, escapes, which bring about much more confusion, more violence and so on. So we are going this morning to investigate together into this question of suffering, whether the human mind can ever be free from it totally; and also we are going to talk about the whole question of death.

Why do we accept suffering, why do we put up with it psychologically? Physical suffering can be controlled or put up with; and it is important that such physical suffering does not distort clarity of thought. We went into that. Because for most of us, when there is physical pain, a continued suffering, it distorts our thinking, it prevents objective thinking, which becomes personal, broken up, distorted. If one is not actively aware of this whole process of physical suffering, whether remembered in the past, or the fear of having it again in the future, then neurotic habits, neurotic activities take place. We spoke of that briefly the other day.

We are asking if it is at all possible for human beings to end suffering at all levels of their existence, psychological suffering. And when we go into it in ourselves deeply, we see one of the major factors of this suffering is attachment—attachment to ideas, to conclusions, to ideologies, which act as security; and when that security is threatened there is a certain kind of suffering. Please, as we said the other day, we are sharing this together, we are looking into this question of suffering together. You are not merely listening to a talk, if I may point out, and gathering a few ideas and agreeing or disagreeing, but rather we are in communication, sharing the problem, examining the question, the issue, actively; and so it becomes our responsibility, yours as well as the speaker's, to go into this question.

There is also attachment to persons; in our relationships there is a

结束苦难。因为如果不终结苦难，我们就会生活在黑暗中，我们就会接受各种各样的信仰、教条和逃避的途径，而这会带来更多的混乱、更多的暴力，等等。所以我们今天早上要一起来探索痛苦这个问题，人类的心灵究竟能否彻底从中解脱；同时我们也要探讨整个死亡的问题。

为什么我们接受了痛苦，为什么我们要从心理上忍受它？身体上的痛苦可以控制或者忍受；重要的是这种身体上的痛苦不会扭曲思维的清晰。这一点我们探讨过了。因为对我们大多数人来说，当身体上有了疼痛，持续的痛苦，它就会扭曲我们的思维，妨碍客观的思考，思维会变得个人化、破碎和扭曲。如果一个人没能有效地觉察身体上的痛苦这整个过程，无论是过去留下了记忆，还是害怕将来会再次遭受痛苦，那么神经质的习惯、神经质的行为就会发生。前几天我们简要地说到了这一点。

我们问，人类究竟有没有可能结束他们生活所有层面上的痛苦，心理上的痛苦。当我们在自己身上深入探究这个问题，我们会看到这种痛苦的主要因素之一是依附——依附于观念、结论、意识形态，它们充当着安全的保障；当这种安全受到了威胁，就会产生某种痛苦。请注意，就像我们那天说的，我们是在一起分担，我们是在一起审视痛苦这个问题。你并不是在单纯地听一场讲座——如果我可以指出的话——收集一些概念然后表示同意或者不同意，而是我们在一起交流，在分担这个问题，积极地审视这个问题、这件事情；所以探究这个问题变成了我们的责任，你和讲话者共同的责任。

此外还有对他人的依附；在我们的关系中存在着大量的痛苦。也

great deal of suffering. That is, the one may be free from this conditioning of fear and so on, and the other may not be and hence there is a tension. The word attachment means "holding on", not only physically but psychologically, depending on something. In a relationship, one may be free and the other may not be free and hence the conflict; one may be a Catholic and the other may not be a Catholic, or a Communist and so on. Hence the conflict that breeds continuous strain and suffering.

Then there is the suffering of the unknown, of death; the suffering of losing something that you were attached to in the past, as memory. I do not know if you have not noticed all these things in yourself? And is it possible to live in complete relationship with another without this tension, which is brought about through self-interest, through self-centred activity, desire pulling in different directions, and live in a relationship in which there may be contradictions, for one may be free, the other may not be? To live in that situation demands not only what is called tolerance—that absurd intellectual thing that man has created - but it demands a much greater thing, which is affection, love, and therefore compassion. We are going to go into that.

We are asking whether man can end suffering. There are various explanations: how to go beyond it, how to rationalize it, how to suppress it, how to escape from it. Now we are asking something entirely different: not to suppress it, not to evade it, nor rationalize it, but when there is that suffering to remain totally with it, without any movement of thought, which is the movement of time and measure.

One suffers: one loses one's son, or wife, or she runs away with somebody else; and the things that you are attached to, the house, the name, the form, all the accumulated conclusions, they seem to fade away, and you suffer. Can one look at that suffering without the observer? We went into

就是说，一个人也许摆脱了恐惧等的制约，而另一个人也许就没有，因而就有一种紧张。"依附"这个词的意思是"紧抓不放"，不仅从身体上而且从心理上依赖某个东西。在关系中，一个人也许是自由的，另一个也许就不自由，因而就有了冲突；一个人也许是个天主教徒，而另一个人也许不是天主教徒或者共产主义者等，于是就有了会滋生不断的紧张和痛苦的冲突。

然后还有来自未知和死亡的痛苦；失去了你过去依附的某种东西，也就是记忆，因而产生的痛苦。我不知道你有没有从自己身上注意到所有这些事情？那么，有没有可能生活在与他人完整的关系中，生活在一种也许存在矛盾的关系中——因为一个人也许是自由的，另一个人也许不自由——而没有这种紧张？这种紧张是由自私、自我中心的行为和往不同方向拉扯的欲望带来的。活在那样的处境中，需要的不仅仅是所谓的"宽容"——人类捏造出来的这种荒唐的智力上的东西——而且需要一种更伟大的东西，那就是关怀、爱，进而是慈悲。我们会探讨这个问题的。

我们问人类是否能够终结痛苦。对此有各种各样的解释：如何超越它，如何把它合理化，如何压制它，如何逃避它。而我们现在问的是截然不同的事情：不是压抑它，不是逃避它，不是把它合理化，而是当出现痛苦时，完全与之共处，没有任何思想活动，也就是时间和衡量的活动。

一个人在受苦：他失去了自己的儿子或者妻子，或者她跟别人私奔了；你依附的那些东西，房子、名声、外形、积累起来的所有结论，

that question of what the observer is. We said the observer is the past, the accumulated memory, experience and knowledge. And with that knowledge, experience, memory, one observes the suffering, so one dissociates oneself from suffering: one is different from suffering and therefore one can do something about it. Whereas the observer is the observed.

This requires a little care and attention, the statement that, "the observer is the observed". We don't accept it. We say the observer is entirely different; and the observed is something out there separate from the observer. Now if one looks very closely at that question, at that statement that the observer is the observed, it seems so obvious. When you say you are angry, you are not different from anger, you are that thing which you call anger. When you are jealous, you are that jealousy. The word separates; that is, through the word we recognise the feeling and the recognition is in the past; so we look at that feeling through the word, through the screen of the past, and so separate it. Therefore there is a division between the observer and the observed.

So we are saying that when there is this suffering, either momentary, or a continuous endless series of causes that bring about suffering, to look at it without the observer. You are that suffering; not, you are separate from suffering. Totally remain with that suffering. Then you will notice, if you go that far, if you are willing to observe so closely, that something totally different takes place: a mutation. That is, out of that suffering comes great passion. If you have done it, tested it out, you will find it. It is not the passion of a belief, passion for some cause, passion for some idiotic conclusion. It is totally different from the passion of desire. It is something which is of a totally different kind of energy; not the movement of thought, which is mechanical.

它们似乎都在消逝，于是你感到痛苦。你能不能没有观察者地看着那种痛苦？我们探讨过了观察者是什么这个问题。我们说过观察者就是过去，就是积累起来的记忆、经验和知识。一个人带着那些知识、经验和记忆去观察痛苦，所以他把自己和痛苦分离了开来：他与痛苦是不同的，因而可以对痛苦做些什么。然而观察者就是被观察者。

　　"观察者就是被观察者"这个说法需要一点关心和关注。我们不接受它。我们说观察者是完全不同的，被观察之物是某种外在的、与观察者分开的事物。然而，如果你非常仔细地看看这个问题，看看"观察者就是被观察者"这个说法，这看来真是太显而易见了。当你说你很生气时，你与愤怒并无不同，你就是那个你叫作愤怒的东西。当你嫉妒时，你就是那个嫉妒。是词语造成了分裂；也就是说，通过词语我们认出了那种感受，而这种识别来自过去；所以我们是透过那个词、透过过去的屏障在看那种感受的，因而把它分离了开来。所以观察者和被观察者之间就有了分裂。

　　所以我们说，当痛苦存在时，无论是暂时的还是有一系列连续不断的原因造成了痛苦，不带着观察者地看着它。你就是那种痛苦；而不是你与那种痛苦是分开的。与那种痛苦完全待在一起。然后你就会注意到，如果你已经走了这么远，如果你愿意如此密切地观察，某种截然不同的事情就发生了：一种突变。也就是说，巨大的激情从那种痛苦中到来了。如果你这么做过，如果你检验过，你会发现的。那不是来自信仰的激情，不是对某种事业的激情、对某个愚蠢结论的激情。它与欲望的激情完全不同。那是一种截然不同的能量，而不是机械的思想运动。

We have a great deal of suffering in what is called love. Love, as we know it now, is pleasure, sexual, the love of a country, the love of an idea, and so on—all derived from pleasure. And when that pleasure is denied there is either hatred, antagonism, or violence. Can there be love, not just something personal between you and me or somebody else, but the enormous feeling of compassion—passion for everything, for everybody. Passion for nature, compassion for the earth on which we live, so that we don't destroy the earth, the animals, the whole thing... Without love, which is compassion, suffering must continue. And we human beings have put up with it, we accept it as normal. Every religion has tried to find a way out of this, but organized religions have brought tremendous suffering.

Religious oganizations throughout the world have done a great deal of harm, there have been religious wars endless persecution, tortures, burning people, especially in the West—it wasn't the fashion in those days in the East. And we are speaking of—not the acceptance of suffering, or the putting up with suffering—but remaining motionless with that suffering; then there comes out of it great compassion. And from that compassion arises the whole question of creation.

What is creation, what is the creative mind? Is it a mind that suffers and through that suffering has learnt a certain technique and expresses that technique on paper, in marble, with paint—that is, is creativeness the outcome of tension? Is it the outcome of a disordered life? Does creativeness come through the fragmentary activity of daily life? I don't know if you are following all this? Or must we give a totally different kind of meaning to creativeness, which may not need expression at all?

So one has to go into this question within oneself very deeply, because one's consciousness is the consciousness of the world. I do not know if you

　　我们在所谓的爱之中经受了大量的痛苦。爱，就我们如今所了解的，是性欢愉，是对国家的爱，对理念等的爱——这些都从欢愉衍生而来。当这种欢愉遭到了拒绝，就会产生仇恨、对抗或者暴力。爱能否存在，它不是仅限于你和我或者其他人之间的某种个人化的东西，而是那种浩瀚的慈悲感——对一切、对所有人的激情。对自然的激情，对我们所生活的地球的慈悲，这样我们就不会破坏地球、动物和整个世界……没有爱，也就是慈悲，痛苦必然会继续。而我们人类容忍了痛苦，我们接受它是正常的。每一种宗教都试图找到摆脱痛苦的途径，但组织化的宗教却带来了巨大的苦难。

　　全世界的宗教组织造成了巨大的伤害，有各种宗教战争、无尽的迫害、折磨、火刑，特别是在西方——这在当时的东方并不流行。而我们所说的——不是接受痛苦或者容忍痛苦——而是一动不动地与那种痛苦待在一起；然后伟大的慈悲就会从中到来。从那种慈悲中就会出现整个创造的问题。

　　什么是创造，什么是创造性的心灵？它是一颗受苦然后从那种痛苦中学到了某种技巧并把它表达在纸上、大理石上、绘画上的心吗？也就是说，创造性是紧张的产物吗？它是失序的生活的产物吗？创造性来自日常生活中破碎的行为吗？我不知道你有没有跟上这些？还是说，我们必须赋予创造性一种截然不同的含义，而它也许根本不需要表达？

　　所以你必须从自己的内在非常深入地探索这个问题，因为你的意识就是全世界的意识。我不知道你有没有意识到这一点？从根本上来说，你的意识就是讲话者的意识，或者全世界其他人的意识，从根本上

realize that? Fundamentally your consciousness is the consciousness of the speaker, of the rest of the world, basically. Because in that consciousness there is suffering, there is pain, there is anxiety, there is fear of tomorrow, fear of insecurity, which every man goes through wherever he lives. So your consciousness is the consciousness of the world, and if there is a mutation in that consciousness it affects the total consciousness of human beings. It is a fact. So it becomes tremendously important that human beings bring about a radical transformation, or mutation in themselves, in their consciousness.

Now we can go into this thing called death, which is one of the major factors of suffering. As with everything else in life we want a quick, definite answer, an answer which will be comforting, which will be totally satisfactory, intellectually, emotionally, physically, in every way. We want immortality, whatever that may mean, and we want to survive, both physically and psychologically. We avoid death at any price, put it as far away as possible. So we have never been able to examine it closely. We have never been able to face it, understand it, not only verbally, intellectually, but completely. We wait until the last moment, which may be an accident, disease, old age, when you can't think, when you can't look, you are just "gaga". Then you become a Catholic, a Protestant, believe in this or that. So we are trying this morning to understand, not verbally, but actually what it means to die—which doesn't mean we are asking that we should commit suicide. But we are asking, what is the total significance of this thing called death, which is the ending of what we know as life.

In enquiring into this we must find out whether time has a stop. The stopping of time may be death. It may be the ending and therefore that which ends has a new beginning, not that which has a continuity. So first

就是如此。因为那个意识中有苦难，有痛苦，有焦虑，有对明天的恐惧，对不安全的恐惧，无论生活在何处，每个人都经历着这些。所以你的意识就是全世界的意识，而如果那个意识能够发生突变，它就会影响人类的整个意识。这是一个事实。所以，人类为自身或者他们的意识带来一场彻底的转变或者突变，就变得无比重要。

接下来我们可以探究这件叫作死亡的事情了，它是痛苦的主要因素之一。就像对待生命中其他的事情一样，我们想要一个快速的、明确的答案，一个令人感到欣慰的答案，一个从智力上、情感上、身体上，从各方面都令人完全满意的答案。我们希望不朽，无论那是什么意思，我们希望从身体上和心理上都继续存活下去。我们不惜一切代价避开死亡，把它推得越远越好。所以我们从来没能仔细地审视它。我们从来没能面对它、了解它，不是仅仅从语言上、智力上，而是彻底地了解。我们一直等到最后一刻，那也许是一场意外、疾病或者老去，当你已经无法思考、无法去看，你已经"老糊涂"的时候。于是你成为一名天主教徒、新教徒，相信这个或那个。所以我们今天早上要试着了解，不是从语言上，而是真正地了解死亡意味着什么——这并不是说我们在问是否应该自杀。而是我们在问，这件被称为死亡的事情，也就是我们所了解的生命的结束，它全部的含义是什么。

在探询这个问题的过程中，我们必须弄清楚时间能否停止。时间的停止也许就是死亡。它也许就是结束，因而结束的东西，而不是有延续性的东西，就会有一个新的开始。所以首先，时间能否存在一个终点，时间能否停止？——不是钟表上的物理时间，比如，昨天、今天和

can there be an ending to time, can time stop?—not chronological time by the watch, as yesterday, today, and tomorrow, the twenty-four hours, but the whole movement of time as thought and measure. That movement, not chronological time, but that movement as thought, which is the whole process of comparing, of measurement, can all that process stop? Can thought, which is the response of memory, and can experience as knowledge—knowledge is always in the past, knowledge is the past—can that whole momentum come to an end? Not in the technological field, we don't even have to discuss that, that is obvious. Can this movement come to an end? Time as hope, time as something that has happened to which the mind clings, attachment to the past, or a projection from the past to the future as a conclusion, and time as a movement of achievement from alpha to omega—this whole movement in which we are caught. If one said there is no tomorrow, psychologically, you would be shocked, because tomorrow is tremendously important: tomorrow you are going to be happy, tomorrow you will achieve something, tomorrow will be the fulfilment of yesterday's hopes, or today's hopes, and so on. Tomorrow becomes extraordinarily significant—the tomorrow which is projected from the past as thought.

So we are asking, can all that momentum come to an end? Time has created, through centuries, the centre which is the "me". Time is not only the past as attachment, hope, fulfilment, the evolving process of thought until it becomes more and more refined. But also that centre around which all our activities take place, the "me", the mine, we and they, both politically, religiously, economically and so on. So the "me" is the conclusion of time, adding to itself and taking away from itself, but there is always this centre which is the very essence of time. We are asking, can that movement come to an end. This is the whole problem of meditation, not sitting down and

明天，24 小时，而是作为思想和衡量的整个时间运动。这种运动，不是物理时间，而是思想这种运动，也就是整个比较和衡量的过程，所有这些过程能够停止吗？思想，也就是记忆的反应能否结束，还有作为知识的经验——知识始终属于过去，知识就是过去——这整个动力能够结束吗？不是在技术领域，这一点我们甚至都不用讨论，这是显而易见的。这种运动能够结束吗？时间就是希望，时间是心智抓住不放的过去发生的事情，是对过去的依附，或者从过去投射到未来的一个结论，时间是从低到高取得成就的一系列活动——我们就困在这整个运动中。如果有人说心理上没有明天，你会感到震惊，因为明天无比重要：明天你会很开心，明天你会达成某个目标，明天会实现昨天的希望或者今天的希望，等等。明天变得格外重要——而这个明天是从过去即时间中投射出来的。

所以我们问，所有这些动力能够结束吗？时间经过千百年建立了"我"这个中心。时间不仅仅包括作为依附、希望、成就的过去，以及变得越来越精良的思想的进化过程，还包括我们发生的所有活动所围绕的中心：政治上、宗教上、经济上等方面的"我"、"我的"、我们和他们。所以"我"就是时间的总和，在它自己身上加加减减，但始终存在这个中心，也就是时间的本质。我们在问，这种运动能否终止？这就是整个冥想的问题，而不是坐下来重复某些咒语、某些字词以及做某些把戏——那都是些愚蠢的无稽之谈。我并不是不宽容，而是那些就是很荒唐。而搞清楚这些问题，探究这些，就变得格外有趣了。

那么死亡是什么？这个问题能用言语回答吗？还是说你必须不仅

repeating some mantra, some words, and doing some tricks—that is all silly nonsense. I am not being intolerant but it is just absurd. And it becomes extraordinarily interesting to find this out, enquire into this.

Then what is death? Can that be answered in terms of words, or must one look at it not only verbally but non-verbally? There is death, the organism dies, by misuse, by abuse, by overindulgence, drink, drugs, accident, all the things that the flesh is heir to - it dies, comes to an end, the heart stops, the brain with all its marvellous machinery comes to an end. We accept it—we are not afraid of the physical organism coming to an end but we are afraid of something totally different. And being afraid of that basically, we want to resolve that fear through various beliefs, conclusions, hopes.

The whole of the Asiatic world believes in reincarnation, they have proof for it—they say so at least. That is—watch this, it is extraordinary —the thing that has been put together by time as the "me", the ego, that incarnates till that entity becomes perfect and is absorbed into the highest principle, which is Brahman, or whatever you like to call it. Time has created the centre, the "me", the ego, the personality, the character, the tendencies, and so on, and through time you are going to dissolve that very entity, through reincarnation. You see the absurdity? Thought has created something as the "me", the centre, and through the evolutionary process, which is time, you will ultimately dissolve that and be absorbed into the highest principle. And yet they believe in this tremendously. The other day I was talking to somebody who is a great believer in this. He said, "If you don't believe it you are not a religious man", and he walked out. And Christianity has its own form of continuity of the "me", the resurrection —Gabriel blowing the trumpet and so on (laughter). When you believe in reincarnation, what is important is that you are going to live another

用语言去看，而且要以非语言的方式去看这个问题？死亡确实存在，有机体会死去，因为滥用、误用、放纵、饮酒、药物、意外，血肉之躯所承载的一切——它会死去、终结，心脏停止跳动，大脑连同它所有不可思议的机能都结束了。我们接受了它——我们不害怕有机体终结，而是害怕某种完全不同的东西。由于从根本上害怕那种结束，我们希望通过各种信仰、结论和希望来解决那种恐惧。

整个亚洲世界都相信转世，对此他们还有证据——至少他们是这么说的。也就是说——看看这个说法，真是不可思议——由时间，也就是"我"、自我拼凑出来的那个东西会转世重生，直到那个实体变得完美，然后被最高法则——也就是大梵天或者无论你喜欢叫它什么——所吸纳。时间制造了这个中心，这个"我"、自我、人格、个性、倾向等，然后你要借助时间、借助转世来消除那个实体。你看到这其中的荒唐了吗？思想造就了"我"、这个中心，然后通过进化过程，也就是时间，你最终将消除那个东西，并被最高法则吸纳。然而他们却无比坚信这一点。有一天我和一个坚信这些的人谈话。他说，"如果你不相信这个，你就不是一个宗教人士"，然后他就离开了。而基督教也有他们自己延续"我"的方式，复活——加百列吹响了号角……诸如此类。（笑声）当你相信转世，那么重要的是你会再活一世，而你此生因为过去的行为而受苦。所以重要的是，如果你真的完全坚信那个信仰的话，那就意味着你现在就必须带着巨大的关怀正确地、恰当地行动。可我们不这么做。这么做需要非凡的能量。

这其中涉及几个问题。不朽是什么，永恒是什么——超越时间的

life and you suffer in this life because of your past actions. So what is important is, if one is actually basically committed wholly to that belief, it means that you must behave rightly, accurately, with tremendous care now. And we don't do that. That demands superhuman energy.

There are several problems involved in this. What is immortality and what is eternity—which is a timeless state—and what happens to human beings who are still caught in this movement of time? We human beings live extraordinarily complex, irresponsible, ugly, stupid lives, we are at each other's throats, we are battling about beliefs, about authority, politically and religiously, and our daily lives are a series of endless conflicts. And we want that to continue. And because our lives are so empty, so full of meaningless words, we say there is a state where there is no death, immortality—which is a state where there is no movement of time. That is, time through centuries has created the idea of the self, of the "me" evolving. It has been put together through time, which is a part of evolution. And inevitably there is death and with the ending of the brain cells thought comes to an end. Therefore one hopes that there is something beyond the "me", the super-consciousness, a spark of God, a spark of truth, that can never be destroyed and that continues. And that continuity is what we call immortality. That is what most of us want. If you don't get it through some kind of fame, you want to have it sitting near God, who is timeless. The whole thing is so absurd.

Is there something which is not of time, which has no beginning and no end, and is therefore timeless, eternal? Our life being what it is, we have this problem of death; and if I, a human being, have not totally understood the whole quality of myself, what happens to me when I die? You understand the question? Is that the end of me? I have not understood, if I have understood myself totally, then that is a different problem, which

状态是什么——还有依然困在这种时间运动中的人类会怎么样？我们人类过着极其复杂、不负责任、丑陋、愚蠢的生活，我们争个你死我活，我们为政治上、宗教上的信仰和权威而战，我们的日常生活是一系列无尽的冲突。而我们希望这一切继续下去。因为我们的生活如此空虚，充满了毫无意义的词语，我们说存在一种没有死亡、有着不朽的状态——那是一种没有时间运动的状态。也就是说，时间用千百年建立了进化的自我、"我"这个概念，它是由时间，也就是进化过程的一部分拼凑起来的。而死亡是不可避免的，随着脑细胞的死亡，思想也结束了。所以你希望存在某种超越"我"的东西，存在超级意识、上帝的火花、真理的火花，它永远不会被扑灭，永远会继续存在下去。而这种延续性就是我们所说的不朽。这就是我们大多数人想要的。如果你没有通过某种名望得到它，你就会希望通过坐在永恒的上帝旁边来得到它。这整件事情是如此荒唐。

有没有一种东西是不属于时间的，它没有开始也没有结束，因而是超越时间的、永恒的？我们的生活就是现在的样子，我们有死亡这个问题；如果我，人类的一员，没有完全了解自己的全部品质，那么当我死去时，我身上会发生什么？你明白这个问题吗？那是我的结束吗？我没有了解自己，如果我完全了解了自己，那就是另外一个问题了，我们会讲到的。如果我没有完全了解自己——我用"了解"这个词指的并不是智力上——而是真正毫无选择地觉察到我自己，觉知我意识的所有内容——如果我没有深入探究我自身的结构和意识的本质，然后我就死了，那会发生什么？

we will come to. If I have not understood myself totally—I am not using the word "understand" intellectually - but actually to be aware of myself without any choice, all the content of my consciousness—if I have not deeply delved into my own structure and the nature of consciousness and I die, what happens?

Now who is going to answer this question? (laughter). No, I am putting it purposefully. Who is going to answer this question? Because we think we cannot answer it we look to someone else to tell us, the priest, the books, the people who have said, "I know", the endless mushrooming gurus. If one rejects all authority—and one must, totally, all authority—then what have you left? Then you have the energy to find out—because you have rejected that which dissipates energy, gurus, hopes and fears, somebody to tell you what happens —if you reject all that, which means all authority, then you have tremendous energy. With that energy you can begin to enquire what actually takes place when you have not totally resolved the structure and the nature of the self, the self being time, and therefore movement, and therefore division: the "me" and the "not me" and hence conflict.

Now what happens to me when I have not ended that conflict? You and I and the rest of the world, if the speaker has not ended it, what happens to us? We are all going to die—I hope not soon but sometime or other. What is going to happen? When we live, as we are living, are we so fundamentally different from somebody else? You may be cleverer, have greater knowledge or technique, you may be more learned, have certain gifts, talents, inventiveness; but you and another are exactly alike basically. Your colour may be different, you may be taller, shorter, but in essence you are the same. So while you are living you are like the rest of the world, in the same stream, in the same movement. And when you die you go on in

　　那么由谁来回答这个问题呢？（笑声）不，我是故意提出这个问题的。谁来回答这个问题？因为我们认为自己回答不了，所以就指望别人来告诉我们，牧师、书本、那些说"我知道"的人，还有如雨后春笋般涌现的数不清的古鲁。如果你拒绝了所有的权威——而你必须彻底拒绝所有权威——那么你还剩下什么？然后你就拥有了发现真相的能量——因为你摒弃了耗费能量的东西：古鲁、希望和恐惧，有人来告诉你会怎么样——如果你摒弃了那一切，也就是所有的权威，那么你就拥有了巨大的能量。有了那种能量，你就可以开始探询当你没有完全解除自我的结构和本质时实际上会发生什么了，而自我就是时间，因而是运动，进而是分裂："我"和"非我"，于是就有了冲突。

　　那么，当我没有终结那种冲突时，我身上会发生什么？如果讲话者没有结束这种冲突，你和我以及全世界其他人身上会发生什么？我们都会死——我希望不要那么快，但迟早会的。那会发生什么？当我们活着的时候，我们从根本上与别人有那么不同吗？你也许聪明一些，有更多的知识或者技能，你也许更博学，有某些天分、才能、发明能力；但你和别的人从根本上是极其相似的。你的肤色也许不同，你也许高一点儿、矮一点儿，但本质上你是一样的。所以当你活着的时候，你就像世界上的其他人一样，处在同一股洪流中，同一种运动中。而当你死去时，你依然继续着同一种运动。我想知道你有没有明白我说的话？只有完全觉察自己的制约、自己的意识及其内容的人，行动起来并且消除了它的人，才不在那股洪流中。这点我说清楚了吗？也就是说，我贪婪、嫉妒、野心勃勃、无情、暴力——你也一样。而这就是我们的日常生

the same movement. I wonder if you understand what I am saying? It is only the man who is totally aware of his conditioning, his consciousness, the content of it, and who moves and dissipates it, who is not in that stream. Am I making this clear? That is, I am greedy, envious, ambitious, ruthless, violent—so are you. And that is our daily life, petty, accepting authority, quarrelling, bitter, not loved and aching to be loved, the agonies of loneliness, irresponsible relationship—that is our daily life. And we are like the rest of the world, it is a vast endless river. And when we die we'll be like the rest, moving in the same stream as before when we were living. But the man who understands himself radically, has resolved all the problems in himself psychologically, he is not of that stream. He has stepped out of it.

The man who moves away from the stream, his consciousness is entirely different. He is not thinking in terms of time, continuity, or immortality. But the other man or woman is still in that. So the problem arises: what is the relationship of the man who is out to the man who is in? What is the relationship between truth and reality? Reality being, as we said, all the things that thought has put together. The root meaning of that word reality is, things or thing. And living in the world of things, which is reality, we want to establish a relationship with a world which has no thing—which is impossible.

What we are saying is that consciousness, with all its content, is the movement of time. In that movement all human beings are caught. And even when they die that movement goes on. It is so; this is a fact. And the human being who sees the totality of this—that is the fear, the pleasure and the enormous suffering which man has brought upon himself and created for others, the whole of that, and the nature and the structure of the self, the "me", the total comprehension of that, actually—then he is

活，卑劣琐碎，接受权威，争讼不休，苦楚不堪，没有人爱而又极度渴望被爱，孤独的痛苦，不负责任的关系——这就是我们的日常生活。而我们就像世界上的其他人一样，这是一条宽阔无边、无尽流淌的河流。当我们死去时，我们还会像其他人一样，像我们以前活着的时候一样在同一条河里流动。但是彻底了解了自己、解决了自己心理上的所有问题的人，他不属于那股洪流，他走了出来。

离开了那股洪流的人，他的意识是完全不同的。他不从时间、延续性或者不朽的角度来思考。但其他的男人或者女人依然身处其中。所以问题就出现了：洪流之外的人和洪流之中的人有什么关系？真理与现实之间的关系如何？如我们之前所说，现实即为思想所造的一切物品。"现实"这个词的词根义是物品。活在这个充满了物品即现实的世界上，我们想要与空无一物的世界建立联系——这是不可能的。

我们说的是，那个意识连同它所有的内容，就是时间的运动。所有人类都困在那种运动中。即使他们死去时，那种运动还在继续着。确实是这样，这是一个事实。而看到了这个整体的人——也就是恐惧、欢愉以及人类加诸自身与他人之上的巨大痛苦，这个整体，自我、"我"的本质和结构，对这一切实实在在的彻底的领悟——然后他就迈出了那股洪流。而这就是意识中的危机。我们一直试图在那个意识的领域内通过时间来解决我们人类所有的经济、社会和政治问题。我想知道你有没有明白这点？因此我们永远也解决不了。我们似乎接受了政客、牧师、分析师或者别的什么人，认为他们会拯救世界。然而，正如我们所说，意识的突变就是时间的终结，也就是经由时间产生的"我"的终结。这

out of that stream. And that is the crisis in consciousness. We are trying to solve all our human problems, economic, social, political, within the area of that consciousness in time. I wonder if you see this? And therefore we can never solve it. We seem to accept the politician as though he was going to save the world, or the priest, or the analyst, or somebody else. And, as we said, the mutation in consciousness is the ending of time, which is the ending of the "me" which has been produced through time. Can this take place? Or is it just a theory like any other?

Can a human being, can you actually do it? When you do it, it affects the totality of consciousness. Which means in the understanding of oneself, which is the understanding of the world—because I am the world—there comes not only compassion but a totally different kind of energy. This energy, with its compassion, has a totally different kind of action. That action is whole, not fragmentary.

We began by talking about suffering, that the ending of suffering is the beginning of compassion; and this question of love, which man has reduced to mere pleasure; and this great complex problem of death. They are all interrelated, they are not separate. It isn't that I am going to solve the problem of death, forgetting the rest. The whole thing is interrelated, inter-communicated. It is all one. And to see the totality of all that, wholly, is only possible when there is no observer and therefore freedom from all that.

Questioner: I'd like to ask a question. You said towards the beginning that it is important for each individual to transform his consciousness. Isn't the fact that you say that it is important an ideal, which is the very thing to be avoided ?

Krishnamurti: When you see a house on fire, isn't it important that you put it out? In that there is no ideal. The house is burning, you are there,

能够发生吗？还是说这只是像其他所有理论一样的另一个理论？

一个人能不能，你能不能实际做到这一点？当你这么做了，就会影响这个意识的整体。也就是说，在对自己的了解之中，也就是对全世界的了解之中——因为我就是世界——出现的不仅仅是慈悲，还有一种截然不同的能量。这种能量，连同它的慈悲，就会产生一种完全不同的行动。这种行动是完整的，不是支离破碎的。

我们一开始谈的是痛苦，痛苦的终结即为慈悲的开始；还有爱这个问题，人类已经把它降低成了欢愉；以及死亡这个非常复杂的问题。它们都是相互关联的，它们不是分开的。并不是我要解决死亡的问题，同时忘掉其他的问题。这整件事情是相互关联、相互交织的，它们都是一个整体。而只有当观察者不存在进而从那一切中解脱出来之时，才有可能完全看到这个整体。

提问者：我想问一个问题。你一开始说过重要的是每个人转变他自身的意识。你所说的重要事实，难道不是一个恰恰需要避免的理想吗？

克里希那穆提：当你看到一座房子着火了，你去把它扑灭，这难道不重要吗？那里面是没有理想的。房子着火了，你就在那里，你必须对此做些什么。但是如果你睡着了，并且在讨论放火烧房子的人头发是什么颜色的……

问：着火的房子是在这个现实世界中的，不是吗？这是一个事实。我们谈的是心理世界。

克：那难道不也是一个实际存在的世界吗？你受苦，这难道不是

and you have to do something about it. But if you are asleep and discussing the colour of the hair of the man who has set the house on fire...

Q: The house on fire is in the world of reality, isn't it? It is a fact. We are talking about the psychological world.

K: Isn't that also a factual world? Isn't it a fact that you suffer? Isn't it a fact that one is ambitious, greedy, violent—you may not be, but the rest —that is a fact. We say the house is a fact, but my anger, my violence, my stupid activities are something different; they are as real as the house. And if I don't understand myself, dissolve all the misery in myself, the house is going to become the destructive element.

Q: Sir, as I understand it, your message and the message of Jesus Christ seem to reach towards the same thing, although stated differently. I had always understood your message and Jesus Christ's message to be quite different in content. About two years ago I was a Christian, so it is very difficult to get rid of statements that Jesus made, such as, "No man cometh to the Father but by me". Although I find more sense in your message at the moment, how do you equate this?

K: It is very simple. I have no message. I am just pointing out. That is not a message.

Q: But why are you doing it?

K: Why am I doing it? Why do we want a message? Why do we want somebody to give us something? When everything is in you.

Q: It is wonderful.

K: No, it is not wonderful (laughter). Please do look at it. You are the result of all the influences, of the culture, the many words, propaganda, you are that. And if you know how to look, how to read, how to listen, how to see, the art of seeing, everything is there, right in front of you. But we don't

一个事实吗？人野心勃勃、贪婪、暴力，这难道不是事实吗——你也许不是这样的，但其他人是——这是一个事实。我们说房子是个事实，但我的愤怒、我的暴力、我愚蠢的行为是不同的事情；它们实际上跟房子一样真实。而如果我不了解自己，不消除我自己身上的所有痛苦，房子就会成为具有破坏性的因素。

问：先生，就我的理解，你的信息和耶稣基督的信息似乎指向了同样的事情，尽管说法不同。我之前一直认为你的信息和耶稣基督的信息在内容上是不同的。大约两年前我还是个基督教徒，所以很难抛开耶稣说的话，比如，"没人能接近天父，除了通过我"。尽管我现在发现你的信息更有道理，然而你是如何把这两者相提并论的？

克：这很简单。我没有任何信息，我只是在指出来，这并不是什么信息。

问：可你为什么要这么做呢？

克：我为什么这么做？我们为什么想得到某种信息？我们为什么希望别人给我们什么东西，当一切都在你自己身上的时候？

问：这很了不起。

克：不，这没什么了不起的。（笑声）请仔细看一看。你就是所有的影响、文化、各种说法和宣传的产物，你就是那些。然而如果你知道如何去看、如何去读、如何聆听、如何观察，如果你懂得看的艺术，一切就都在那里了，一切就在你面前。但是我们没有那种能量、意愿或者兴趣。我们希望有人来告诉我们纸上写了什么。然后我们把那个告诉我们的人变成了一个了不起的人。我们崇拜他，或者摧毁他，这都是一

have the energy, the inclination, or the interest. We want somebody to tell us what there is on the page. And we make that person who tells us into an extraordinary human being. We worship him, or destroy him, which is the same thing. So it is there. You don't need a message. Do look at it please. Is the book important, or what you find in the book? What you find in the book, and after you have read it you throw it away. Now in these talks, you listen, find out, go into it, and throw away the speaker. The speaker is not at all important. It is like a telephone.

The other question is, "Why do you speak?" Does that need answering? Would you say to the flower on the wayside, "Why do you flower?" It is there for you to look, to listen, to see the beauty of it and come back again to look at the beauty of it. That is all.

Q: (partly inaudible) We have the same message, the same words, we have it in ourselves, the guru.

Q: (repeating) We have a guru in ourselves.

K: Have you? Guru means in Sanskrit, the root meaning of that word means "heavy".

Q: He said heaven.

K: Heaven, it is the same thing, sir. Have you a heaven in yourself? My lord, I wish you had! (laughter). In yourself you are so confused, so miserable, so anxious—what a set of words to use—heaven! You can substitute God into heaven, heaven as God and you think you are quite different. People have believed that you had God inside you, light inside you, or something else inside you. But when you see actually that you have nothing, just words, then if there is absolutely nothing there is complete security. And out of that, everything happens, flowers.

回事。所以说它就在那里，你不需要什么信息。请务必看看这一点。是书本重要，还是你在书中的发现更重要？你在书中有所发现，而当你读过之后，就得把它扔掉。那么从这些讲话中，你聆听、探索、发现了真相，然后就把讲话者扔掉。讲话者根本不重要，他就像一部电话机一样。

另一个问题是："你为什么讲话？"这还需要回答吗？你会对路边的一朵花说"你为什么开放"吗？它就在那里等你去看、去听、去看到它的美，然后回来再看看它的美。仅此而已。

问：（部分模糊不清）我们拥有同样的信息、同样的话语，它就在我们自己身上，那个古鲁。

问：（重复）我们自己内心就有古鲁。

克：你有吗？古鲁在梵文里的意思是，那个词的词根义是"沉重"。

问：他说的是天堂。

克：天堂，那是一回事，先生。你自己内心有天堂吗？我的天，我真希望你有！（笑声）你自己的内心是如此困惑、如此不幸、如此焦虑——这都是一套什么样的用词啊——天堂！你可以把神换成天堂，天堂就是神，然后你就认为自己很不一样了。人们相信你的内心有神，你的内心有光明，或者有别的什么。但是，当你实实在在地看到你除了言辞之外一无所有，如果真的彻底一无所有，那么就有了彻底的安全。然后从那里一切都会发生，一切都会绽放。

CHAPTER 9
第 9 章

THE SACRED , RELIGION,
MEDITATION

神圣、宗教与冥想

I would like this morning to talk about the question of what is sacred, what is the meaning of religion and of meditation. First we must examine what is reality and what is truth. Man has been concerned throughout the ages to discover, or live in truth; And he has projected various symbols, conclusions, images made by the mind or by the hand and imagined what is truth. Or he has tried to find out through the activity and the movement of thought. And I think we should be wise if we would differentiate between reality and truth and when we are clear what reality is then perhaps we shall be able to have an insight into what is truth.

The many religions throughout the world have said that there is an enduring, everlasting truth, but the mere assertion of truth has very little significance. One has to discover it for oneself, not theoretically, intellectually, or sentimentally, but actually find out if one can live in a world that is completely truthful. We mean by religion the gathering together of all energy to investigate into something: to investigate if there is anything sacred. That is the meaning we are giving it, not the religion of belief, dogma, tradition or ritual with their hierarchical outlook. But we are using the word "religion" in the sense: to gather together all energy, which will then be capable of investigating if there is a truth which is not controlled, shaped, or polluted by thought.

The root meaning of the word reality is thing or things. And to go into the question of what is reality, one must understand what thought is. Because

"我们要一起观察现实是什么，思想的局限是什么，思想究竟能否洞察真理。还是说真理在思想的领域之外？

"一个人必须拥有这种冥想的心灵品质，不是偶尔才有，而是整天都有。而这种神圣将不仅仅在醒着的时候影响我们的生活，在睡眠时也是一样。"

今天早上我想谈谈什么是神圣的、宗教和冥想的意义这些问题。首先我们必须检视什么是现实，什么又是真理。人类世世代代以来一直都注重探索真理或者活在真理中；于是他投射出了由头脑或者双手制造的各种各样的符号、结论和形象，并且想象真理是什么。或者他试图通过行为和思想的活动来弄清真相。而我认为，如果我们想区分现实与真理，我们就应该具有智慧，而当我们清楚了现实是什么，然后或许我们就能够洞察真理是什么。

全世界的许多宗教都说存在着持久的、永恒的真理，但仅仅坚称真理存在没什么意义。你必须自己去发现它，不是从理论上、智力上或情感上，而是真正弄清楚人能不能活在一个完全真实的世界上。我们所说的宗教指的是聚集所有的能量去探究：探究有没有什么神圣的事物。这就是我们赋予它的含义，而不是信仰、教条、传统或仪式及其等级化

our society, our religions, our so-called revelations are essentially the product of thought. It is not my opinion or my judgement, but it is a fact. All religions when you look at them, observe without any prejudice, are the product of thought. That is, you may perceive something, have an insight into truth, and you communicate it verbally to me and I draw from your statement an abstraction and make that into an idea; then I live according to that idea. That is what we have been doing for generations: drawing an abstraction from a statement and living according to that abstraction as a conclusion. And that is generally called religion. So we must find out how limited thought is and what are its capacities, how far it can go, and be totally aware that thought doesn't spill over into a realm in which thought has no place.

I don't know if you can see this? Please, we are not only verbally communicating, which means thinking together, not agreeing or disagreeing, but thinking together, and therefore sharing together; not the speaker gives and you take, but together we are sharing, therefore there is no authority. And also there is a non-verbal communication, which is much more difficult, because unless we see very clearly the full meaning of words, how the mind is caught in words, how words shape our thinking, and can go beyond that, then there is no non-verbal communication, which becomes much more significant. We are trying to do both: to communicate verbally and non-verbally. That means we must both be interested at the same time, at the same level, with the same intensity, otherwise we shan't communicate. It is like love; love is that intense feeling at the same time, at the same level. Otherwise you and I don't love each other. So we are going to observe together what is reality, what are the limitations of thought, and whether thought can ever perceive truth. Or is it beyond the realm of thought?

I think we all agree, at least most of us do, even the scientists, that

的世界观这种宗教。我们是在这个意义上使用"宗教"这个词的：把所有的能量聚集到一起，于是能够探究有没有一种真理是没有受到思想的控制、塑造或污染的。

"现实"这个词的词根义是东西或物品。若要探究什么是现实这个问题，我们就必须了解思想是什么。因为我们的社会、我们的宗教、我们所谓的启迪本质上都是思想的产物。这不是我的观点或者我的判断，而是事实。所有的宗教，当你毫无偏见地看着它们、观察它们，就会发现它们是思想的产物。也就是说，你也许洞察到了什么，对真理有了洞见，然后你用语言把它传达给我，而我从你的说法中得出了一个抽象的结论，并且把它变成了一个概念，然后根据那个概念生活。这就是我们世世代代以来所做的事：从一个说法得出抽象的结论，然后根据那个抽象的结论来生活，而这就是我们通常所说的宗教。所以我们必须弄清楚思想有多么局限，它有哪些能力，它能走多远，并且完全警觉思想不会溢出到一个思想没有位置的领域中。

我不知道你有没有明白这一点？请注意，我们不是仅仅从语言上沟通，也就是说我们是在一起思考，不是同意或者不同意，而是一起思考，因而一起分享；不是讲话者给你然后你接受，而是我们在一起分担，因此不存在任何权威。还有一种非语言的交流，而这要困难得多，因为除非我们非常清楚语言的全部含义，心智是如何受困于语言之中的，语言是如何塑造了我们的思维，并且超越这一切，否则就不存在非语言的沟通，而这实际上要重要得多。我们正试着两者都做到：语言和非语言的沟通。也就是说我们必须在同一时间、在同一层面上，带着同

thought is a material process, is a chemical process. Thought is the response of accumulated knowledge as experience and memory. So thought is essentially a thing. There is no sacred thought, no noble thought, it is a thing. And its function is in the world of things, which is technology, learning, learning the art of learning, the art of seeing and listening. And reality is in that area. Unless we understand this rather complex problem we shall not be able to go beyond it. We may pretend, or imagine, but imagination and pretension have no place in a human being who is really serious and is desirous to find out what is truth.

As long as there is the movement of thought, which is time and measure, in that area truth has no place. Reality is that which we think and the action of thought as an idea, as a principle, as an ideal, projected from the previous knowledge into the future modified and so on. All that is in the world of reality. We live in that world of reality—if you have observed yourself you will see how memory plays an immense part. Memory is mechanical, thought is mechanical, it is a form of computer, a machine, as the brain is. And thought has its place. I cannot speak if I have no language; if I spoke in Greek you wouldn't understand. And learning a language, learning to drive a car, to work in a factory and so on, there thought is necessary. psychologically, thought has created the reality of the "me". "Me", "my", my house, my property, my wife, my husband, my children, my country, my God - all that is the product of thought. And in that field we have established a relationship with each other which is constantly in conflict. That is the limitation of thought.

Unless we put order into that world of reality we cannot go further. We live a disorderly life in our daily activities; that is a fact. And is it possible to bring about order in the world of reality, in the world of thought, socially,

样强烈的热情，否则我们就无法沟通。这就像爱：爱就是在同一时间、同一层面上的那种热烈的感情，否则你我就不爱对方。所以我们要一起观察现实是什么，思想的局限是什么，思想究竟能否洞察真理。还是说真理在思想的领域之外？

我想我们都同意，至少我们大部分人，甚至科学家都会同意思想是一个物质过程，是一个化学过程。思想是积累起来的知识也就是经验和记忆的反应。所以说思想本质上是一种物品。不存在神圣的思想，也不存在高尚的思想，它就是一种物品。而在这个物质世界、科技世界上，它的功能在于学习，学习学习的艺术、看和听的艺术。而现实也在这个领域。除非我们懂得了这个相当复杂的问题，否则我们就无法超越它。我们可以假装或者想象，但想象和伪装在一个真正认真并渴望发现真理的人身上毫无一席之地。

只要存在思想的运动，也就是时间和衡量的活动，真理在那个领域中就没有位置。现实是我们所思考的，是概念、原则、理想这些思想的行动，这些思想从先前的知识投射到未来并稍做调整，等等。这一切都处于现实世界中。我们就生活在这个现实世界上——如果你观察自己，你就会发现记忆起到了多么重要的作用。记忆是机械的，思想是机械的，它是一种形式的计算机，是一台机器，就像大脑一样。而思想有它的位置。如果我不懂语言，我就无法讲话；如果我说希腊语，你就听不懂。学习语言，学习驾驶汽车、在工厂工作等，这里是需要思想的。思想从心理上制造了"我"这个现实。"我""我的"，我的房子、我的财产、我的妻子、我的丈夫、我的孩子、我的国家、我的神——这一

morally, ethically and so on? And who is to bring about order in the world of reality? I live a disorderly life—if I do—and being disorderly, can I bring about order in all the activities of daily life? Our daily life is based on thought, our relationship is based on thought, because I have an image of you and you have an image of me, and the relationship is between those two images. The images are the product of thought, which is the response of memory, experience and so on. Now can there be order in the world of reality? This is really a very important question. Unless order is established in the world of reality there is no foundation for further enquiry. In the world of reality, is it possible to behave orderly, not according to a pattern set by thought, which is still disorder? Is it possible to bring about order in the world of reality? That is, no wars, no conflict, no division. Order implies great virtue, virtue is the essence of order —not following a blueprint, which becomes mechanical. So who is to bring order in this world of reality? Man has said, "God will bring it. Believe in God and you will have order. Love God and you will have order." But this order becomes mechanical because our desire is to be secure, to survive, to find the easiest way of living—let us put it that way.

So we are asking, who is to bring order in this world of reality, where there is such confusion, misery, pain, violence and so on. Can thought bring about order in that reality—a world of reality which thought has created? Do you follow my question? The Communists say control the environment, then there will be order in man. According to Marx the State will wither away—you know all that. They have tried to bring order but man is in disorder, even in Russia! So one has to find out, if thought is not to bring about order, then what will? I don't know if this is a problem to you, if it really interests you? So one has to ask, if thought, which has made such a mess of life, cannot bring clarity into this world of reality, then is there

切都是思想的产物。而就在那个领域中，我们彼此建立了一种冲突不断的关系。这就是思想的局限。

除非我们把这个现实世界纳入秩序，否则我们就寸步难行。我们在日常活动中过着一种失序的生活，这是一个事实。有没有可能从社会、道德、伦理等方面为这个现实世界、这个思想的世界带来秩序？而又由谁来为这个现实世界带来秩序？我过着一种失序的生活——如果是这样的话——在自身混乱的情况下，我能够为日常生活的所有行为带来秩序吗？我们的日常生活以思想为基础，我们的关系以思想为基础，因为我对你抱有形象，你对我也抱有形象，关系就是那两个形象之间的关系。形象是思想的产物，而思想是记忆、经验等的反应。那么，现实世界中能够存在秩序吗？这真的是一个非常重要的问题。除非在这个现实世界中建立起秩序，否则就没有进一步探询的基础。在现实世界中，有没有可能有序地行动，而不是根据思想设下的模式？那依然是失序。有没有可能在这个现实世界上建立秩序？也就是说，没有战争、没有冲突、没有分裂。秩序意味着伟大的美德，美德就是秩序的核心——而不是遵循某幅蓝图，那会变得机械。那么谁要在这个现实世界上带来秩序？人类说了："上帝会带来秩序的。相信上帝，你就会拥有秩序。热爱上帝，你就会拥有秩序。"但这种秩序会变得机械，因为我们想要的是得到安全、生存下去并找到最简单的生活方式——让我们这样来表达。

所以我们问，谁来为这个有着如此之多混乱、不幸、痛苦和暴力等的世界带来秩序？思想能为这种现实，为思想所造的这个现实世界带来秩序吗？你明白我的问题吗？共产主义者说控制环境，然后人类之中

an observation in the field of reality, or of the field of reality, without the movement of thought. Are we meeting each other about this? A human being has exercised thought, he says there is disorder, I will control it, I will shape it, I will make order according to certain ideas—it is all the product of thought. And thought has created disorder. So thought has no place in order, and how is this order to come about?

Now we will go into it a little bit. Can one observe this disorder in which one lives, which is conflict, contradiction, opposing desires, pain, suffering, fear, pleasure and all that, this whole structure of disorder, without thought? You understand my question? Can you observe this enormous disorder in which we live, externally as well as inwardly, without any movement of thought? Because if there is any movement of thought, then it is going to create further disorder, isn't it? So can you observe this disorder in yourself without any move, ment of thought as time and measure—that is, without any movement of memory?

We are going to see whether thought as time can come to an end. Whether thought as measure, which is comparison, as time, from here to there —all that is involved in the movement of time—whether that time can have a stop? This is the very essence of meditation. You understand? So we are going to enquire together if time has a stop, that is, if thought as movement can come to an end. Then only is there order and therefore virtue. Not cultivated virtue, which requires time and is therefore not virtue, but the very stopping, the very ending of thought is virtue. This means we have to enquire into the whole question of what is freedom. Can man live in freedom? Because that is what it comes to. If time comes to an end it means that man is deeply free. So one has to go into this question of what is freedom. Is freedom relative, or absolute? If freedom is the outcome of thought then it is relative. When freedom is not

就会出现秩序。根据马克思的说法，国家将会消亡——你知道那些。他们试图建立秩序，但人类依然混乱，哪怕在俄国也是如此！所以你必须弄清楚，如果思想无法带来秩序，那么什么可以？我不知道这对你来说是不是一个问题，它是不是真的让你感兴趣？所以你必须问一问，如果思想让生活如此混乱，它无法将清晰带入这个现实世界，那么现实的领域中有没有一种观察，或者说有没有一种对现实领域的观察，是没有思想运动的？关于这一点我们明白对方的意思了吗？一个人运用了思想，他说存在失序，我要控制它，我要塑造它，我要根据某些理念来建立秩序——这全都是思想的产物。而正是思想造成了失序。所以思想在秩序中没有地位，那么这种秩序如何才能到来？

现在我们来稍稍探讨一下这个问题。你能不能观察自己所处的这种失序，也就是冲突、矛盾、互相对立的欲望、痛苦、不幸、恐惧、欢愉以及那一切，这整个失序的结构，而没有思想？你理解我的问题吗？你能不能观察我们所处的这种外在和内在皆有的巨大混乱，而没有任何思想活动？因为如果存在丝毫的思想活动，就会造成进一步的失序，不是吗？所以你能不能观察自己内心的这种失序，而没有任何思想活动也就是时间和衡量的活动——也就是说，没有任何记忆的活动？

我们这就来看一看思想即时间能不能终止。思想就是衡量，而衡量即比较，思想就是由此及彼的时间——这一切都包含在时间运动中——这种时间能否停止？这就是冥想的本质，你明白吗？所以我们要一起来探询时间能否停止，也就是说思想活动能否终止。只有此时才会有秩序，进而有美德。不是培养出来的美德，那需要时间因而并非美德，而

bound by thought then it is absolute. We are going to go into that.

Outwardly, politically, there is less and less freedom. We think politicians can solve all our problems and the politicians, especially the tyrannical politicians, assume the authority of God, they know and you don't know. That is what is going on in India, freedom of speech, civil rights, have been denied, like in all tyrannies. Democratically we have freedom of choice, we choose between the Liberal, Conservatives, Labour or something else. And we think that having the capacity to choose gives us freedom. Choice is the very denial of freedom. You choose when you are not clear, when there is no direct perception, and so you choose out of confusion, and so there is no freedom in choice—psychologically, that is. I can choose between this cloth and that cloth, and so on; but psychologically we think we are free when we have the capacity to choose. And we are saying that choice is born out of confusion, out of the structure of thought, and therefore it is not free. We accept the authority of the gurus, the priests, because we think they know and we don't know. Now if you examine the whole idea of the guru, which is becoming rather a nuisance in this country and in America, the world over—I am sorry I am rather allergic to gurus (laughter), I know many of them, they come to see me (laughter). They say, "What you are saying is the highest truth"—they know how to flatter! But we are dealing, they say, with people who are ignorant and we are the intermediaries: we want to help them. So they assume the authority and therefore deny freedom. I do not know if you have noticed that not one single guru has raised his voice against tyranny.

A man who would understand what freedom is must totally deny authority, which is extraordinarily difficult, it demands great attention. We may reject the authority of a guru, of a priest, of an idea, but we establish

是思想的停止本身、思想的终结本身就是美德。这意味着我们必须探询"自由是什么"这整个问题。我们能活在自由中吗？因为那将是自然发生的事情。如果时间终止，那就意味着那个人获得了深刻的自由。所以你必须探究"自由是什么"这个问题。自由是相对的还是绝对的？如果自由是思想的结果，那它就是相对的。当自由不被思想所限，那它就是绝对的。我们这就来探讨这个问题。

外在的、政治上的自由正变得越来越少。我们以为政客能够解决我们所有的问题，而政客，特别是专制的政客，接管了上帝的权威，我们知道而我们不知道。这就是在印度发生着的事情，言论自由、公民权被剥夺了，就像在所有的专制政权下一样。在民主方面我们拥有选择的自由，我们在自由党、保守党、工党或者别的什么之间进行选择。而我们认为拥有选择的能力给了我们自由。选择正是对自由的否定。当你不清晰时，当你没有直接的洞察时，你才会选择，所以你的选择出自困惑，因而选择中没有自由——从心理上讲正是如此。我在这块布和那块布等之间选择；但是我们以为当我们拥有选择的能力时，我们在心理上是自由的。而我们说选择脱胎于困惑，脱胎于思想的结构，所以它不自由。我们接受了古鲁、牧师的权威，因为我们认为他们知道而我们不知道。然而，如果你审视古鲁的整个概念——古鲁正在这个国家、在美国以及全世界变成一种相当令人厌恶的东西——抱歉我对古鲁非常过敏（笑声），我认识很多古鲁，他们会来见我（笑声）。他们说，"你说的是至高无上的真理"——他们知道如何阿谀奉承！但我们面对的——他们说——是愚昧的人们，我们是媒介：我们想帮助他们。所以他们掌

an authority in ourselves—that is "I think it is right, I know what I am saying, it is my experience. All that gives one the authority to assert, which is the same thing as the guru and the priest.

Can the mind be free of authority, of tradition, which means accepting another as your guide, as somebody to tell you what to do, except in the technological field? And man must be free if he is not to become a serf, a slave, and deny the beauty and depth of the human spirit. Now can the mind put aside all authority in the psychological sense?—if you put aside the authority of the policeman you will be in trouble. That requires a great deal of inward awareness. One obeys and accepts authority because in oneself there is uncertainty, confusion, loneliness, and the desire to find something permanent, something lasting. And is there anything lasting, anything that is permanent, created by thought? Or does thought give to itself permanency? The mind desires to have something it can cling to, some certainty, some psychological security. This is what happens in all our relationships with each other. I depend on you psychologically - because in myself I am uncertain, confused, lonely— and I am attached to you, I possess you, I dominate you. So living in this world is freedom possible, without authority, without the image, without the sense of dependency? And is it freedom from something or freedom per se?

Now can we have freedom in the world of reality? You understand my question?—can there be freedom in my relationship with you? Can there be freedom in relationship between man and woman, or is that impossible? —which doesn't mean freedom to do what one likes, or permissiveness, or promiscuity. But can there be a relationship between human beings of complete freedom? I do not know if you have ever asked this question of yourself? You might say it is possible or not possible. The possibility or the impossibility of it is not an answer, but to find out whether freedom can

握了权威进而否定了自由。我不知道你有没有注意到没有任何一个古鲁扬声抗议过专制统治。

一个想了解自由是什么的人，必须完全否定权威，而这极为困难，需要巨大的注意力。我们也许拒绝了某个古鲁、某个牧师、某个概念的权威，但我们在自己内心建立了另一个权威——那就是"我认为这是对的，我知道我在说什么，这是我的经验"。这一切都给了你断言什么的权威，而这跟古鲁和牧师是一回事。

心智能不能摆脱权威、摆脱传统，除了在技术领域以外？权威意味着接受别人做你的向导，接受别人来告诉你怎么办。而人必须自由，如果他不想成为一个仆从、一个奴隶，不想拒绝人类精神的美与深度的话。那么心智能不能摒弃心理上的所有权威？——如果你置警察的权威于不顾，你就会有麻烦。那需要大量的内在觉察。人服从和接受权威是因为他自身不确定、困惑、孤独，渴望发现某种永恒、持久的东西。然而存在任何持久的、永恒的由思想所造的东西吗？还是说思想赋予了其自身以永久性？心智渴望拥有某种它可以紧紧依附的东西，某种确定性，某种心理上的安全感。这就是发生在我们与彼此的一切关系中的事情。我从心理上依赖你——因为我自己内心是不确定的、困惑的、孤独的——于是我依附于你，我占有你，我控制你。所以，活在这个世界上，没有权威、没有意象、没有依赖感的自由可能吗？那是从某事中解脱的自由还是自由本身？

那么，我们能够在这个现实世界上拥有自由吗？你理解我的问题吗？——我与你的关系中能否存在自由？自由能否在男人和女人之间的

exist, absolute freedom in our relationships. That freedom can only exist in relationship when there is order: order not according to you, or another, but order in the sense of the observation of disorder. And that observation is not the movement of thought, because the observer is the observed; only then there is freedom in our relationship.

Then we can go to something else. Having observed the whole nature of disorder, order comes into being in our life. That is a fact, if you have gone into it. From there we can move and find out whether thought can end, can realize its own movement, see its own limitation and therefore stop. We are asking, what place has time in freedom. Is freedom a state of mind in which there is no time?—time being movement of thought as time and measure. Thought is movement, movement in time. That is, can the brain, which is part of the mind—which has evolved through centuries with all the accumulated memories, knowledge, experience—is there a part of the brain which is not touched by time? Do you understand my question? Our brain is conditioned by various influences, by the pursuit of desires; and is there a part of the brain that is not conditioned at all? Or is the whole brain conditioned and can human beings therefore never escape from conditioning? They can modify the conditioning, polish, refine it, but there will always be conditioning if the totality of the brain is limited, and therefore no freedom.

So we are going to find out if there is any part of the brain that is not conditioned. All this is meditation, to find out. Can one be aware of the conditioning in which one lives? Can you be aware of your conditioning as a Christian, a Capitalist, a Socialist, a Liberal, that you believe in this and you don't believe in that?—all that is part of the conditioning. Can a human being be aware of that conditioning? Can you be aware of your consciousness?—not as an observer, but that you are that consciousness.

关系中存在，还是说那是不可能的？——那种自由并不意味着为所欲为、放纵或者滥交的自由，而是说，人与人之间能不能存在一种完全自由的关系？我不知道你究竟有没有问过自己这个问题？你也许会说这是可能的或者是不可能的。它可能或者不可能并不是答案，而是要去弄清楚自由能否存在，绝对的自由在我们的关系中能否存在。只有当秩序存在时，那种自由才能存在：秩序并不是就你或者别人而言的秩序，而是"观察到失序"这个意义上的秩序。而那种观察不是思想的运动，因为观察者就是被观察之物；只有此时我们的关系中才存在自由。

接下来我们就可以探讨其他的事情了。观察到了失序的整个本质，秩序就会在我们的生活中出现。这是一个事实，如果你探究过这个问题的话。从这里我们就可以出发了，去弄清楚思想能否终止，能否意识到它自己的运动，看到它自身的局限并进而停下来。我们问，时间在自由中有什么位置。自由是不是一种没有时间的心灵状态？——时间就是思想即时间和衡量的活动。思想就是运动，时间中的运动。也就是说，大脑，心智的一部分——它带着积累起来的所有记忆、知识和经验已经进化了千百年——大脑有没有一个部分是时间没有触及的？你明白我的问题吗？我们的大脑被各种影响、被对欲望的追求所制约；而大脑有没有一个部分根本没有受到制约？还是说，整个大脑受到了制约，乃至人类永远都无法逃脱制约？他们可以调整制约，粉饰它，提炼它，但是如果整个大脑是局限的，那么制约就会一直存在，因而没有自由。

所以我们要搞清楚大脑是不是有一个部分并没有受到制约。这些就是冥想，也就是去发现真相。你能不能觉察自己所身处的制约？你能

And if you are aware, who is it that is aware? Is it thought that is aware that it is conditioned? Then it is still in the field of reality, which is conditioned. Or is there an observation, an awareness in which there is pure observation? Is there an act, or an art of pure listening?

Do listen to this a little bit. The word "art" means to put everything in its right place, where it belongs. Now can you observe without any interpretation, without any judgement, without any prejudice—just observe, see purely? And can you listen, as you are doing now, without any movement of thought. It is only possible if you put thought in the right place. And the art of learning means not accumulating—then it becomes knowledge and thought—but the movement of learning, without the accumulation. So there is the art of seeing, the art of listening, the art of learning—which means to put everything where it belongs. And in that there is great order.

Now we are going to find out if time has a stop. This is meditation. As we said at the beginning, it is all in the field of meditation. Meditation isn't something separate from life, from daily life. Meditation is not the repetition of words, the repetition of a mantra, which is now the fashion and called transcendental meditation, or the meditation which can be practised. Meditation must be something totally unconscious. I wonder if you see this? If you practise meditation, that is follow a system, a method, then it is the movement of thought, put together in order to achieve a result, and that result is projected as a reaction from the past and therefore still within the area of thought.

So can there be a mutation in the brain? It comes to that. We say it is possible. That is, a mutation is only passible when there is a great shock of attention. Attention implies no control. Have you ever asked whether you can

不能觉察自己作为一个基督教徒、资本主义者、社会主义者、自由党人所受的局限，你相信这个但不相信那个制约？——所有这些都是制约的一部分。一个人能不能觉察这种制约？你能不能觉知自己的意识？——不是作为一个观察者，而是你就是那个意识。如果你是觉知的，那么那个觉知的人又是谁？是思想觉察到自己身受制约吗？那样的话它就依然处在局限的现实领域中。还是说，存在一种观察，一种只有纯然观察的觉知？是不是有一种行动，或者一种纯然聆听的艺术？

请务必认真听一听这些。"艺术"这个词的意思是把一切都放在合适的位置上，放在它所属的地方。那么，你能不能观察而不做任何诠释，不做任何评判，也没有任何偏见——只是纯粹地观察和看？你能不能像现在这样聆听，而没有任何思想活动？只有当你把思想放在了合适的位置上，这才有可能。而学习的艺术指的不是积累——那样的话就变成了知识和思想——而是指没有积累的学习活动。所以就有了看的意思、听的艺术、学习的艺术——那意味着把一切都放在它所属的位置上。而这其中就有着非凡的秩序。

现在我们要来弄清楚时间能否停止。这就是冥想。正如我们一开始所说的，这些都属于冥想的领域。冥想并不是某种与生活、与日常分开的东西。冥想不是重复词句、反复诵念咒语，而如今这成为时尚，被称为超验冥想或者可以练习的冥想。冥想必须是某种完全无意而为的事情。我想知道你有没有明白这一点？如果你练习冥想，也就是遵循某个体系、某种方法，那就是思想的运动，是为了取得某个结果而编造出来的，而那个结果是从过去作为一个反应投射出来的，因而依然在思想的

live in this world without a single control?—of your desires, of your appetites, of the fulfilment of your desires and so on, without a single breath of control? Control implies a controller: and the controller thinks he is different from that which he controls. But when you observe closely the controller is the controlled. So what place has control? In the sense of restraint, suppression, to control in order to achieve, to control to change yourself to become something else—all that is the demand of thought. Thought by its very nature being fragmentary, divides the controller and the controlled. And we are educated from childhood to control, to suppress, to inhibit—which does not mean to do what you like; that is impossible, that is too absurd, too immature.

But to understand this whole question of control demands that you examine the desire which brings about this fragmentation; the desire to be and not to be. To find out whether you can live without comparison, therefore without an ideal, without a future—all that is implied in comparison. And where there is comparison there must be control. Can you live without comparison and therefore without control— do you understand? Have you ever tried to live without control, without comparison? Because comparison and control are highly respectable. The word "respect" means to look about. And when we look about we see that all human beings, wherever they live, have this extraordinary desire to compare themselves with somebody, or with an idea, or with some human being who is supposed to be noble, and in that process they control, suppress. Now if you see this whole movement, then one will live without a single breath of control. That requires tremendous inward discipline. Discipline means actually to learn, not to be disciplined to a pattern like a soldier. The word "discipline" means to learn. Learn whether it is possible to live without a single choice, comparison, or control. To learn about it;

领域内。

那么大脑中能不能发生一种突变？这个问题自然而然就出现了。我们说这是可能的。也就是说，只有当出现了关注带来的巨大震撼，突变才是可能的。关注意味着没有控制。你可曾问过你能不能没有丝毫控制地活在这个世界上？——不控制你的欲望、对你欲望的满足等，没有一丝一毫的控制？控制隐含着一个控制者，而控制者认为他与他所控制的对象是不同的。然而当你仔细观察，你就会发现控制者就是被控制对象。那么控制有什么意义？在克制、压抑的意义上，为了成就而控制，为了把自己变成别的什么而控制——这一切都是思想的欲求。思想的本质是支离破碎的，它划分了控制者和被控制对象。而我们从小受到的教育就是要控制、压抑和约束——并不是说你要为所欲为，那是不可能的，那太荒唐、太幼稚了。

而若要理解这整个控制的问题，你就需要审视造成这种破碎状况的欲望，成为什么和不成为什么的欲望。要弄清楚你能不能毫无比较地活着，因而没有理想、没有未来——那些都包含在比较之中。你能不能毫无比较地活着进而没有丝毫控制——你明白吗？你可曾尝试过没有控制、没有比较地活着？因为比较和控制是非常令人尊敬的。"尊敬"这个词的意思是查看四周。而当我们查看四周，我们发现所有的人类，无论他们住在哪里，都有"比较"这种强烈的欲望——拿自己跟别人比，或者跟某个理念、某个应该很高尚的人进行比较，而在这个过程中他们就会控制和压抑。然而，如果你看到了这整个活动，你就能够没有丝毫控制地活着了。这需要非凡的内在纪律。纪律的意思实际上是学习，而

not to accept it, not to deny it, but to find out how to live.

Then out of that comes a brain which is not conditioned. Meditation then is freedom from authority, putting everything in its right place in the field of reality, and consciousness realizing its own limitation and therefore bringing about order in that limitation. When there is order there is virtue, virtue in behaviour.

From there we can go into the question, whether time has a stop. Which means, can the mind, the brain itself, be absolutely still?—not controlled. If you control thought in order to be still, then it is still the movement of thought. Can the brain and the mind be absolutely still, which is the ending of time? Man has always desired throughout the ages to bring silence to the mind, which he called meditation, contemplation and so on. Can the mind be still?—not chattering, not imagining, not conscious if that stillness, because if you are conscious of that stillness there is a centre which is conscious, and that centre is part of time, put together by thought; therefore you are still within the area of reality and there is no ending in the world of reality of time.

Man has made, whether by the hand or by the mind, what he thinks is sacred, all the images in churches, in temples. All those images are still the product of thought. And in that there is nothing sacred. But out of this complete silence is there anything sacred? We began by saying that religion is not belief, rituals, authority, but religion is the gathering of all energy to investigate if there is something sacred which is not the product of thought. We have that energy when there is complete order in the world of reality in which we live—order in relationship, freedom from authority, freedom from comparison, control, measurement. Then the mind and the brain become completely still naturally, not through compulsion. If one sees that anything which thought has created is not sacred, nothing—all the churches, all the temples, all the mosques in

不是像一名士兵一样约束自己。"纪律"这个词意味着学习。学习有没有可能活着而没有丝毫的选择、比较或控制。去了解它，不是接受它，也不是拒绝它，而是去弄清楚该如何生活。

然后从中就产生了一颗未被制约的头脑。此时冥想即为从权威中解脱的自由，把现实世界中的一切都放在恰当的位置上，同时意识也认识到了自身的局限，因而为那种局限带来了秩序。当有了秩序，就有了美德，行为中的美德。

从这里我就可以探究这个问题了：时间能否停止。也就是说，心智、大脑本身能不能完全安静？——但不是受到了控制而安静。如果你为了变得安静而控制思想，那就依然是思想的活动。大脑和心灵能不能彻底寂然不动？那就是时间的终止。人类世世代代以来一直想为心灵带来安宁，他们称之为冥想、沉思，等等。心灵能够寂然不动吗？没有喋喋不休，没有想象，也没有意识到那种寂静，因为如果你意识到了那种寂静，就出现了一个有意识的中心，而那个中心是时间的一部分，是由思想拼凑出来的；因此你依然处于现实的领域中，时间并没有在这个现实世界中终止。

人类制造出他认为神圣的东西，无论用双手还是头脑，制造出了教堂里、寺庙里的所有神像。所有那些神像依然是思想的产物，其中没有任何神圣可言。然而，从这种彻底的寂静之中能不能出现某种神圣的东西？我们一开始就说过宗教并不是信仰、仪式、权威，而是聚集所有的能量去探究是否存在某种并非思想产物的神圣事物。当我们所生活的这个现实世界中有了彻底的秩序——关系中的秩序，摆脱了权威，摆脱

the world have no truth—then is there anything sacred?

In India, when only Brahmins could enter Temples and Ghandi was saying that all people can enter temples—I followed him around one year —and I was asked, "What do you say to that"? I replied, God is not in temples, it doesn't matter who enters. That was of course not acceptable. So in the same way we are saying that anything created by thought is not sacred, and is there anything sacred? Unless human beings find that sacredness, their life really has no meaning, it is an empty shell. They may be very orderly, they may be relatively free, but unless there is this thing that is totally sacred, untouched by thought, life has no deep meaning. Is there something sacred, or is everything matter, everything thought, everything transient, everything impermanent? Is there something that thought can never touch and therefore is incorruptible, timeless, eternal and sacred? To come upon this the mind must be completely, totally still, which means time comes to an end; and in that there must be complete freedom from all prejudice, opinion, judgement—you follow? Then only one comes upon this extraordinary thing that is timeless and the very essence of compassion.

So meditation has significance. One must have this meditative quality of the mind, not occasionally, but all day long. And this something that is sacred affects our lives not only during the waking hours but during sleep. And in this process of meditation there are all kinds of powers that come into being: one becomes clairvoyant, the body becomes extraordinarily sensitive. Now clairvoyance, healing, thought transference and so on, become totally unimportant; all the occult powers become so utterly irrelevant, and when you pursue those you are pursuing something that will ultimately lead to illusion. That is one factor. Then there is the factor of

了比较、控制和衡量——我们就拥有了那种能量。此时心灵和大脑就会自然而然地变得完全安静,而不是通过强制。如果你看到了思想所造的一切都不是神圣的,毫无神圣可言,世界上所有的教堂、所有的庙宇、所有的清真寺都没有真理——那么究竟有没有任何神圣的事物?

在印度,当只有婆罗门能够进入寺庙,而甘地说所有人都可以进入寺庙——有一年我跟着他四处走了走——然后有人问我:"你对此有什么看法?"我回答说,神并不在寺庙中,谁进去并不重要。当然这种说法他们无法接受。所以同样的,我们说思想所造的一切都不是神圣的,那么究竟存在任何神圣的事物吗?除非人类找到了那种神圣,否则他们的生命真的没有任何意义,那是一具空壳。他们也许非常有序,他们也许相对自由,然而,除非有了这种完全神圣、未被思想沾染的东西,否则生命没有深刻的意义。有没有什么神圣的事物,还是说一切都是物质,一切都是思想,一切都是短暂的、不永恒的?有没有什么是思想永远无法触及进而是不会腐败的、超越时间的、永恒的、神圣的东西?若要遇见它,心灵必须彻底地、完全地静止不动,那意味着时间停止了;其中必定会有从所有的偏见、观点和评判中彻底解脱的自由——你明白吗?只有此时你才能邂逅这种永恒的非凡事物,而那就是慈悲的精髓。

所以冥想具有重要的意义。一个人必须拥有这种冥想的心灵品质,不是偶尔才有,而是整天都有。而这种神圣将不仅仅在醒着的时候影响我们的生活,在睡眠时也是一样。在这个冥想的过程中,会出现各种各样的能力:具有透视的能力,身体变得极其敏感。而透视、疗愈、思想转移等这些能力,会变得完全不重要;所有神秘的能力都会变得完全无

sleep. What is the importance of sleep? Is it to spend the sleeping hours dreaming? Or is it possible not to dream at all? What are dreams, why do we dream, and is it possible for a mind not to dream, so that during sleep, the mind being utterly restful, a totally different kind of energy is built in?

If during waking hours we are completely attentive to our thoughts, to our actions, to our behaviour, totally aware, then are dreams necessary? Or are dreams a continuation of our daily life, in the form of pictures, images, incidents—a continuity of our daily conscious or unconscious movements? So when the mind becomes totally aware during the day, then you will see that dreams become unimportant, and being unimportant they have no significance and therefore there is no dreaming. There is only complete sleep; that means the mind has complete rest: it can renew itself. Test it out. If you accept what the speaker is saying, then it is futile; but not if you enquire and find out if during the day you are very very awake, watchful, aware without choice—we went into what it is to be aware—then out of that awareness when you do sleep, the mind becomes extraordinarily fresh and young. Youth is the essence of decision, action. And if that action is merely centred round itself, round the centre of myself, then that action breeds mischief, confusion and so on. But when you realize the whole movement of life as one, undivided, and are aware of that, then the mind rejuvenates itself and has immense energy. All that is part of meditation.

关紧要，而当你追求那些，你就是在追求某种最终会导致幻觉的东西。这是一个因素，然后还有一个因素是睡眠。睡眠具有什么重要性？它是把睡觉的时间用来做梦吗？或者有没有可能根本不做梦？梦是什么，我们为什么做梦，一个人有没有可能不做梦，于是在睡眠期间，心变得极其安详，因而注入了一种截然不同的能量？

如果醒着的时候我们能够全然关注我们的思想、我们的活动、我们的行为，对它们完全觉知，那么还需要做梦吗？还是说，梦是我们白天的生活以画面、形象和事件等形式的延续——延续我们白天有意识或无意识的活动？所以，当心灵白天的时候变得完全觉知，那么你就会发现梦变得完全不重要了，因为不重要所以它们毫无意义，因而晚上就不会做梦。于是只有彻底的睡眠，那意味着心灵得到了彻底的休息：它可以让自己崭新如初。去检验一下。如果你接受了讲话者说的话，那是徒劳无益的；除非你探询并弄清楚白天的时候你能不能非常清醒、非常警觉，毫无选择地觉察——我们之前探讨过觉察是什么——那么出于那份觉察，当你确实睡着时，心就会变得格外清新和年轻。年轻是决断和行动的核心。而如果那种行动仅仅以自身为中心，只围绕着自我这个中心，那么那个行动就会导致伤害和困惑，等等。然而，当你认识到生命的整个运动是一个不可分割的整体，觉察到了这一点，那么心灵就能让自己新生进而拥有无尽的能量。所有这些都是冥想的一部分。

PART 3
第三部分

Some Questions and Answers
问与答

CHAPTER 10
第 10 章

RIGHT LIVELIHOOD
正确的谋生之道

Questioner: Is a motive necessary in business? What is the right motive in earning a livelihood?

Krishnamurti: What do you think is the right livelihood?—not what is the most convenient, not what is the most profitable, enjoyable, or gainful; but what is the right livelihood? Now, how will you find out what is right? The word "right" means correct, accurate. It cannot be accurate if you do something for profit or pleasure. This is a complex thing. Everything that thought has put together is reality. This tent has been put together by thought, it is a reality. The tree has not been put together by thought, but it is a reality. Illusions are reality—the illusions that one has, imagination, all that is reality. And the action from those illusions is neurotic, which is also reality. So when you ask this question, "What is the right livelihood", you must understand what reality is. Reality is not truth.

Now what is correct action in this reality? And how will you discover what is right in this reality?—discover for yourself, not be told. So we have to find out what is the accurate, correct, right action, or right livelihood in the world of reality, and reality includes illusion. Don't escape, don't move away, belief is an illusion, and the activities of belief are neurotic, nationalism and all the rest of it is another form of reality, but an illusion. So taking all that as reality, what is the right action there?

Who is going to tell you? Nobody, obviously. But when you see reality without illusion, the very perception of that reality is your intelligence, isn't

提问者：动机在事业中是必要的吗？谋生的正确动机是什么？

克里希那穆提：你认为什么是正确的谋生之道？——不是最方便的是什么，也不是最有利可图、最愉快、最有收获的是什么，而是正确的谋生之道是什么？那么，你要如何发现什么是正确的？"正确"这个词意味着恰当、精确。如果你做某件事是为了利益或者快感，那它就不可能是正确的。这是一件很复杂的事情。思想所造的一切都是现实，这顶帐篷由思想所造，它是一个现实存在。这棵树并非由思想所造，但它也是一个现实存在。幻觉也是现实——人抱有的各种幻觉、想象，这一切都是现实。而从这些幻觉中产生的行动是神经质的，这也是现实。所以，当你提出"什么是正确的谋生之道"这个问题时，你必须了解什么是现实。现实并非真理。

那么，在这样的现实中，什么是正确的行动？而你又如何去发现在这样的现实中什么是正确的？——你自己去发现，而不是由别人告诉你。所以，我们必须弄清楚精确、恰当、正确的行动是什么，或者在现实世界中正确的谋生之道是什么，而现实也包括了幻觉。不要逃避，不要躲开，信仰是一种幻觉，信仰产生的行为是神经质的，国家主义以及诸如此类的一切是另一种形式的现实，但也是幻觉。所以认识到了这一切都是现实，那么此时正确的行动是什么？

由谁来告诉你答案呢？显然没有人告诉你。但是，当你毫无幻觉地看到现实，对那现实的洞察本身就是你的智慧，不是吗？智慧之中不存在现实与幻觉的混合物。所以，当你观察到了现实，树的现实，帐篷的现实，思想所造的现实，包括幻象和错觉，当你看到了所有的现实，那洞察本身就是你的智慧——不是吗？所以你的智慧会告诉你该怎么办。我想知道你有没有明白这一点？智慧就是洞察现在如何与现在并非如何——洞察"现在如何"并看到"现在如何"这个现实，那意味着你没有任何心理活动，没有任何心理需求，那些都是各种形式的幻觉。看到这一切就是智慧；无论你身在何处，那智慧都会起作用，因此它会告诉你怎么办。

那么什么是真理？现实与真理之间有什么关联？其间的关联就是这种智慧——智慧看清了现实的整体因而不会把它带入真理。然后真理就会通过智慧对现实产生作用。

it? in which there is no mixture of reality and illusion. So when there is observation of reality, the reality of the tree, the reality of the tent, reality which thought has put together, including visions, illusions, when you see all that reality, the very perception of that is your intelligence—isn't it? So your intelligence says what you are going to do. I wonder if you understand this? Intelligence is to perceive what is and what is not—to perceive "what is" and see the reality of "what is", which means you don't have any psychological involvement, any psychological demands, which are all forms of illusion. To see all that is intelligence; and that intelligence will operate wherever you are. Therefore that will tell you what to do.

Then what is truth? What is the link between reality and truth? The link is this intelligence. Intelligence that sees the totality of reality and therefore doesn't carry it over to truth. And the truth then operates on reality through intelligence.

CHAPTER 11
第 11 章

WILL

意志

Questioner: I wish to know if effort of will has a place in life.

Krishnamurti: Has the will a place in life? What do we mean by life? - going to the office every day, having a profession, a career, the everlasting climbing the ladder, both religiously and mundanely, the fears, the agonies, the things that we have treasured, remembered, all that is life, isn't it? All that is life, both the conscious as well as the hidden. The conscious of which we know, more or less; and all the deep down hidden things in the cave of one's mind, in the deepest recesses of one's mind. All that is life: the illusion and the reality, the highest principle and the "what is", the fear of death, fear of living, fear of relationship - all that. What place has will in that? That is the question.

I say it has no place. Don't accept what I am saying; I am not your authority, I am not your guru. All the content of one's consciousness, which is consciousness, is created by thought which is desire and image. And that is what has brought about such havoc in the world. Is there a way of living in this world without the action of will? That is the present question.

I know this, as a human being I am fully aware of what is going on within my consciousness, the confusion, the disorder, the chaos, the battle, the seeking for power, position, safety, security, prominence, all that; and I see thought has created all that. Thought plus desire and the multiplication of images. And I say, "What place has will in this?" It is will that has created this. Now can I live in this without will? Biologically, physiologically, I have

提问者：我希望知道运用意志的努力在生活中是否具有某种地位。

克里希那穆提：意志在生活中可有地位？我们所说的生活是什么？——每天去办公室上班，有一份工作、一份职业，不停地攀爬宗教或者世俗的阶梯，还有恐惧和痛苦，我们所珍视、所怀念的事物，这一切都是生活，不是吗？这一切就是生活，既包括有意识的部分，也包括隐藏的潜意识。有意识的部分我们或多或少都知道；此外还有在我们内心深处最隐蔽的洞穴和密室中所深深潜藏的那些东西。那一切就是生活：幻觉和现实，最高原则和"现在如何"，对死亡的恐惧，对生活的恐惧，对关系的恐惧——这一切。意志在这里有什么位置？这就是那个问题。

我说它没有任何位置。不要接受我说的话；我不是你的权威，也不是你的古鲁。人意识的所有内容，也就是意识本身，都由思想即欲望和意象所造。而这就是导致这个世界如此混乱的肇因。那么有没有一种生活在这个世界上的方式是没有意志力行为的？这就是我们现在的问题。

我知道这一点，作为一个人，我完全明白自己的意识中所发生的事情：困惑、失序、混乱、斗争，追逐权力、地位、安全、保障以及声望等；我发现是思想造成了这一切——思想加上欲望以及无数的意象。于是我问："意志在这里起了什么作用？"正是意志造成了这一切。那么我能活在这种状况中而没有任何意志吗？从生理上、身体上，我必须

to exercise a certain form of energy to lean a language, to do this and that. There must be a certain drive. I see all this. And I realise—not as a verbal realization, as a description, but the, actual fact of it, as one realizes pain in the body—I realize that this is the product of thought as desire and will. Can I, as a human being, look at aU this, and transform this without will?

Now what becomes important is what kind of observation is necessary. Observation to see actually what is. Is the mind capable of seeing actually "what is"? Or does it always translate into "what should be", "what should not be", "I must suppress", "I must not suppress", and all the rest of it? There must be freedom to observe, otherwise I can't see. If I am prejudiced against you, or like you, I can't see you. So freedom is absolutely necessary to observe—freedom from prejudice, from information, from what has been learned, to be able to look without the idea. You understand: to look without the idea. As we said the other day, the word "idea" comes from Greek; the root meaning of that word is to observe, to see. When we refuse to see, we make an abstraction and make it into an idea.

There must be freedom to observe, and in that freedom will is not necessary; there is just freedom to look. Which means, to put it differently, if one makes a statement, can you listen to it without making it into an abstraction? Do you understand my question? The speaker makes a statement such as, "The ending of sorrow is the beginning of wisdom". Can you listen to that statement without making an abstraction of it?　the abstraction being: "Is that possible?", "What do we get from it?", "How do we do it?". Those are all abstractions—and not actually listening. So can you listen to that statement with all your senses, which means with all your attention? Then you see the truth of it. And the perception of that truth is action in this chaos.

运用某种形式的能量去学习一门语言，去做这做那。这时必须有某种驱动力，我明白这些。而且我也认识到——不是作为语言上的认识，也不是描述，而是认识到了这个实际的事实，就像我意识到身体上的痛苦一样——我认识到那一切都是思想即欲望和意志的产物。那么，我作为一个人，能不能看到并转化这一切而不动用任何意志？

那么现在变得重要的就是：哪一种观察是必需的？观察以看到现在实际如何。心智能否看到实际的"现在如何"？抑或它总是把它诠释成"应该如何""不应如何""我必须压抑""我不可以压抑"等诸如此类的一切？我必须拥有观察的自由，否则我就看不到。如果我对你抱有偏见，或者我喜欢你，我就看不到你。所以若要观察，自由是绝对必要的——摆脱了偏见、知识和所学东西的自由，能够不带着观念去看。你知道：要不带着观念去看。正如我们前几天说过的，"观念"这个词来源于希腊语，这个词的词根义是去观察、去看。当我们拒绝去看，我们就会进行抽象并且把它变成一个观念。

我们必须拥有观察的自由，在那份自由中意志是多余的，只有去看的自由。也就是，换句话说，如果有人做了一句陈述，你能聆听它而不把它变成一个抽象的概念吗？你理解我的问题吗？讲话者说了这样一句话："悲伤的终结就是智慧的开始。"你能聆听这句话而不把它变成一个抽象的概念吗？——抽象的过程就是这样的："这可能吗？"，"我们从中能得到什么？"，"我们如何才能做到？"。这些都是抽象的过程，而非实际在聆听。所以，你能用你所有的感官，也就是用你所有的注意力去聆听这句话吗？然后你就会发现其中蕴含的真理，而对那真理的洞察就是在这混乱之中的行动。

CHAPTER 12
第 12 章

EMOTIONS AND THOUGHT
情感与思想

Questioner: Are emotions rooted in thought?

Krishnamurti: What are emotions? Emotions are sensations, aren't they? You see a lovely car, or a beautiful house, a beautiful woman or man, and the sensory perception awakens the senses. Then what takes place? Contact, then desire, Now thought comes in. Can you end there and not let thought come in and take over? I see a beautiful house, the right proportions, with a lovely lawn, a nice garden: all the senses are responding because there is great beauty—it is well kept, orderly, tidy. Why can't you stop there and not let thought come in and say, "I must have" and all the rest of it? Then you will see emotions, or sensations, are natural, healthy, normal. But when thought takes over, then all the mischief begins.

So to find out for oneself whether it is possible to look at something with all the senses and end there and not proceed further—do it! That requires an extraordinary sense of awareness in which there is no control; no control, therefore no conflict. Just to observe totally that which is, and all the senses respond and end there. There is great beauty in that. For after all what is beauty?

提问者：情感的根源在于思想吗？

克里希那穆提：什么是情感？情感就是感受，不是吗？你看到一辆漂亮的车，或者一座美丽的房子、一个漂亮的女人或男人，然后感官知觉就唤起了感受。接下来发生了什么？接触，然后有了欲望，此时思想就介入了进来。你能在那里就打住，不让思想进来接管吗？我看到一座漂亮的房子，比例匀称，有美丽的草地、精致的花园：所有的感官都在回应，因为它太美了——被照料得很好，整洁有序。你为什么不能在那里就停下，不让思想进来说"我必须拥有它"以及诸如此类的话？然后就会发现感情或者感受是自然的、健康的、正常的。但是当思想接管时，所有的不幸就都开始了。

所以，要亲自去发现有没有可能用所有的感官看着某样东西，然后就此打住不再往前走一步——去这么做！这需要毫无控制的非凡的觉察感；没有控制，因而没有冲突。只是全然观察现状，所有的感官做回应然后就此结束。这其中有着巨大的美，因为归根结底，美是什么呢？

CHAPTER 13
第 13 章

BEAUTY

美

Is beauty in the world of reality? Or is it not within the movement of thought as time? Please follow this carefully because we are investigating together. I am not laying down the law. I am just asking myself: does beauty lie within the movement of thought as time? That is, within the field of reality. There are beautiful paintings, statues, sculpture, marvellous cathedrals, wonderful temples. If you have been to India, some of those ancient temples are really quite extraordinary: they have no time, there has been no entity as a human being who put them together. And those marvellous old sculptures from the Egyptians, from the Greeks, down to the Moderns. That is, is it expression and creation? Does creation need expression? I am not saying it does, or does not, I am asking, enquiring. Is beauty, which is both expression outwardly and the sense of inward feeling of extraordinary elation, that which comes when there is complete cessation of the "me", with all its movements?

To enquire what is beauty, we have to go into the question of what is creation. What is the mind that is creative? Can the mind that is fragmented, however capable, whatever its gifts, talent, is such a mind creative? If I live a fragmented life, pursuing my cravings, my selfishness, my self-centred ambitions, pursuits, my pain, my struggle—is such a mind (I am asking) creative?—though it has produced marvellous music, marvellous literature, architecture and poetry—English and other literature is filled with it. A mind that is not whole, can that be creative? Or is creation only possible when there is total wholeness and therefore no fragmentation? A mind that is fragmented is not a beautiful mind, and therefore it is not creative.

美存在于这个现实世界中吗？抑或，它不在思想即时间的运动中？请仔细听听这一点，因为我们正在一起探索。我并不是在定下什么规矩，而只是在问我自己：美存在于思想即时间的运动中吗？也就是说，在现实的领域中。现实中有美丽的绘画、雕刻、塑像，有壮丽的大教堂和庄严的庙宇。如果你去过印度，那些古老的寺庙中有一些真的非常令人惊奇，它们没有时间感，你不会感觉到自己是造就它们的人类的一员。还有那些来自古埃及、古希腊的令人叹为观止的古老雕塑，一直留存到了现代。然而这是美的表达和创造吗？创造需要表达吗？我并没有说需要还是不需要，我在问，我在探询。美，既包括外在的表达，也包括内心非凡的喜悦感，它是不是在"我"及其所有活动彻底止息时才会到来？

若要探询美是什么，我们就必须探究"创造是什么"这个问题。什么是具有创造性的心灵？支离破碎的心，无论它如何才华横溢、天赋异禀、能力非凡，这样的一颗心是创造性的吗？如果我过着一种支离破碎的生活，追逐我的欲望、我的自私、我自我中心的野心、目标，还有我的痛苦、我的挣扎——这样的一颗心（我在问）是创造性的吗？——尽管它能做出美妙的音乐、美妙的文学、建筑和诗歌——它们充斥着英国以及各国文学。一颗不完整的心，它可能具有创造性吗？一颗破碎的心不是一颗美丽的心，因而不是创造性的。

CHAPTER 14
第 14 章

THE STREAM
OF "SELFISHNHSS"
"自私" 的洪流

One can see that thought has built the "me", the "me" that has become independent, the "me" that has acquired knowledge, the "me" that is the observer, the "me" that is the past and which passes through the present and modifies itself as the future. It is still the "me" put together by thought, and that "me" has become independent of thought. That "me" has a name, a form. It has a label called X or Y or John. It identifies with the body, with the face; there is the identification of the "me" with the name and with the form, which is the structure, and with the ideal which it wants to pursue. Also with the desire to change the "me" into another form of "me", with another name. This "me" is the product of time and of thought. The "me" is the word: remove the word and what is the "me"?

And that "me" suffers: the "me", as you, suffers. The "me" in suffering is you. The "me" in its great anxiety is the great anxiety of you. Therefore you and I are common; that is the basic essence. Though you may be taller, shorter, have a different temperament, different character, be cleverer, all that is the peripheral field of culture; but deep down, basically we are the same. So that "me" is moving in the stream of greed, in the stream of selfishness, in the stream of fear, anxiety and so on, which is the same as you in the stream. Please don't accept what I am saying—see the truth of it. That is, you are selfish and another is selfish; you are frightened, another is frightened; you are aching, suffering, with tears, greed, envy, that is the common lot of all human beings. That is the stream in which we are

　　你可以发现是思想造就了"我"，那个变得独立存在的"我"，那个获取了知识的"我"，那个身为观察者的"我"，那个本身即是过去并穿过现在改头换面变成未来的"我"。但它依然是由思想拼凑而成的那个"我"，并且那个"我"变得独立于思想而存在。那个"我"有个名字，有个外形，它贴了个标签，叫作"甲"或"乙"，或者"约翰"。它与身体、与相貌相认同，"我"把自己与名字和外形这些结构等同起来，与它希望追求的理想等同起来，也和把"我"变成另一个形式的"我"这个愿望、和另一个名字相认同。这个"我"是时间和思想的产物，这个"我"就是这个词：把这个词拿掉，那个"我"又是什么？

　　而那个"我"遭受着痛苦：这个"我"，也就是你，受着苦。身处痛苦的那个"我"就是你。身处巨大焦虑的那个"我"就是极其焦虑的你。所以你和我是一样的，这是最基本的核心。尽管你也许个子高一些或者矮一些，有着不同的脾气、不同的秉性，或者聪明一些，但那一切都属于文化的边缘地带；在内心深处，我们从根本上都是一样的。所以是那个"我"在贪婪的洪流、自私的洪流、恐惧、焦虑等的洪流之中运动，你在这洪流中的运动也是一样的。请不要接受我说的话——看看其中包含的真相。也就是说，你自私，其他人也自私；你恐惧，别人也恐惧；你在受苦、感觉到痛苦，满含泪水、贪婪和羡妒，而这也是全

living, the stream in which we are caught, all of us. We are caught in that stream while we are living; please see that we are caught in this stream as an act of life. This stream is "selfishness"—let us put it that way—and in this stream we are living—the stream of "selfishness"—that expression includes all the descriptions of the "me" which I have just now given. And when we die the organism dies, but the selfish stream goes on. Just look at it, consider it.

Suppose I have lived a very selfish life, in self-centred activity, with my desires, the importance of my desires, ambitions, greed, envy, the accumulation of property, the accumulation of knowledge, the accumulation of all kinds of things which I have gathered—all of which I have termed as "selfishness". And that is the thing I live in, that is the "me", and that is you also. In our relationships it is the same. So while living we are together flowing in the stream of selfishness. This is a fact, not my opinion, not my conclusion; if you observe you will see it, whether you go to America, to India, or all over Europe, modified by the environmental pressures and so on, but basically that is the movement. And when the body dies that movement goes on... That stream is time. That is the movement of thought, which has created suffering, which has created the "me" from which the "me" has now asserted itself as being independent, dividing itself from you; but the "me" is the same as you when it suffers. The "me" is the imagined structure of thought. In itself it has no reality. It is what thought has made it because thought needs security, certainty, so it has invested in the "me" all its certainty. And in that there is suffering. In that movement of selfishness, while we are living we are being carried in that stream and when we die that stream exists.

Is it possible for that stream to end? Can selfishness, with all its

人类共同的命运。这是我们身处其中的洪流，我们所有人都困在其中的洪流。我们在生活的同时，就困在那股洪流之中；请看到这一点：我们受困于这股洪流之中，这就是我们生活的运动。这股洪流就是"自私"——让我们这么来表达——而我们就生活在这股洪流中——"自私"的洪流——这个表达包含了我刚刚对于那个"我"给出的所有描述。当我们死去时，机体也死去了，但自私的洪流却继续着。请务必来看一看，思考一下这一点。

假设我过着一种非常自私的生活，活在自我中心的活动里，带着我的各种欲望，给予我的欲望、野心、贪婪、妒忌、财富的积累、知识的积累，我收集起来的各种事物等积累以重要性——我把这些都叫作"自私"。而我就活在自私当中，自私就是"我"，自私也是你。在我们的关系中，也是同样的情况。所以在生活中，我们就是一起流动在这自私的洪流之中。这是一个事实，不是我的观点，也不是我的结论。如果你观察一下的话，你就会看到这一点，无论你去美国、印度还是整个欧洲，你都会看到它在环境之类的压力之下会稍做调整，但从根本上来说，还是那种运动在继续。而当身体死去，这种运动还会继续下去……这股洪流就是时间。它就是思想的运动，是它造成了痛苦，产生了"我"，经由这种思想运动，现在这个"我"声称自己是独立的，然后把自己和"你"区分开来，但是当它受苦时，这个"我"和你是一样的。这个"我"是思想所想象出来的结构，它本身没有任何真实性。是思想造就了它，因为思想需要安全感、确定性，于是把自己所有的确定性都投注在那个"我"之中，而在这之中就有着痛苦。当我们生活的时

decorations, with all its subtleties, come totally to an end? And the ending is the ending of time. Therefore there is a totally different manifestation after the ending, which is: no selfishness at all.

When there is suffering, is there a "you" and "me"? Or is there only suffering? I identify myself as the "me" in that suffering, which is the process of thought. But the actual fact is you suffer and I suffer, not "I" suffer something independent of you, who are suffering. So there is only suffering... there is only the factor of suffering. Do you know what it does when you realize that? Out of that non-personalised suffering, not identified as the "me" separate from you, when there is that suffering, out of that comes a tremendous sense of compassion. The very word "suffering" comes from the word "passion".

So I have got this problem. As a human being, living, knowing that I exist in the stream as selfishness, can that stream, can that movement of time, come totally to an end? Both at the conscious as well as at the deep level? Do you understand my question, after describing all this? Now, how will you find out whether you, who are caught in that stream of selfishness, can completely step out of it?—which is the ending of time. Death is the ending of time as the movement of thought if there is the stepping out of that. Can you, living in this world, with all the beastliness of it, the world that man has made, that thought has made, the dictatorships, the totalitarian authority, the destruction of human minds, destruction of the earth, the animals, everything man touches he destroys, including his wife or husband. Now can you live in this world completely without time?—that means no longer caught in that stream of selfishness.

You see there are many more things involved in this; because there is such a thing as great mystery. Not the thing invented by thought, that is not

候，我们被那种自私的运动，被那股洪流所卷走，而当我们死去时，那股洪流却仍然继续存在着。

那么这股洪流有可能结束吗？自私，以及它所有的装点、所有的微妙之处，能够彻底结束吗？而那种结束就是时间的结束，因而结束之后就会有一种完全不同的显现——不再有丝毫的自私。

当痛苦出现时，存在一个"你"和一个"我"吗？抑或只有痛苦而已？我在那种痛苦中将自己等同为"我"，这是思想的过程。然而实际的事实是你在受苦，我也在受苦，而不是"我"独立于你在遭受痛苦，你也在受苦。所以只有痛苦而已……只存在受苦这个事实。你知道当你认识到了这一点会发生什么吗？从那种非个人化的痛苦中，并没有一个与你分离的"我"，当那种痛苦出现时，从中就会产生一种浩瀚的慈悲感。"痛苦"这个词本身就来自"激情"。

所以我就有了这个问题：作为一个人，活着并且知道我处在自私的洪流当中，那么这股洪流，这种时间的运动能够彻底结束吗？在意识层面以及更深的层面上都结束？在我描述了这一切之后，你明白我的问题了吗？那么，你要如何弄清楚，困在自私的洪流中，你能否彻底从中走出来？——也就是时间能否终结。如果能够从中走出来，死亡就是时间即思想运动的终结。活在这个野蛮残酷的世界上，活在这个人类一手造就、思想一手造就的世界上——有着各种独裁和专制的权威，人类的心灵遭到了破坏，地球、动物遭到了破坏，人类摧毁着他所碰触的一切，包括自己的妻子或丈夫——你能否活在这个世界上却没有任何时间感？——那意味着不再受困于这股时间的洪流中。

mysterious. The occult is not mysterious, which everybody is chasing now, that is the fashion. The experiences which drugs give are not mysterious. There is this thing called death, and the mystery that lies where there is a possibility of stepping out of it.

That is, as long as one lives in the world of reality, which we do, can there be the ending of suffering in that world of reality? Think about it. Look at it. Don't say yes, or no. If there is no ending of suffering in the world of reality—which brings order—if there is no ending of selfishness in the world of reality—it is selfishness that creates disorder in the world of reality—if there is no ending to that then you haven't understood, or grasped, the full significance of ending time. Therefore you have to bring about order in the world of reality, in the world of relationships, of action, of rational and irrational thinking, of fear and pleasure. So can one, living in the world of reality as we are, end selfishness? You know it is a very complex thing to end selfishness, it isn't just, "I won't think about myself".... This selfishness in the field of reality is creating chaos. And you are the world and the world is you. If you change deeply you affect the whole consciousness of man.

　　你知道这其中涉及了很多事情，因为巨大的奥秘这回事确实存在。它并不是思想发明的东西，思想发明的东西并不神秘。神秘学并不神秘，可如今所有人都在追逐它，这已成为一种时尚。药物带来的体验也并不神秘。存在这种叫作死亡的事物，而奥秘就在从那股洪流中走出来的可能性之中。

　　也就是说，只要一个人活在现实世界中，我们也确实如此，那么在这个现实世界中苦难能够结束吗？好好想一想，不要说"能"或者"不能"。如果现实世界中的苦难无法结束——而这种结束将会带来秩序——如果现实世界中的自私无法终结——正是自私造成了现实世界中的失序——如果这一切无法终结，那么你就没有懂得或者理解终结时间的全部意义。所以你必须在现实世界中，在关系、行动、理性或不理性的思考、恐惧和欢愉的世界中建立秩序。那么，就像我们现在这样活在现实世界中的一个人，能够终结自私吗？你知道，终结自私是一件非常复杂的事情，它不是仅仅说一句"我不会再考虑我自己了"……现实领域中的这种自私正制造着混乱，而你就是世界，世界就是你。如果你深刻地改变了，你就会影响整个人类的意识。

CHAPTER 15
第 15 章

THE UNIFYING FACTOR
统一的因素

What is the unifying factor in meditation? Because that is one of the most necessary and urgent things. Politicians are not going to bring this unity however much they may talk about it. It has taken them thousands of years just to meet each other. What is that factor? We are talking about a totally different kind of energy, which is not the movement of thought with its own energy; and will that energy, which is not the energy of thought, bring about this unity? For God's sake, this is your problem, isn't it? Unity between you and your wife or husband, unity between you and another. You see, we have tried to bring about this unity; thought sees the necessity of unity and therefore has created a centre. As the sun is the centre of this world, holding all things in that light, so this centre created by thought hopes to bring mankind together. Great conquerors, great warriors, have tried to do this through bloodshed. Religions have tried to do it, and have brought about more division with their cruelty, with their wars, with their torture. Science has enquired into this. And because science is the accumulation of knowledge, and the movement of knowledge is thought, being fragmentary it cannot unify.

Is there an energy which will bring about this unity, this unification of mankind? We are saying, in meditation this energy comes about, because in meditation there is no centre. The centre is created by thought, but something else, totally different, takes place, which is compassion. That is the unifying factor of mankind. To be—not to become compassionate,

　　冥想中统一的因素是什么？因为这是最为必要和紧迫的事情之一。政客是不会带来这种统一的，无论他们对此如何高谈阔论。仅仅是面对彼此，就已经花了他们几千年的时间。那个因素是什么？我们说的是一种截然不同的能量，它不是带有自身能量的思想运动；那种能量并非思想的能量，它能带来这种统一吗？看在老天的分上，这是你的问题，不是吗？——你和你的妻子或丈夫之间的统一，你和他人之间的统一。你知道，我们一直试图带来这种统一；思想看到了统一的必要性，并进而建造了一个中心。就像太阳是这个世界的中心，将一切聚拢在它的光辉之下，所以思想建造的这个中心也希望把人类团结起来。伟大的征服者、伟大的战士试图通过流血牺牲来实现这一点。各派宗教也试图实现这一点，却通过他们的残忍、他们的战争、他们的酷刑造成了更多的分裂。科学界也探究过这个问题，但由于科学是对知识的积累，而知识的运动就是思想，所以本身就支离破碎的科学也无法带来统一。

　　有没有一种能量可以带来人类的这种统一、这种团结？我们说，从冥想中这种能量就会产生，因为冥想中不存在中心。中心由思想所造，但在冥想中有另一种截然不同的事物发生，那是慈悲。那就是统一人类的因素。心怀慈悲——不是变得慈悲，那又是另一种欺骗了——而

that is again another deception—but to be compassionate. That can only take place when there is no centre, the centre being that which has been created by thought—thought which hopes that by creating a centre it can bring about unity, like a fragmentary government, like a dictatorship, like autocracy, all those are centres hoping to create unity. All those have failed, and they will inevitably fail. There is only one factor, and that is this sense of great compassion. And that compassion is when we understand the full width and depth of suffering. That is why we talked a great deal about suffering, the suffering not only of a human being, but the collective suffering of mankind. Don't understand it verbally or intellectually but somewhere else, in your heart, feel the thing. And as you are the world and the world is you, if there is this birth of compassion you will inevitably bring about unity, you can't help it.

只是心怀慈悲。只有当思想所造的中心不复存在时,这件事才能够发生——思想希望借助建造一个中心就能带来统一,就像一个支离破碎的政府、一个独裁政权、专制政权一样,所有这些都是希望实现统一的中心。这一切都已经失败了,它们也注定会失败。只有一个因素,那就是这种浩瀚的慈悲感,而这种慈悲出现于我们充分懂得了痛苦的广度和深度之时。这就是我们就痛苦谈了那么大篇幅的原因,不仅仅是个人的痛苦,还有人类集体遭受的痛苦。不要从字面上或者智力上去理解它,而是从别处,从你的内心去理解它,去感受这样东西。因为你就是世界,世界就是你,如果这种慈悲得以诞生,你就必然会带来统一,你挡都挡不住。